LANCHESTER THEORY
Science to Win the Competition
Translated by Jay Tabrizi

by

Dr. T. Onoda

Lanchester Press, Inc.
P. O. Box 60621
Sunnyvale, CA 94086
http://www.lanchester.com

Lanchester Press, Inc., Sunnyvale, California, USA
Copyright © Lanchester Press, Inc.
With permission of Kaihatsusha Publishing Company, Tokyo Japan.
All rights reserved. No part of this book may be reproduced, stored in a retrieval system, or transmitted in any form or by any means, electronic, mechanical, photocopying, recording, holographic, or otherwise without the prior written permission of the copyright holder.
Published 1999
Printed in the United States of America by Patson's Press, Inc. Sunnyvale, CA.

Library of Congress Catalog Card Number: 99-71492

ISBN: 1-57321-015-3

Lanchester Press, Inc.
P. O. Box 60621
Sunnyvale, CA 94086
http://www.lanchester.com

Contents

Foreword by the Publisher — ix

Introduction by Dr. N. Taoka — x

Preface by Dr. T. Onoda — xii

Chapter 1
Competition Model and its Historical Background — 1

1.1 Science of competition
  1.1.1 Differences between strategy and tactics — 1
  1.1.2 Consumption of forces and depreciation — 2
  1.1.3 Continuous fixed-sum method — 3
  1.1.4 Fixed-rate method — 4
  1.1.5 Continuous fixed-rate method — 6
  Summary — 12

1.2 Equations of competition for survival
  1.2.1 Predator and prey — 12
  1.2.2 Predator model — 14
  1.2.3 Solving the predator model — 15
  1.2.4 Numeric solution using a calculator — 18

1.3. Conflict models
  1.3.1 Richardson model — 20
  1.3.2 Structural model and the phenomenological model — 23
  1.3.3 Linear model and non-linear model — 26
  1.3.4 Certainty models and probability models — 27

Chapter 2
Science of Competition and Lanchester Laws — 31

- 2.1 The basic forms of competition
  - 2.1.1 The legacy of F. W. Lanchester — 31
  - 2.1.2 Lanchester's N-Squared Law — 35
  - 2.1.3 Two basic models for competition — 50
  - 2.1.4 Contributions of the U.S. Navy Operations Research team — 53

- 2.2 Lanchester's Linear Law
  - 2.2.1 Single combat and the ratio of force in duels — 54
  - 2.2.2 Differential equations in single combat and duels — 58
  - 2.2.3 Conditions to win a single combat — 64

- 2.3 Lanchester's N-Squared Law
  - 2.3.1 The ratio of forces in group-to-group combat or total war — 67
  - 2.3.2 Differential equations in group-to-group combat or total war — 68
  - 2.3.3 Winning: Conditions for victory in a total war — 86
  - 2.3.4 Pacific war examples — 93

- 2.4 Lanchester Law based on the theory of probability
  - 2.4.1 Why the probability approach is required — 106
  - 2.4.2 Binomial distribuition — 109
  - 2.4.3 The case of Lanchester's Linear Law — 114
    - Summary — 136
  - 2.4.4 Lanchester's Square Law and the exchange rate — 138
    - Summary — 161

Chapter 3
The Lanchester Strategy Model — 163

- 3.1 Generalization of Lanchester's square law
  - 3.1.1 Introducing the concept of supply and demand — 163

3.1.2	Boulding's supply model (logistics)	165
3.1.3	Generalized Lanchester model	169
3.1.4	Relationship between fighting strength, production, and supply	180
3.2	Separation of strategic and tactical components of strength	
3.2.1	Attack and destruction against production and supply	185
3.2.2	The B17, B29, and the birth of strategic air force	187
3.2.3	Strategic and tactical forces	196
3.2.4	Strategic and tactical forces: The generalized Lanchester model	198
3.3	The principles of decision-making and Game theory	
3.3.1	Certainty and uncertainty in relation to cause and effect	200
3.3.2	Game theory as seen in the game of scissors-paper-rock	203
3.3.3	Mixed-strategy game and basic solution	206
3.3.4	Pure strategy game and saddle point/solution of equilibrium	211
3.4	Lanchester strategy model and distribution of fighting strength	
3.4.1	Application of the min-max principle	214
3.4.2	Solving a system of partial differential equations	215
3.4.3	Two equilibrium conditions	219
3.4.4	Relationship between strategic and generalized models	222
	Summary	225

Chapter 4
Strategy Model and Marketing Applications   229

4.1	The principle and theory of the 40% market share	
4.1.1	Military problems in relation to marketing	229
4.1.2	The science of market share – condition for the top position	231
4.1.3	Why Kirin beer remains at the top	234
4.1.4	Why the Liberal Democratic Party stays in power	238

4.2	Shooting range theory: the weak and the strong	
4.2.1	Inferiority fraction: the top ranker is also in danger	242
4.2.2	Top position monopoly – absolute safety	244
4.2.3	Shooting range: Single combat and total war	246
4.2.4	Separation of attack target and competition target	249
4.3	The change process of market share	
4.3.1	Five patterns of market share	251
4.3.2	Fiercely - fought absolute oligopoly (case of W. Germany)	256
4.3.3	Concentration and the HH index	257
4.3.4	The real market share in competition	262
4.4	Strategic area and tactical area in marketing	
4.4.1	The "Law of Quantity" or the logic of the strong	267
4.4.2	Decision-making area and the communication area	268
4.4.3	Establishment of marketing tactical equations	271
4.4.4	Customer retention and new market development	274

Chapter 5
Marketing Development and Establishment of Strategy and Tactics   277

5.1	The law as seen in newspaper circulation market share	277
5.2	Regulations against super stores in Matsumoto City, and the ratio of city modernization and store floor space	281
5.3	Studying the conformity between customer visitation and receiving order planning, the equations and tactics	287
5.4	Consequences	301
	Index	303

Foreword

We are very pleased to publish this English language edition of Dr. T. Onoda's seminal volume on the mathematical derivation of the Lanchester strategy in sales and marketing. This book is important as it draws together the threads of theory beginning with Lanchester in 1914, Koopman in the United States from 1943, and the body of knowledge developed in Japan since the mid–'50s by Dr. Taoka and others. Dr. Onoda has woven this theory from diverse areas of game theory, ecology, probability, and rigorous mathematicals to demonstrate the key concepts of the Lanchester strategy in sales and marketing. This book also illustrates the applicability of the Lanchester strategy in previously well–known areas such as military science, and in new areas such as marketing and politics. After all, what more does a political party do than peddle a product called candidate? Finally, we have a unified theory of sales and marketing based on scientific reality and not on subjective hype.

We would also like to take this opportunity to thank all our colleagues and associates in the production of this book. Jay Trabrizi for his care and attention in translating the original text, to Costas Schuler for preparing the figures, diagrams, and numerous pages of mathematics, editor Donna Lee Braunstein, and John Hessler and staff at our printer, Patson's Press, Inc.

Lanchester Press, Inc.
February 1999.

Introduction

Taikobo Onoda has been a close friend of mine for over twenty years. That is, we were both researchers at the Social Psychology Research Center sponsored by Dr. Minami of Hitotsubashi University in around 1955. Dr. Kato of Gakushuin University, Dr. Ishikawa of Seijo University, Mr. Niki, president of Japan Research Center, among many others, were all members of this research center, aiming to establish a new social science for the postwar Japan.

After 4 years, we left the research center for two reasons. One was that we were not satisfied with the science of social psychology. We were skeptic about the scientific veracity of the survey and application of the statistics with respect to the science of social psychology.

The reason concerned the effectiveness of the science of social psychology. Our interests began to move toward the science of economics and marketing with new applications in the postwar Japan. The book that piqued my interest in the Lanchester Law was *Competition Among Corporations and Technology* published in 1960 by technocrats of the time. This book, which conducted a very important historical study of the exchange of energy resources and innovation-driven competition among industries and resulting life cycles, referred to the Lanchester Law in only five lines.

In those days, I believed that in the science of social psychology, the scientific research of competition was one of the least attended subjects. I also predicted that it would inevitably be linked with the science of military. I was determined to study the subject of competition scientifically and based on rules, and found that the Lanchester Law was the most systematic and logical principle for the subject of my research.

In the summer of 1962, I and Dr. Onoda, while attending a seminar sponsored by the Sales Promotion Bureau (SPB), made a vow to thoroughly research and study the Lanchester Law and its logical structure. Since then, 17 years has past in the blink of an eye.

And the ultra growth we have experienced in our economy and the following stagnation caused by the oil shock not only proves the veracity of the Lanchester Law but several other rules that we have developed. Presently, regarding the significance of the Lanchester Law, borrowing Dr. Deming's line, we can say, "managers who don't know of Lanchester, their names will disappear from the telephone directory."

Dr. Onoda's *The Science to Win Competition*, brings all the basic principles and theories that form the calculus and statistics of Lanchester Law together in a single volume. Although reading this book requires some special knowledge of mathematics and statistics, I strongly recommend it as a required textbook for the study of Lanchester. I would like to express my deepest praises to Dr. Onoda for his hard work over so many years.

Dr. Nobuo Taoka

Preface

The best way to read this book is to start from Chapter 4, finish Chapter 5, and then start reading again from Chapter 1. Chapters 2 and 3 include many mathematical equations; therefore, skipping these chapters, as well as Chapter 1, which lays the ground work for the other two chapters, and reading the results and the actual examples first is recommended.

Issues involving the competition have been treated in various fields since ancient times. Conflicts cause tension and at times sorrow. But everyone agrees that competition is the driving force behind progress. There are winners and losers in any competition. The winner gains satisfaction and the loser awaits the next chance. People admire the winner and cannot help sympathizing with the loser.

To win the competition, force (strength) is needed. Does this mean that always the strong wins and the weak loses? But the weak may beat the strong. To win, strategy is also needed. Those who join the competition all expect to win, and it is possible to open the door of victory through the right strategy.

One extreme form of competition is war. In a war, one must eliminate the enemy or face elimination. Retreat also means defeat. In such an extreme environment during World War I, Lanchester analyzed two basic forms of combat quantitatively. These are Lanchester's linear and N-squared laws, which showed that depending on the fighting strategy, the fighting strength could affect the outcome differently.

Throughout World War II, Lanchester laws incorporated research from mathematics and biology, adopting the idea of logistics, and were generalized. Furthermore, the fighting strength was divided into the tactical force, to fight the enemy, and the strategic force, to destroy production and supply; it incorporated the game theory and gave birth to the Lanchester Strategy Model.

After the war, as the role of marketing activity that brought together supply and demand expanded, and competition began to heat up, interest in Lanchester's works began to increase. It goes without saying that wars and market competition are quite different. Parties can freely join the competition or leave it. The object of competition is gaining and maintaining customers. As a result, the market share can be correlated to the fighting strength.

In 1969, the author introduced the Lanchester Strategy Model in a newspaper article. I boldly stipulated that achieving 41.7% of the market as the condition for the top (runaway) position, and together with other theories offered the science of market share. There were some criticisms on the simplistic explanation of human affairs in terms of mathematical models. However, separate from the issue of human personality, there are certainly regularity and principles in many human activities.

Social sciences differ from natural sciences in that they do not verify hypotheses through experiments. Only accumulation of social facts can verify them. Throughout the 1970s, the Lanchester Strategy Model has seen widespread popularity in the marketing field. Laws governing opposing forces also apply to the voting rates in elections. A fact that gives me the greatest satisfaction if the Lanchester Strategy Model is understood as a general science to win any type of competition.

Special thanks are due to all those who made this book possible. A special note of appreciation is extended to Dr. Taoka, Mr. Shima, Mr. Moriguchi, and Mr. Nakagawa, who helped with the cover design, and Miss. Otomo, who helped with cleaning up the manuscript. To Mr. S. Matsubara, President, Kaihatsu Publishing, I also offer my very sincere thanks.

July 29, 1979
Dr. Taikoubo Onoda.

Chapter 1

Competition model and its historical background

1.1 Science of competition

1.1.1 Differences between strategy and tactics

Strategy and tactics were originally military terms; however, they are being used daily without their real meaning being called into question.

Although price strategy and discount strategy may not sound quite familiar, price tactic and discount tactic are recognized. Rather than regional tactic and distribution tactic, regional strategy and distribution strategy are commonly used. Another example would be decoy tactic and knock-off tactic, not decoy strategy and knock-off strategy. Because words are like living things, such usage of strategy and tactic cleverly describes the real feel of these expressions and their contents.

What issues are common to the strategy of pricing, region, and distribution, and to the tactic of discount, decoy, and knock-off? Let's consider pricing first. Pricing is determined appropriately prior to the sale of a product based on the competition, quality, features, and demand. The same thing is true for a geographic region. A company may have some strengths or weaknesses or have totally undeveloped areas in a region. Under current low-growth conditions where there are imbalances in regional demands, it is common sense not to sell a product nationwide. Also, in the case of distribution, it is necessary to decide whether to stay with existing channels or come up with new channels. That is, regarding all issues of strategy, prior to the execution of strategy, data must be collected in advance and one of the many actual options must be acted upon.

On the other hand, in the case of tactic, discount, decoy, or knock-off are not thought out from the outset. Frankly, these measures are taken because the competition is taking similar measures. These issues are raised in the heat of competition and marketing battle. To win over the customer, at times flexibility is allowed. However, without a clear pricing strategy, resorting to such tactics is like not being able to see the forest for the trees, which could lead to large-scale price collapse and cause the whole campaign to spiral out of control.

That is, strategy is advance decision-making, an invisible function, while tactic is communication, and essentially visible. This is why strategy has precedence and importance over tactic, and in order to win in a competition, it is so important to have a strategy along with an effective matrix of tactics.

1.1.2 Consumption of forces and depreciation

Both strategy and tactic presume a battle or a competition, a clash of forces between friends and foes. Inflicted damages should consume forces as long as they are not produced or replenished. The science of competition, therefore, begins with the quantification of the consumption of forces for both friends and foes.

An example of this can be seen in the idea of depreciation in accounting. Depreciation has two kinds: fixed-sum method and fixed-rate method.

Let the acquired cost be 100,000 yen (A) and the depreciation period 5 years (t).

First, in the fixed-sum method, let's consider the annual remaining book value after depreciation (S_t).

Here, the annual depreciation (a) is equal to the remaining book value after the depreciation period (by law, this is 1/10 of the acquired cost) subtracted from the acquired cost; that is, a = (9/10)A/t = 90/5 = 18,000 yen.

[Fixed-sum method]	(t)	Depreciation period (accumulated)	Remaining book value after depreciation (St=A-at)
Acquisition date	0 Year	0×1,000 yen	A = 100 × 1,000 yen
After 1 year	1	a=18 (18)	A - a=82
After 2 years	2	a=18 (36)	A - 2a=64
After 3 years	3	a=18 (54)	A - 3a=46
After 4 years	4	a=18 (72)	A - 4a=28
After 5 years	5	a=18 (90)	A - 5a=10

As shown in the above table, in the fixed-sum method, $S_t = -at + A$ is a linear equation.

1.1.3 Continuous fixed-sum method

In accounting, depreciation is calculated on a 6-month or yearly basis; however, depreciation begins with the acquisition; that is, the ratio of the depreciation period for a very short time (Δt) to the depreciated value (ΔS) is represented as:

$$\frac{\Delta S}{\Delta t} = \frac{S_{t+\Delta t} - S_t}{\Delta t} = \frac{[A - a(t + \Delta t)] - [A - at]}{\Delta t}$$
$$= \frac{A - at - a \cdot \Delta t - A + at}{\Delta t} = \frac{-a \cdot \Delta t}{\Delta t} = -a$$

We can also find the limit of this ratio as Δt $\left[\lim_{\Delta t \to 0}\right]$ approaches zero and have the differential equation as follows:

$$\lim_{\Delta t \to 0} \frac{\Delta S}{\Delta t} = \lim_{\Delta t \to 0} \frac{S_{t+\Delta t} - S_t}{\Delta t} = -a \quad \therefore \frac{dS}{dt} = -a$$

By separating the variables and integrating both sides, we will have the general solution:

$$dS = -adt$$
$$\int dS = -a\int dt$$
$$\therefore \int 1 dS = -a\int 1 dt$$
$$x^0 = 1, \quad \int x^n dx = \frac{1}{n+1}x^{n+1} + C \text{ (where C is constant)}$$
$$S_t = -at + C \qquad \therefore C = S_t + at$$

Because we know the initial t value (at t = 0); that is, we know the acquisition value ($S_0 = A$), then: $C = S_0 + a \times 0 = A$ and we get the particular solution $S_t = A - at$.

In the fixed-sum method, therefore, the ratio of depreciation in value is always a constant, whether depreciation is continuous or otherwise.

1.1.4 Fixed-rate method

In the fixed-rate method, the annual depreciation rate (r) is multiplied by (S_t); that is:

At acquisition $\quad t = 0 \quad$ Acquisition value $S_0 = A$
After 1 year $\quad t = 1 \quad$ Remaining book value $S_1 = A - Ar = A(1-r)$
After 2 years $\quad t = 2 \quad$ Remaining book value $S_2 = A(1-r) - A(1-r)r = A(1-r)(1-r)$
$$= A(1-r)^2$$
After 3 years $\quad t = 3 \quad$ Remaining book value $S_3 = A(1-r)^2 - A(1-r)^2 r = A(1-r)^2(1-r)$
$$= A(1-r)^3$$
After 4 years $\quad t = 4 \quad$ Remaining book value $S_4 = A(1-r)^3 - A(1-r)^3 r = A(1-r)^3(1-r)$
$$= A(1-r)^4$$
After 5 years $\quad t = 5 \quad$ Remaining book value $S_5 = A(1-r)^4 - A(1-r)^4 r = A(1-r)^4(1-r)$
$$= A(1-r)^5$$

After t years $\quad$ Remaining book value $\quad S_t = A(1-r)^t$

Because by law the remaining book value after depreciation is 1/10 of the acquisition value, then we have for $\frac{1}{10}A$

$$\frac{1}{10}A = A(1-r)^t, \quad \frac{1}{10} = (1-r)^t \quad \therefore r = 1 - \sqrt[t]{0.1}$$

if $t = 5$, then $r = 1 - \sqrt[5]{0.1} \approx 1 - 0.631 = 0.369$ (annual depreciation rate)

Fixed – rate method	(t)	Depreciation $\{A(1-r)^{t-1}r\}$	remaining book value after accumulated depreciation $\{St = A(1-r)^t\}$
At acquisition	0	0x1000 yen	$A = 100 \times 1000$ yen
After 1 year	1	$Ar = 37(37)$	$A(1-r) = 63$
After 2 years	2	$A(1-r)r = 23(60)$	$A(1-r)^2 = 40$
After 3 years	3	$A(1-r)^2 r = 15(75)$	$A(1-r)^3 = 25$
After 4 years	4	$A(1-r)^3 r = 9(84)$	$A(1-r)^4 = 16$
After 5 years	5	$A(1-r)^4 r = 6(90)$	$A(1-r)^5 = 10$

Accumulated depreciation $A\{1-(1-r)^t\}$

Subtraction of the depreciation from the acquisition cost is called conversion of the depreciation value to the acquisition cost. In our calculation, the frequency of conversion is once a year, if it is twice a year, then the remaining book value S_t after t years and the annual depreciation rate (r) change as follows:

$$S_t = A\left(1 - \frac{r}{2}\right)^{2t}$$

$$\frac{1}{10}A = A\left(1 - \frac{r}{2}\right)^{2t}, \quad \frac{1}{10} = \left(1 - \frac{r}{2}\right)^{2t} \quad \therefore r = 2\left(1 - \sqrt[2t]{0.1}\right)$$

if $t = 5$, $r = 2\left(1 - \sqrt[10]{0.1}\right) \approx 2(1 - 0.794) = 0.411$ (annual depreciation rate)

Generally, if the frequency of conversion is n, then the remaining book value S_t after t years and the annual depreciation rate r are represented as follows:

$$S_t = A\left(1-\frac{r}{2}\right)^{nt}$$

$$\frac{A}{10}A = \left(1-\frac{r}{n}\right)^{nt}, \quad \frac{1}{10} = \left(1-\frac{r}{n}\right)^{nt} \quad \therefore \quad r = n\left(1-\sqrt[nt]{0.1}\right)$$

Here, r changes with n and therefore it is called nominal depreciation rate. The real depreciation rate is r/n; however, when n changes, if the time lapse remains the same, then the remaining book value would be equal.

1.1.5 Continuous fixed-rate method

As seen in the fixed-sum method, value depreciation begins at acquisition ; therefore, when n approaches infinity, the remaining book value after continuous fixed-rate depreciation would be as follows:

$$\lim_{n \to \infty} S_t = \lim_{n \to \infty} A\left(1-\frac{r}{n}\right)^{nt}$$

Here, let $-\dfrac{r}{n} = h, \ n \to \infty$ thus $h \to 0$

$$\lim_{n \to \infty} S_t = \lim_{n \to \infty} A(1+h)^{-\frac{r}{h}t} \quad \therefore \ n = -\frac{r}{h}$$

$$= \left[\lim_{n \to \infty}(1+h)^{\frac{1}{h}}\right]^{-rt}$$

$$= Ae^{-rt} \qquad e = 2.718281...\text{(base of natural logarithms)}$$

(Note 1):

if $h = \dfrac{1}{m}$, then $m = \dfrac{1}{h}$. If $h \to 0$, then $m \to \infty$,

$$\lim_{h \to 0}(1+h)^{\frac{1}{h}} = \lim_{m \to \infty}\left(1+\frac{1}{m}\right)^{m}$$

It is evident that by entering various values for m, a convergence occurs as follows:

m		$(1+\frac{1}{m})^m$
0.1	$(1+10)^{0.1}$	$= 1.2709\ 8161\ 5$
1	$(1+1)^1$	$= 2.$
10	$(1+0.1)^{10}$	$= 2.5937\ 4246\ 0$
100	$(1+0.01)^{100}$	$= 2.7048\ 1382\ 9$
1,000	$(1+0.001)^{1,000}$	$= 2.7169\ 2393\ 2$
10,000	$(1+0.0001)^{10,000}$	$= 2.7181\ 4592\ 7$
100,000	$(1+0.00001)^{100,000}$	$= 2.7182\ 6823\ 7$
1,000,000	$(1+0.000001)^{1,000,000}$	$= 2.7182\ 8046\ 9$
10,000,000	$(1+0.0000001)^{10,000,000}$	$= 2.7182\ 8169\ 3$
100,000,000	$(1+0.00000001)^{100,000,000}$	$= 2.7182\ 8181\ 5$

We can prove that the converging constant does not exceed 3 by using an expansion based on the binomial theorem:

(Note 2)

When $x = k^y$, then $y = \log_k x$, where k is the base.

Here, we have the following:

$$\frac{\Delta y}{\Delta x} = \frac{\log_k(x+\Delta x) - \log_k x}{\Delta x} = \frac{\log_k(x/x + \Delta x/x)}{\Delta x}$$

$$= \frac{\log_k(1+\Delta x/x)}{\Delta x}$$

Now, let $\frac{\Delta x}{x} = h$, then $\Delta x = hx$.

When $\Delta x \to 0$, then $h \to 0$

$$\frac{dy}{dx} = \lim_{h \to 0} \frac{\log_k(1+h)}{hx} = \lim_{h \to 0} \left\{ \frac{1}{x} \cdot \frac{1}{h} \log_k(1+h) \right\}$$

$$= \frac{1}{x} \lim_{h \to 0} \left\{ \log_k(1+h)^{\frac{1}{h}} \right\}$$

$$\therefore \quad \frac{dy}{dx} = \frac{1}{x} \log_k \left\{ \lim_{h \to 0} (1+h)^{\frac{1}{h}} \right\} = \frac{1}{x} \log_k e$$

Let k be e, then $\log_e = 1$
Hence:

$$x = e^y, \quad y = \log_e x, \quad \frac{dy}{dx} = \frac{d}{dx}(\log_e x) = \frac{1}{x}$$

Normally, base e is not written in $\log_e$.

We can also obtain the general solution through the following differential equation:

$$y' = \frac{1}{x}, \quad \frac{dy}{dx} = \frac{1}{x}, \quad \int dy = \int \frac{1}{x} dx$$
$$y = \log x + C \quad (C \text{ is a constant})$$

(Note 3). *Differentiating e^x*:

Let $y = e^x$, we take the natural logarithm of both sides.
Let $\log y = x$, $\log y = z$, we differentiate the composite function:

(left – hand side) $\quad \dfrac{dz}{dx} = \dfrac{dz}{dy} \cdot \dfrac{dy}{dx} = \dfrac{d}{dy}(\log y) \dfrac{dy}{dx} = \dfrac{1}{y} \cdot \dfrac{dy}{dx}$

(right – hand side) $\quad \dfrac{d}{dy}(x) = 1$

$$\therefore \quad \frac{1}{y} \cdot \frac{dy}{dx} = 1, \quad \frac{dy}{dx} = y, \quad \therefore \quad \frac{dy}{dx} = e^x$$

That is, differentiating e^x with respect to x and integrating it yields no differences.

Let k be a constant. Let the differential of e^{kx} be $kx = u$.

Differentiating both sides with respect to x and we get $k = \dfrac{du}{dx}$,

$$(e^{kx})' = \dfrac{d}{du}(e^u)\dfrac{du}{dx} = e^u \cdot k = ke^{kx}$$

Taking the limits of the depreciation rates at each instance, and analyzing them in the same way as in the fixed rate method, we obtain:

$$\lim_{\Delta t \to 0} \dfrac{\Delta S}{\Delta t} = \lim_{\Delta t \to 0} \dfrac{S_{t+\Delta t} - S_t}{\Delta t} = \lim_{\Delta t \to 0} \dfrac{Ae^{-r(t+\Delta t)} - Ae^{-rt}}{\Delta t}$$

$$= \lim_{\Delta t \to 0} \dfrac{Ae^{-rt} \cdot e^{-r\Delta t} - Ae^{-rt}}{\Delta t} = Ae^{-rt} \left[\lim_{\Delta t \to 0} \dfrac{e^{-r\Delta t} - 1}{\Delta t} \right]$$

Let $e^{-r\Delta t} - 1 = u$. If $\Delta t \to 0$, then $e^{-r\Delta t} \to e^0 = 1$, $u \to 0$.
Or, $e^{-r\Delta t} = 1 + u$, Taking logarithm of both sides, rearranging, and substituting $\Delta t = -\dfrac{1}{r}\log(1+u)$ and we get

$$= Ae^{-rt} \left[\lim_{u \to 0} \dfrac{u}{-\{\log(1+u)\}/r} \right] = Ae^{-rt} \left[-r \lim_{u \to 0} \dfrac{1}{\{\log(1+u)\}/u} \right]$$

$$= Ae^{-rt} \left[-r \cdot \dfrac{1}{\log\left\{ \lim_{u \to 0}(1+u)^{\frac{1}{u}} \right\}} \right]$$

$$= Ae^{-rt} \left[-r \dfrac{1}{\log e} \right] = Ae^{-rt} \left[-r \dfrac{1}{1} \right]$$

$$\lim_{\Delta t \to 0} \dfrac{\Delta S}{\Delta t} = Ae^{-rt}(-r), \qquad Ae^{-rt} = S \quad \text{thus,} \quad \text{(Note: Character added for time is arbitrary and therefore is deleted)}$$

$$\therefore \frac{dS}{dt} = -rS$$

That is, in the case of continuous fixed-rate depreciation, (dS/dt) is also proportionate to S. We can also obtain the general and particular solutions as follows:

$$\frac{dS}{dt} = -rS \quad \text{Separate values,} \quad \frac{1}{S}dS = -rdt,$$

$$\int \frac{1}{S}dS = -r\int dt, \quad \log S = -rt + C$$

$$S = e^{-rt+C} = e^C \cdot e^{-rt}, \quad e^C \quad (C \text{ is constant}),$$

(General solution) $\quad S = Ce^{-rt}$

When $t = 0$, since $S_0 = A$, $\quad A = C \cdot e^{-rt}$

Thus $\quad C = A$

(Particular solution) $\quad S = Ae^{-rt}$

In the fixed-rate method, assuming n to be the number of annual conversions, the annual depreciation rate was $r = n\left(1 - \sqrt[nt]{0.1}\right)$; if $n = 1$ and $t = 5$, then $r = 0.369$; if $n = 2$, then $r = 0.411$ (again, if $t = 5$).

In the case of continuous depreciation:

$$\frac{1}{10}A = Ae^{-rt}, \quad \frac{1}{10} = \frac{1}{e^{rt}}, \quad e^{rt} = 10, \quad rt = \log 10,$$

$$\therefore r = \frac{2.302585}{t},$$

$$\text{if } t = 5, \quad r = \frac{2.302585}{5} \approx 0.4605$$

The following graph shows the fixed-sum method and the fixed-rate method. Both in the fixed-rate depreciation method where n = 1 and in the continuous depreciation method, if time (t) is the same, then remaining book values would be equal.

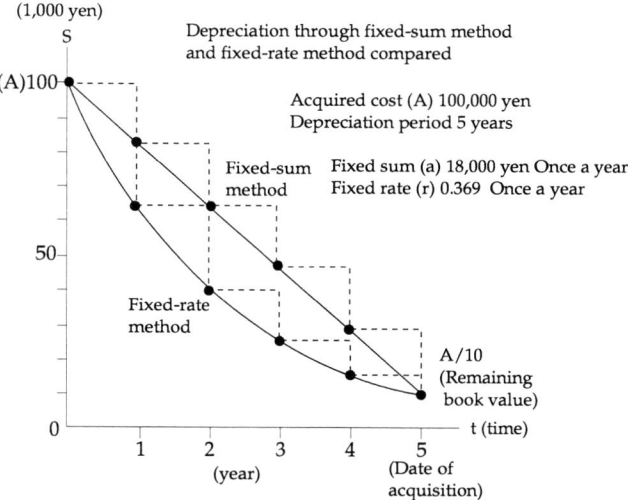

In equation $S = A(1-r)^t$, if the + sign is used, then we get the equation for principle (A) with interest (r) compounded after t years.

Furthermore, in the continuous fixed-rate method, if r is turned to plus, then, (dS/dt) = rS, and we get the steep exponential curve.

Other typical examples of the equation $S = Ae^{-rt}$ involve the decay of uranium and radium. In these cases, $\dfrac{dS}{dt} = -rS$ represent the rate of decay that is proportional to the remaining amount (S) and r is the radioactive material's characteristic half-life proportional constant ($log2/t$).

Summary

Let acquisition cost be A (yen), depreciation period, t (year), and the remaining book value after period t, S (yen), then for the continuous fixed-sum depreciation case:

Depreciation sum $a = 0.9A/t$

Depreciation rate: $\dfrac{dS}{dt} = -a$

Remaining book value after period t (particular solution) $S = A - at$

Depreciation rate $r = 2.302585/t$

Depreciation rate: $\dfrac{dS}{dt} = -rS$

Remaining book value after period t (particular solution) $S = Ae^{-rt}$

1.2 Equations of competition for survival

1.2.1 Predator and prey

The important fact to keep in mind is that in any competition there is always "the other side." The process of depreciation does not take this into account. However, in competitive situations, the effects of changes in the balance of power on both sides must always be considered.

In nature, predator and prey maintain a surprising balance without leading to the depletion of prey or an uncontrollable increase of the predator.

During World War I (1914 – 1918), in the Adriatic sea, many fishermen were conscripted, and to make matters worse, German U boats put an end to their business of fishing. Professor Vito Volterra (1860 – 1940) of Rome University analyzed the fish population.

Some fish eat other fish. When the population of shark increases, the population of their prey fish start to decline. This reduces the shark population, which in turn results in an increase in the population of their prey fish. D'Ancona, a zoologist, studied this relationship and actually compared the number of predator fish, Selachians (shark family), in the following table:

Region	1905	1910	1911	1912	1913	1914	1915	1916
Trieste	—	5.7	8.8	9.5	15.7	14.6	7.6	16.2
Fiume	—	—	—	—	—	11.9	21.4	22.1
Venice	21.8	—	—	—	—	—	—	—

Region	1917	1918	1919	1920	1921	1922	1923
Trieste	15.4		19.9	15.8	13.3	10.7	10.2
Fiume	21.2	36.4	27.3	21.0	15.9	11.8	10.7
Venice			30.9	25.3	25.9	26.8	26.6

Trieste, Venice, and Fiume are famous fishing harbors at the northern base of the Adrian sea. There is no data for Venice prior to World War I (–1913) and during World War I (1914 – 1918).

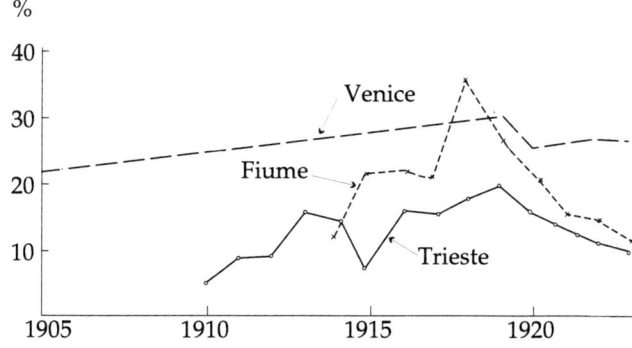

Percentage of Selachians (shark family) compared to the total of fish harvest

It is evident that the shark population increased during the war and decreased afterward then returned to its original level. It seems that the shark population rose because people stopped fishing during those years. Professor Volterra's study was an attempt to find an answer to d'Ancona's question (Volterra, V., 1926. *System Ecology* translated by Yasuo Shimazu, Kyoritsu Publications, 1973).

1.2.2 Predator model

Let the number of predators be x and the number of their prey be y. If y dies completely, as in the continuous fixed rate depreciation, x will die out at a fixed rate of (a)

$$\text{(Predator)} \quad \frac{dx}{dt} = -ax \quad (1.1)$$

Then, the general solution would be $x = C_1 e^{-at}$

If x dies completely, as in the continuous compounded interest case, y will multiply at a fixed rate of (b)

$$\text{(Prey)} \quad \frac{dy}{dt} = by \quad (1.2)$$

Then, the general solution would be $y = C_2 e^{bt}$

This will lead to the total elimination of predator and an infinite number of prey. But in reality both predator and prey "coexist" and none of the above cases actually occur in practice.

When there is only y number of prey, the above equations modified by Volterra look as follows:

$$\text{(Predator)} \quad \begin{cases} \dfrac{dx}{dt} = -(a-cy)x & (1.3) \\[6pt] \text{(Prey)} \quad \dfrac{dy}{dt} = (b-dx)y & (1.4) \end{cases}$$

a,b>0, constants.
c,d>=0, These are sometimes called appetite constants.

That is, with y, the rate of decrease for predator is reduced from a to a-cy. If y>(a/c), then the number of predator x will actually increase.

On the other hand, with x, the rate of increase for prey is reduced from b to b-dx. If x>(b/d), then the number of prey x will actually decrease. That is:

(Predator) $\dfrac{dx}{dt} = -ax + cxy$

(Prey) $\dfrac{dy}{dt} = by - dxy$

Where x y is the rate that the predator finds prey, compared to equations (1.1) and (1.2), this shows that the number of predators increase and the prey decrease.

1.2.3 Solving the predator model

Solving the predator model devised by Volterra is rather complicated.

The ratio of equations (1.3) and (1.4) is

$$\dfrac{dy}{dx} = -\dfrac{(b-dx)}{x} \cdot \dfrac{y}{(a-cy)}$$

Now we can separate variables:

$$\left(\dfrac{a-cy}{y}\right) dy = -\left(\dfrac{b-dx}{x}\right) dx$$

$$\left(a\dfrac{1}{y} - c\right) dy = -\left(b\dfrac{1}{x} - d\right) dx$$

Rearranging terms:
$$\left(b\frac{1}{x}-d\right)dx+\left(a\frac{1}{y}-c\right)dy=0$$

Integrating both sides
$$b\log x - dx + a\log y - cy = C \quad (C \text{ is constant})$$
and converting to antilogarithm, the right side becomes e^c, a constant.
$$x^b e^{-dx} \cdot y^a e^{-cy} = C, \quad (C \text{ is constant}) \quad C \geq 0 \quad (1.5)$$
and by introducing x and y, we will have
$$x^b e^{-dx} = \frac{1}{X} = X^{-1}, \quad x^{-b}e^{dx} = X,$$
$$y^a e^{-cy} = Y$$
$$X^{-1}Y = C, \quad \therefore Y = CX$$

To find the maximum and minimum values of Y, we differentiate Y with respect to x and equate it to zero.

We then have:
$$\frac{dY}{dx} = C(X)' = C(x^{-b}e^{dx})'$$

From the differential equation $(uv)' = u'v+uv'$ we get
$$\frac{dY}{dx} = C\{(x^{-b})'e^{dx} + x^{-b}(e^{dx})'\}$$
$$= C(-bx^{-b-1}e^{dx} + dx^{-b}e^{dx}) = 0$$

$C \neq 0$ we then have
$$-bx^{-b-1}e^{dx} + dx^{-b}e^{dx} = 0$$
$$\therefore \quad bx^{-b-1}e^{dx} = dx^{-b}e^{dx}$$
$$bx^{-1} = d, \quad \frac{b}{x} = d,$$
$$\therefore x = \frac{b}{d}$$

Therefore, the maximum and minimum values of Y will be

$$Y = C\left(\frac{b}{d}\right)^{-b} e^{d(\frac{b}{d})}$$

$$y^a e^{-cy} = C\left(\frac{b}{d}\right)^{-b} e^{b}$$

$$= C\left(\frac{d}{b}e\right)^{b} \qquad (1.6)$$

Similarly, with respect to X, we will have $y = \dfrac{a}{c}$

$$X^{-1} = x^b e^{-dx} = C\left(\frac{c}{a}e\right)^{a} \qquad (1.7)$$

By looking at equation (1.5), the multiple of the variable part with respect to x on the left side and the variable part with respect to y is constant.

If the logarithm is taken, the sum will be constant, which means the curve representing x and y is a closed curve. It is similar to the same family of curves as circles $(x-a)^2 + (y-b)^2 = r^2$ and ellipses $\dfrac{x^2}{a^2} + \dfrac{y^2}{b^2} = 1$ (a>b>0). In determining the maximum and minimum values of x and y, we have $X_{MIN.} > 0, Y_{MIN} > 0$ in all cases.

About the same time that Volterra published his theory (circa 1920), Lotka in America published a similar predatory model (Lotka, A.J., *Elements of Physical Ecology*, Williams & Willkins, Baltimore, 1925). Therefore, today, these simultaneous equations are referred to as Lotka-Volterra predatory model and are the basis of quantitative ecology.

1.2.4 Numeric solution using a calculator

In the first half of the 1920s, most of the interest was directed to the problem of solving the predatory model equations. But now we are able to easily perform numeric calculations for differential equations through various software programs (Shin Hitotsumatsu, *Differential Equations for the Competition of Survival*, Modern Mathematics , June 1977).

For example, when $\quad \begin{aligned} a &= 1, \quad c = 2 \\ b &= 3, \quad d = 4 \end{aligned}$

then:
$$\begin{cases} (\text{Predator}) & \dfrac{dx}{dt} = -(1-2y)x \\ (\text{Prey}) & \dfrac{dy}{dt} = (3-4x)y \end{cases}$$

For initial condition ($t = 0$), let $x_0 = 1.2$ and $y_0 = 1.5$, then according to (1.5):
$$x^3 e^{-4x} y e^{-2y} = C \quad (C \text{ is constant})$$

Entering the initial condition

$$C = (1.2)^3 e^{-4 \times 1.2} (1.5) e^{-2 \times 1.5}$$
$$= (1.2)^3 (1.5) e^{-4.8} e^{-3.0} = 2.592 e^{-7.8} = \frac{2.592}{e^{7.8}}$$
$$= 0.001062033$$

Using the Runge-Kutta method, and incrementing t [$\Delta t = 0.05$] by 0.05 approximately, we get the following smooth graph that oscillates periodically:

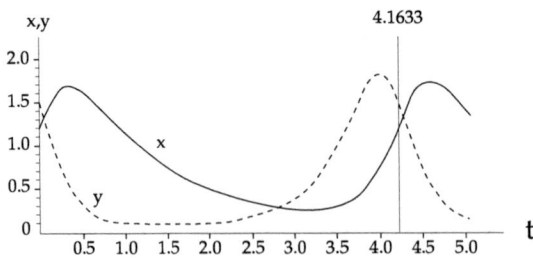

Maximum and minimum values for x,

when $y = \dfrac{a}{c} = \dfrac{1}{2}$ are $x^3 e^{-4x} = C\left(\dfrac{2}{1}e\right) = 0.005773810$

and for y when $x = \dfrac{b}{d} = \dfrac{3}{4}$ are $ye^{-2y} = C\left(\dfrac{4}{3}e\right)^3 = 0.050563566$

Using the software program to solve the polynomial, we get

$$x_{MAX.} = 1.675843, \quad x_{MIN.} = 0.250558,$$
$$y_{MAX.} = 1.780791, \quad y_{MIN.} = 0.056627$$

By plotting x (predator) and y (prey) without t, we obtain the following closed graph around the $\left(\dfrac{b}{d}, \dfrac{a}{c}\right)$ point of balance, the vorticity point:.

This graph shows the functional relationship between x and y.

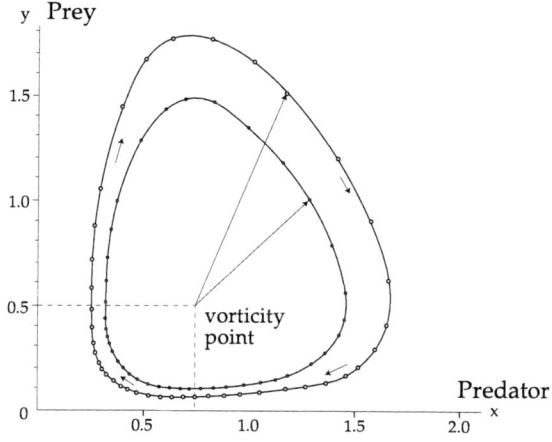

This relationship remains the same when the initial values are changed, for example, to $x_0 = 1.3$, and $y_0 = 1$.

Furthermore, we can expand this model to include two species of predators preying on one species of prey:

$$\begin{cases} \dfrac{dx}{dt} = (a - cy - kx)x & (1.8) \\ \dfrac{dy}{dt} = (b - dx - ly)y & (1.9) \end{cases}$$

(a and b are proliferation rates within species.)
(c and d are coefficients of competition among species.)
(k and l are coefficients of competition within species.)

When two species prey on the same prey, eventually the weaker species dies out and a state of equilibrium is achieved. The probability for the weaker species to survive is very small (Smith, J.M., *Mathematical Ideas in Biology*, Cambridge Univ. Press, London, 1968).

It is a fact that there is a lot of criticism of the predatory model from ecologists. They argue that ecology is different from particle physics, and one must consider the food that is consumed by the prey also. But taking these various factors into account will only lead to a highly complex model that is removed from reality and therefore useless. At any rate, Volterra's model remains an epoch in the development of science of competition.

1.3 Conflict Models

1.3.1 Richardson Model

Conflict is a special case of competition and is experienced not only in nature but also in human society and in daily life. We may proclaim the principles of equality but in fact a fierce competition exists in the background.

Political science studies conflict between nations and the friction between political parties, and economics deals with conflicts between corporations and labor unions, among other topics. Sociology studies conflicts between families, races, and religions, while psychology deals with personal conflicts, and above all, history is mostly preoccupied with wars and conflicts.

The British-born Boulding (1910–), a professor at Colorado University, wondered whether there is a general phenomenon of conflict and whether one can establish a general theory of conflict that could be applied to a full range of phenomena, and published a book (Kenneth E. Boulding, *Conflict and Defense: A General Theory*, Harper & Row, New York, 1962).

In his book such varied mathematical models as the model for the possibility of survival, the ecological model, the model for epidemic diseases are introduced. At the core of all his models resides the Richardson Process Model. This is shown in the following system of differential equations:

$$\begin{cases} \dfrac{dm}{dt} = P + an - cm & (1.10) \\ \dfrac{dn}{dt} = Q + bm - dn & (1.11) \end{cases}$$

Let *m* and *n* be two adversarial countries.

The following models represent cases where these two countries, which are threatened by each others military build-up, further expand or restrain their armaments in order to prevent invasion from their adversary.

m, n	Scale of armaments and hostility based on insecurity and grievance.
$\dfrac{dm}{dt}, \dfrac{dn}{dt}$	Ratio of military build-up, t represents time.
P, Q	Constant of insecurity and grievance.
a, b	Coefficient of defense build-up. (An integer greater than 0).
c, d	Coefficient of military restraint. (An integer greater than or equal to 0).

Note that we allow $ab - cd \neq 0$.

The solution is divided into two sets depending on the state of coefficients.

Case 1. *ab<cd*; that is, in comparison, the coefficient of military restraint is greater than the coefficient of defense build-up. Therefore, although there is the constant of insecurity, a degree of balance is going to be maintained in the armaments of each country.

$$P = 2, \quad a = 1, \quad c = 2$$
$$Q = 3, \quad b = 1, \quad d = 2$$

$$\begin{cases} \dfrac{dm}{dt} = 2 + n - 2m \\ \dfrac{dn}{dt} = 3 + m - 2n \end{cases} \quad \text{Initial condition } (t = 0) \quad \begin{aligned} m_0 &= 5 \\ n_0 &= 3 \end{aligned}$$

And the solution is (the general solution is given in Chapter 3, 3.1.3)

$$\begin{cases} m = 2\dfrac{1}{3} + 1\dfrac{1}{2}e^{-t} + 1\dfrac{1}{6}e^{-3t} \\ n = 2\dfrac{2}{3} + 1\dfrac{1}{2}e^{-t} - 1\dfrac{1}{6}e^{-3t} \end{cases} \quad e = 2.718281.....$$

As time passes ($t \to \infty$), the point of balance $\left(2\dfrac{1}{3}, 2\dfrac{2}{3}\right)$ is approached.

Case 2. *ab>cd*. In this case, the coefficient of defense build-up is greater than the coefficient of military restraint; therefore, the armaments of these two countries expand without restraints, with a great risk of engagement of war at some future point.

For example, let

$$P = 2, \quad a = 2, \quad c = 1$$
$$Q = 3, \quad b = 2, \quad d = 1$$

$$\begin{cases} \dfrac{dm}{dt} = 2 + 2n - m \\ \dfrac{dn}{dt} = 3 + 2m - n \end{cases} \quad \text{Initial condition } (t = 0) \quad \begin{aligned} m_0 &= 5 \\ n_0 &= 3 \end{aligned}$$

And the solution is

$$\begin{cases} m = -2\dfrac{2}{3} + 6\dfrac{1}{2}e^{t} + 1\dfrac{1}{6}e^{-3t} \\ n = -2\dfrac{1}{3} + 6\dfrac{1}{2}e^{t} - 1\dfrac{1}{6}e^{-3t} \end{cases} \quad e = 2.718281.....$$

As time passes ($t \to \infty$), because $e^{t} \to \infty$ and $e^{-3t} \to 0$; therefore, both m and n approach infinity.

Lewis F. Richardson (1881 – 1953) was a British meteorologist who studied the theory of diffusion of particles in the atmosphere and researched the related partial differential equations and their approximate solutions using differential calculus. He also attempted to construct and analyze a mathematical model for national sentiments aroused by conflicts and military race among countries. He left 43 theses beginning with *Mathematical Psychology of War*, 1919, and ending with *Submissiveness of Nations*, 1953. Following his death, his ideas and methodologies were compiled by several scientists into the following two books. Boulding also introduces these books:

1. *Arms and Insecurity*, Pittsburgh, Boxwood, 1960.
2. *Statistics of Deadly Quarrels*, Chicago, Quadrangle, 1960.

1.3.2 Structural Model and Phenomenological Model

Creation of a mathematical model focuses on the cause and effect and attempts to organize apparently complex phenomena (*Mathematical Models*, Kondo Jiro, Maruzen Press, 1976). There are many ways to create a mathematical model; however, in reality they are divided into two:

The cause and effect have a clear relationship.

The cause and effect relationship are converted to a black box, which, although its internal operation is not known, its output from a given input can be experimentally understood.

The former is called the Structural Model and is mostly used in control functions such as inventory management, transportation management (LP), etc. within corporations. For example, with respect to the basic problem of inventory, the optimum volume of order is achieved when inventory and order costs are both at a minimum.

annual cost (Z) = inventory cost + order cost

 inventory cost = average inventory volume x unit inventory cost
 order cost = average order volume x unit order cost

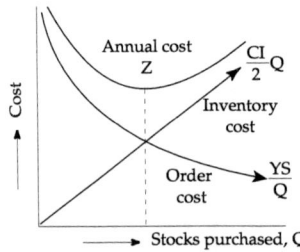

* We assume unit order cost has no relation to inventory volume; we also allow the monthly demand to remain more or less constant

Q: Order (stock) cost   C: Part unit
i: Inventory cost ratio (%)
Y: Annual demand   S: Single order cost
Ci: Annual inventory cost for a part unit

$\dfrac{Y}{Q}$: Order volume (number of orders)

$\dfrac{Q}{2}$ = Average inventory volume

Therefore, the mathematical model will look as follows:

$$Z = \dfrac{Q}{2}Ci + \dfrac{Y}{Q}S = \dfrac{Ci}{2}Q + \dfrac{YS}{Q}$$

The order volume Q must be optimized for minimum annual cost, Z; that is:

$$\frac{dZ}{dQ} = \frac{Ci}{2} - \frac{YS}{Q^2} = 0, \quad \frac{Ci}{2} = \frac{YS}{Q^2}, \quad Q^2 = \frac{2YS}{Ci},$$

$$\therefore \quad Q = \sqrt{\frac{2YS}{Ci}}$$

Here, unit product cost, C, is 400 yen, existing inventory ratio, i, is 30%, single order cost, S, is 3,750 yen, and the annual demand, Y, is 100,000 parts. The optimum order volume, Q, would be

$$Q = \sqrt{\frac{2 \times 100,000 \times 3,750}{400 \times 0.30}} = 2,500 \quad \text{(part/frequency)}$$

The frequency of order would be once every 9 days as Y/Q = 100,000/2,500 = 40 times.

The latter phenomenological model is mostly applied to sales management, advertising planning, and so forth, which are generally activities associated with external corporate management activities.

For example, this applies to the following case: A certain retailer studies sales costs by regional block. Cost, C, per unit sales (cost for sales of 10,000 yen) and sales, V, and surface area, S, for each block can be expressed as

$$C = k + \frac{a}{V} + b\sqrt{S}$$

Here, k is a fixed value, and a and b are constants. Assuming larger areas yield greater sales, the question is how the sales costs can be minimized. In this model, the above equation in itself is an issue. Generally, cost decreases with increased sales; furthermore, greater the area, higher the cost, but since area is a squared value, one can presume that cost is proportional to the square root of sales.

By selecting coefficients k, a, and b specifically from the past data, the cost function, C, can be found. The relationship between cause and effect is not clear, but this is an effort to find a principle that relies on repeating past experience from the existing data, for which another example would be demand forecast. But if this is close to a real application, then the results would be quite acceptable.

1.3.3 Linear Model and Non-Linear Model

The Richardson model also depends on this phenomenological model. $\left(\frac{dm}{dt}\right)$ and $\left(\frac{dn}{dt}\right)$ apply positively according to the national sentiment (P and Q). Furthermore, they apply positively and increase drawn by the size of adversary's armament (n for m, and m for n) in square of arms expansion coefficients (a and b). Finally, this model assumes a negative force that restrains arms expansion as a result of internal constrains and costs in the square of arms reduction coefficients (c and d).

Richardson divided major arms expansions in the twentieth century to the following three phases:

1. Ended in 1914. World War I starts;
2. Ended in 1939. World War II starts; and
3. Ongoing (as of 1951). Cold war and nuclear proliferation.

He then attempted to come up with various coefficients from these data. His results explain the first major arms race up to World War I. They also support the second phase up to World War II. However, the results are totally insufficient when applied to the third phase; consequently, Richardson himself offered the following improved mathematical model:

$$\begin{cases} \dfrac{dm}{dt} = P + an\{1 - k(n-m)\} - cm & (1.12) \\ \dfrac{dn}{dt} = Q + bm\{1 - l(m-n)\} - dn & (1.13) \end{cases}$$

Here, k and l are new constants that represent effects of subservience in response to threat. These constants are greater or equal to 0. If both constants are 0, then we get the previous model. The threat is effective only by the difference in the military forces ($n-m$ for country m and $m-n$ for country n), resulting in a subservient effect.

That is, if m or n are excessively greater than n or m, because k and l are integers, the content of { } becomes negative. This leads to a force reduction, much less expansion, regardless of anxiety parameters, P and Q. These equations can be further arranged as follows:

$$\begin{cases} \dfrac{dm}{dt} = P + an - cm - ak(n^2 - mn) \\ \dfrac{dn}{dt} = Q + bm - dn - bl(m^2 - mn) \end{cases}$$

Compared to the previous mathematical model, with respect to m and n, these equations are no longer linear, and compared to the previous linear differential equations, their general solutions are not known. Using computer software programs, we can only obtain localized, specific numerical solutions for them (*The Mathematics of Nonlinear Phenomena* by Masaya Yamaguchi, Asakura Shoten, 1975, Edition 4).

1.3.4 Certainty Models and Probability Models

Mathematical models could be divided into Certainty Models and Probability Models. Both the previous inventory model and the Richardson Model were certainty models that did not include probability in their problem solutions. The probability models of both inventory and stocks of goods are somewhat different. For example, a retailer stocks certain goods at the beginning of each month. If an item is sold, the profit is 4,000 yen; if not, it will be cleared at the month-end for a loss of 2,000 yen.

The following table is based on the past sales record:

Number of items sold (x)	0	1	2	3	4	5	6	Total
Probability (sales ratio) P(x)	0.0	0.1	0.1	0.2	0.3	0.2	0.1	1.0
Accumulation probability F(x)	0.0	0.1	0.2	0.4	0.7	0.9	1.0	

How many items should be ordered at the beginning of each month?

A probability model applies in this case because the inventory presumes uncertain customers, which is different from the case of a parts warehouse in a factory.

To solve this, we first see what happens if 2 parts are specifically ordered, and calculate the "expectation value" from the number of items sold. When there is a variable (in this case, the number of items sold: 1-6 items); the expectation value corresponds to an average value as the process is repeated many times in which it is the product sum of occurrence probability and values assumed by the variable that is profits or losses.

When 2 items are ordered, the expectation value E of the subtraction of loss from profit (profit balance) can be found below as 7,400 yen.

Number of items sold	0	1	2	3	4	5	6	Expectation value
Profit	0	4,000	8,000	8,000	8,000	8,000	8,000	
Loss	-4,000	-2,000	0	0	0	0	0	
(Expectation value calculation)	-4,000×0	2,000×0.1	8,000×0.1	8,000×0.2	8,000×0,3	8,000×0.2	8,000×0.1	7,400

Similarly, by changing the order volumes to 1, 3, 4, 5, and 6 sequentially, and calculating the expectation values, we get 4,000 yen, 10,200 yen, 11,800 yen, 11,200 yen, and 10,200; therefore, when 4 items are ordered, the expectation value is 11,800 yen, which is the highest.

But this approach is very time consuming. Instead, the following method is used.

Let the profit for one item be "a" yen and the loss for 1 unsold item be "b" yen. "x" in $F(x)$, the accumulation probability, is the optimum order volume when it exceeds $\dfrac{a}{a+b}$ for the first time. In our example,

$$\frac{a}{a+b} = \frac{4,000}{4,000+2,000} = \frac{4}{6} = \frac{2}{3} = 0.67$$

$$F(3) = 0.4 < 0.67 < 0.7 = F(4)$$

Therefore, the optimum order volume is found to be 4. (*Mathematics of Chance* by Ryoichi Takekuma, Kawade Shobo, 1965).

To solve certainty models, algebraic and differential/integral methods are used. The most-commonly used method is Linear Programming (*LP*). Linear programming is used to find the limit values of linear equations under the conditions of linear inequalities. This approach was first devised during World War II to solve a transportation problem. It was an extremely important issue for the United States in transporting massive volumes of men and material across vast areas of the Pacific and Atlantic oceans most efficiently and effectively.

To solve probability models, the probability theory and numerical statistics are used. In addition to LP, various other theories such as information theory and Monte Carlo method, etc. are developed. In particular, The Game Theory established in the 1930s is one of the most effective ways in confrontational and decision-making scenarios. In fact, Boulding has set aside a separate chapter for this case.

It should be kept in mind that all models are abstract. An elegant mathematical model must be kept in perspective and not viewed as a real world model; otherwise, it would be akin to putting the cart before the horse. Simply applying the mathematics does not mean that mistakes can be avoided. One must be constantly mindful of the results so that they do not detach from immediate realities.

Chapter 2

Science of Competition and Lanchester Laws

2.1 The basic forms of competition

2.1.1 The Legacy of F. W. Lanchester

Frederick William Lanchester (1868 – 1946) in 1916 at the age of 48 published *Aircraft in Warfare, the Dawn of the Fourth Arm*, Constable and Co., London, [Reprinted by Lanchester Press, Inc., Sunnyvale 1995, ISBN 1-57321-002-1 -ED]. This book is a compilation of a series of articles he had previously contributed to the British magazine *Engineering*, and was published at his own expense. At the time he was a member of the Advisory Committee for Aeronautics and an engineering consultant to the newly established automobile manufacturers, Daimler and B.S.A., Co. His life history is as follows:

After he graduated from Royal College of Science:

Age 27 – 28, 1895 – 1896.
    Designs and manufactures the first
    British gasoline car.

Age 31, 1889.
    Establishes Lanchester Co.,
    an engineering consulting firm.

Age 39, 1907.
    Publishes *Aerial Flight, Vol. I.*
    Aerodynamics; Vol.II. Aerodonetics.

Age 41 – 52, 1909 – 1920.
Becomes a member of the Advisory Committee for Aeronautics

Age 42 – 62, 1910 – 1930.
Engineering consultant to the automobile manufacturer, Daimler.

Age 60 – 62, 1928 – 1930.
Engineering consultant to the Diesel division of the Beardmore company.

He was also an honorary member of F. R. S., LL. D., and the Royal Aeronautical Society. He died at the age of 78 (1946) in Birmingham, northwest of London, where in nearby Coventry, his papers and notebooks are preserved in the library.

>Lanchester Library
>Priory St.,
>Coventry, CV1 5FB, England.

He married Dorothea, daughter of Thomas Cooper, a priest, in 1919 and had no children. Lanchester made great theoretical and practical contributions to the creation of gasoline engines employed in cars and aircraft as an aeronautics engineer. Specially, his books, *Aerial Flight*, Vol. I., *Aerodynamics*; Vol. II., *Aerodonetics*, published in 1907 were groundbreaking at the time.

Bernoulli's (Swiss mathematician, 1700 – 1782) principles explain the aerodynamic lift that allows an aircraft to fly. When an aircraft flies horizontally at a constant speed, forces of lift and weight, as well as thrust and drag act on the aircraft's center of gravity, as shown in the figure.

Among these forces, thrust and drag come from the air. When all these four forces are balanced, the external forces acting on the aircraft will be equal to zero, and according to Newton's second law, the aircraft then will keep flying.

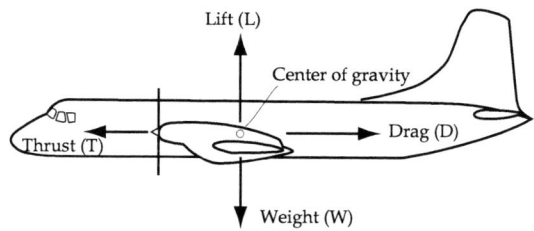

Balance of forces in a horizontal flight.

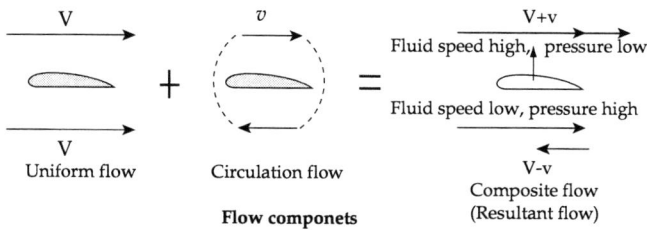

Flow componets

When the wing moves forward through the air, other than a uniform airflow with a velocity of V, it also creates a vortex, which results from air viscosity, that circulates around the wing. Because this vortex adheres to the wing it is called the binding vortex. The velocity of the circulating flow (v) is added to the velocity of the uniform flow (V) at the top surface of the wing and subtracted from the velocity of the uniform flow (V) at the lower surface of the wing. According to Bernoulli's principles, where the fluid speed is high, the pressure is low, and where the fluid speed is low, the pressure is high. Therefore, an upward lift is applied to the wing from below the wing. The same principle is true when a baseball player throws a curve ball. The ball curves in the direction where the spin is applied. The lift (L) is expressed as follows (from *Why Airplanes Fly* by Jiro Kondo — Kodansha Blue Books, P-256, 1975):

C_L is lift coefficient that depends on wing type and wing inclination angle

ρ is air density, V is air velocity

S is wing surface area

$$L = C_L \frac{1}{2} \rho V^2 S \ (kg/m^2)$$

$\frac{1}{2}\rho V^2$ is called dynamic pressure

The above principles apply to wings that are infinitely long (2-dimensional wings); however, actual wings have definite lengths (3-dimensional wings), and the flow of air at the wing edge cannot be ignored. At the wing edge, the high-pressure air below the wing surface attempts to run around into the low-pressure air above the wing surface. This is called the wing-edge vortex.

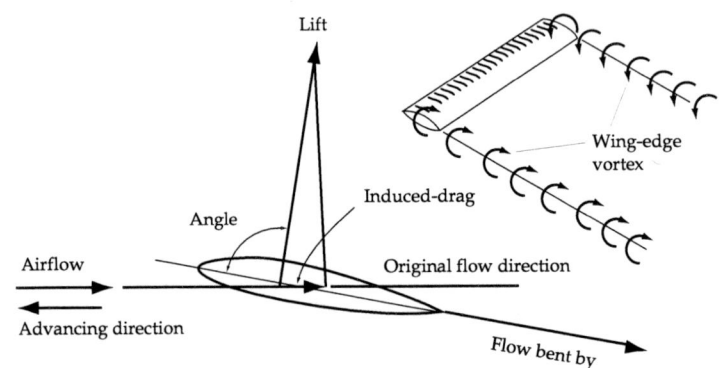

Why is Induced Drag generated?

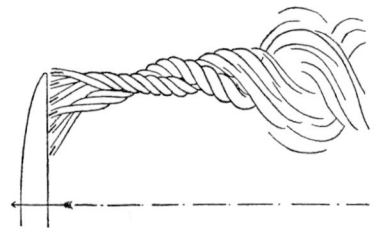

The structure of vortex around the wing as illustrated by Lanchester

When the wing-edge vortex is created, the flow that impacts the wing is affected and becomes somewhat inclined downward. Because the direction of the lift, which is perpendicular to the airflow, is inclined backward against the advancing direction of the airplane, a backward force is created in the thrust. This acts as a drag and is therefore called "induced drag." According to the theory of wings, the induced lift coefficient for a finite (3-dimensional) wing is proportionate to the square of lift coefficient. Because the wing-edge vortex gains lift, a drag is induced. If lift can be likened to revenue, the induced drag is a tax paid on this revenue.

The smaller the interval between the wing edges, the greater the induced drag. A glider has insufficient thrust by itself; therefore, it must have very long and slender wings. Because the wing-edge vortex has no core, it is released from both wing edges in the form of a vortex. This vortex is called a free vortex as compared to a binding vortex. With large jet airplanes, this free vortex can be sufficiently strong to cause a light aircraft to crash.

The person who studied such finite (3-dimensional) wings for the first time was none other than Lanchester. His work was later incorporated by German physicist, Ludwig Prandtl (1875 – 1953), in the *Theory of Wings*, and is know today as the Lanchester-Prandtl Theory of Three Dimensional Wings.

2.1.2 Lanchester's N–Squared Law

Lanchester, who was one of the first aeronautical engineers was also one of the first who recognized the dramatic effects of airplanes on the character and conduct of warfare. Of course, with the start of World War I (July 1914), some progressive military officers also came to the realization that airplanes were going to change the way wars were fought. But Lanchester was the first person to study the effects of airplanes on warfare quantitatively as well as numerically.

He included the result of his studies in his book, *Warfare and Aircraft*. He wrote "Most of warfare tactics that up to this point have been carried out by the army would be carried out by the air force in a similar or even a greater degree. Once this fact is verified, the number of aircraft used by the military is bound to increase a great deal more. This means that the outcome of future warfare will be decided by the air power."

His recommendations in the book, *Aircraft in Warfare*, was adopted by the British army major, David Henderson, on whose suggestion the War Priorities Committee in August 1917 made a recommendation to the war cabinet. Consequently, in April 1918, an independent British Air Force and the Ministry of Air Force was established by the wartime cabinet of Lloyd George. Ironically, Lord Trenchard who was appointed commander in chief of the Royal Air Force was originally opposed to the establishment of an independent British Air Force. However, by the end of World War I (November 1918), large-scale retaliatory air strikes by his new air force hastened Germany's decision to end the war. At least, through psychological effects, they caused interruption in the production of military goods in the Rein region (Liddell Hart, *History of the First World War*, Charles E. Tuttle Co., Inc., 1934. Translated by Tatsuo Uemura, Fuji Publications, 1976).

Lanchester, in order to prove the impact of the aircraft in warfare, was forced to mathematically analyze the balance of power between two opposing forces in a battle. The following are some of the questions he faced.

Under what conditions could a weaker force beat a stronger one?

Could the concentration of fire power be explained in terms of mathematical equations?

That being the case, if mathematical equations that express such processes were used, then what would be the outcome in a battle between forces and what outcome could be expected?

Could such results be expressed mathematically?

He eventually was able to come up with a succinct and simple equation for these problems. This is called Lanchester's N^2 Law. To devise his law, Lanchester conducted a quantitative study of the amount of damage suffered by two fighting parties in several land, sea, and air battles in the past. Lanchester refers to this law in Chapters 5, 6, 14, and 18 of his book, *Warfare and Aircraft*. The following is a summary of the Lanchester Law extracted from his book:

The Law of Concentration.

In the present dire situation, fundamentals of war must be studied in detail both in theory and in practice (from a practical perspective). One of the main issues that lie at the heart of strategy is concentration. This means the concentration of warring nations' total resources into a single target or goal. At the same time, this means the concentration of main forces of navies or armies into a single point within a tactical theater. But the Law of Concentration is not just a strategic law but it is mostly applied to purely tactical operations and is recognized on the logistical side based on facts and scientific method.

This point is somewhat obfuscated by a great number of authorities. That is because, two different aspects — mental concentration (clear and accurate definition and specification of a target) and logistical concentration — are both wrapped into one general expression. Some people try to apply to the word, concentration, a unique nuance. But in reality, the word used in these two different applications has totally different meanings and there is no common basis.

The importance of concentration in logistics is based on the basic laws concerning offense and defense.

To understand the true value and importance of concentration in logistics, one should not pay serious attention to the superficiality of concentration. Attention must rather be directed to the basic principles of concentration. Also, in searching for the control factor of logistical concentration, the more rational basic issues must be considered.

Comparing conditions for ancient wars and modern wars.

There is one major difference between ancient wars and modern wars in the method of defense. Let's use this to explain the problem at hand. In the ancient wars, a weapon corresponded to another weapon one-to-one. Defensive behaviors were direct and positive. If the offense was carried with a sword or an ax, then the defense was put up with a sword or a shield. In modern terms, an artillery gun corresponds to an artillery gun, a rifle attack is defended with a rifle, and an artillery attack is defended with an artillery piece. But defense against modern weapons is indirect. In other words, since eliminating the enemy is to defend oneself, the battle is necessarily conducted through large groups. As a result, through history, the importance of concentration is not recognized.

Under ancient conditions, normally, an individual soldier corresponded to another individual soldier; consequently, there were no strategic planning or tactics other than matching the approximate number of soldiers on the battlefield. Even though applying twice as many soldiers in some areas of a battle field could be considered a general practice, the number of soldiers on the battlefield at any given time remained approximately equal on both sides (as long as the battle was not lost). In modern warfare, however, this is totally different.

Under modern warfare conditions, with the introduction of long-range weapons such as artillery guns, the concentration of a superior force is superior directly from the aspect of force involved in the actual battle. A numerically inferior force, rather than being targeted one soldier at a time, is additionally exposed to severe artillery fire. The importance of this difference is far greater than one can imagine. I would like to describe this subject in great detail because it contains all the issues critical to the questions raised here.

By comparing the ancient and modern conditions, to a certain degree, there is no suggestion that the strength of concentration did not exist in ancient times. For example, when an army is defeated and is on the run, the superiority in number for the victor is decisive. Even prior to a victory or defeat, independent of the attack, the pressure from the superiority in number itself undoubtedly affects the outcome to a great degree. Furthermore, although bow and arrow, and spear are less effective weapons than guns, the more they are available (within a limit), the more effective they can be concentrated on a small army. These conditions are extreme forms in such comparisons, which I brought up here for the purpose of my discussion.

Let's assume under the ancient battle conditions, where soldiers face each other one-on-one, the fire power is equal on both sides; clearly, on average, the whole battle will consist of numerous single battles (duels) and the number of soldiers killed will be roughly equal to the number of soldiers fighting.

And, let's assume 1000 soldiers (army A) fight another 1000 soldiers (army B). Army A (1000) and army B (1000) can either make a one-time battle, or army A can concentrate its 1000 on 500 of army B, and after eliminating them, proceed to destroy the remaining 500 of army B (either way the result would be the same).

Assuming that army B does not lose its will to fight throughout the battle, once army A eliminates half of army B in the first battle, it is already reduced to half its size (see note); thus, the second battle begins with an equal number of soldiers on both sides (army A, 500, and army B, 500).

(Note: Strictly speaking, this is not accurate. As the battle approaches its end, the small number of soldiers remaining in the losing army will come under attack by a greater number of winning soldiers, which means fewer casualties among the winning army. Still, this does not violate the basic principle here).

Studying the modern conditions.

Now let's us consider the modern conditions. Again, even when the fire power is equal on both sides, even when the number of forces (soldiers) are equal, each individual soldier is different (i.e., "is hidden," and so on). Every soldier on average has a certain hit rate that brings down an enemy within a certain amount of time. Therefore, the number of casualties brought down per unit of time would be directly proportionate to the number of opposing soldiers. Expressed mathematically, let b be the number of soldiers in army A and r be the number of soldiers in army B, then:

$$\frac{db}{dt} = -r \times c \quad (1)$$

$$\frac{dr}{dt} = -b \times k \quad (2)$$

Here, t is time, and c and k are proportional constants (c = k, when the fire power of each soldier is equal).

Validity of the mathematical process.

Many people censure the mathematical process of the subject of concentration. They maintain that attempting to calculate anything and everything such as human morale and leadership, the strengths and weaknesses of weapons, which cannot be measured, and "combat chance," which is even more full of ambiguity, is ludicrous just because there are so many unknown factors. The response to this is very simple. It is very common to directly and numerically compare the forces that participate in battles or can be used in wars. They also have been discussed in newspapers in some detail. Furthermore, even though such extreme force calculations tacitly consent to the validity of mathematical principles, they are only limited to special cases. It should be noted, however, that unconditional and simple calculations of fire power, and denying the expanded application of mathematical theories are similar to employing a scale as a precision tool broadly and without discretion, which is an irrational and unintelligent practice. Specially, in the application of mathematical theories, for example, as in the case of the principle of lever, not allowing for any modifications would be too extreme.

Inequality of the unit of fire power.

In equations (1) and (2), we assumed that both k and c are equal. This means, we have assumed the fire power of each unit is equal. This condition, of course, is not met when the training and morale of the fighting forces are not equal. In addition, even if the efficiency of the weapons were different, this condition is still not met. Training and morale, along with other mental factors, cannot be measured in the same way wine or steel are measured in terms of their weight, and cannot be rendered into mathematical equations. However, the problem of the weapons clearly can be studied logically. Also, as shown below, we can study those issues raised here.

The effect of weapon efficiency.

The difference in the efficiency of weapons — for example, accuracy and firing speed of rifles — can be shown through the difference of c and k, constants in the differential equations (1) and (2). In the simple case of a rifle or a machine gun, the efficiency of the weapons can be expressed sufficiently and the comparison values can be easily obtained.

If numerically the forces are equal but the fire power is unequal; that is, even though the number of forces are equal, the numeric balance of power changes, and the result changes as well. Let's assume that army A with a force of 500 equipped with machine guns attacks army B with a force of 1000 equipped with rifles, and after the lapse of a certain amount of time, the loss among army A is 100 against a loss of 200 among army B, and let's assume that there is no change in the balance of force, then (since army A is superior) 100 versus 200 is deemed equal fighting power.

Let M represent the efficiency and value of each unit of army A and N represent the same for army B. Then the ratio of loss for army A and army B can be shown as follows:

$$\frac{db}{dt} = -Nr \times (\text{Proportional constant}) \quad (3)$$

$$\frac{dr}{dt} = -Mb \times (\text{Proportional constant}) \quad (4)$$

Here, the condition for equality is (Note: to obtain a value for each unit; that is, to render a value for each soldier, a division by the number of each force, b and r, is performed):

$$\frac{1}{b} \cdot \frac{db}{dt} = \frac{1}{r} \cdot \frac{dr}{dt}$$

Therefore,

$$\frac{1}{b} \times (-Nr) = \frac{1}{r} \times (-Mb)$$

And as a result, $Nr^2 = Mb^2$ \quad (5)

In other words, the fighting strength of the two forces becomes equal when the fighting value (efficiency) of each unit multiplied by the square of the number of each force are equal.

The result of the study. The N^2 law.

It is easy to rephrase the meaning of equation (5) in a simpler way.

Fighting strength can be defined broadly as proportionate to the fighting value of each unit multiplied by the square of the number of each force.

A numeric example.

As an example of what we discussed here, let's assume an army of 50,000 fights with two armies of 40,000 and 30,000 in that order and with similar equipment. Since $50,000^2 = 40,000^2 + 30,000^2$, therefore the fighting strength is equal on both sides.

If one side, that is, the inferior armies are given the time to join forces, the 50,000 army will be destroyed. This is because the fighting power for the 70,000 army will no longer be equal, and from the actual relation of 49 to 25, the gap in strength will be twice as wide.

To calculate the outcome, many exceptional qualities such as high morale and superior tactics must be factored in; nonetheless, this does not invalidate the numerical explanation.

An example of when the fighting strength is different.

Here, let's give an example where the difference in the fighting value for a unit is a factor. From many experiences, let's assume that a soldier with a machine gun has approximately 16 times as many hits as one with a rifle within a given amount of time. How many soldiers with machine guns are required to replace 1000 infantrymen on a battlefield? Let the fighting value for a rifle be the unit (of measurement), and the required number be n. Because the fighting strength of the infantry battalion is $1,000^2$, then:

$$n = \sqrt{\frac{1,000,000}{16}} = \frac{1,000}{4} = 250$$

Consequently, n is equal to one-forth of the opposing force.

This example provides us with many insights, and at the same time, with effects and strengths of this method. The basic premise calls for the exact concentration of the fire power of each soldier upon the enemy soldier. That is, the enemy concentrates the fire power distributed among four infantrymen upon a machine gunner. Therefore, a machine gunner lasts on average 1/4 of an hour, and during that short period of time, is 16 times more efficient, but in fact, he is merely doing the job of 4 rifle handlers instead of 16 soldiers.

This is a case of sharp shooting one enemy at a time as in the Boer war (see note). That is, this case applies when the battle formation is based on a sniper shooting.

(Note: The Dutch, Huguenot, and German ancestors of the Boers first settled in the Cape of South Africa in 1652. In the 1870s, diamonds and minerals were discovered in two Boer countries, the Transvaal Republic and the Orange Free State. This lead to the British encroachment. On October 11, 1890, these two countries join forces against the British and fighting pursues. The British win a victory against a vastly outnumbered army of 20,000 Boers and subsequently declare the annexation of the two countries. The campaign then turns into a prolonged guerrilla war.

In 1902, all of South Africa falls under the British rule. To clean up the guerrillas, the British begin to hold civilian prisoners, almost all of them women and children, putting them in concentration camps, and burning down farms and villages. Reports about these camps shocks the entire civilized world, bringing criticism against the British. These events eventually lead to the establishment of the South African Republic and the Apartheid policy.)

On the other hand, under circumstances where the possibility of concentration is excluded, such as when searching a territory or a mountain edge from a distance, or volley-firing upon a spot of land or defenseless people, this basic assumption will not be valid. That is, the value of the weapons for each machine gunner is sixteen times greater than the infantryman gunner as represented by the fire power. The same is true when a machine gunner opposes a weapon that targets a spot of land rather than a grenade or an individual.

I would like to call attention to the nature of resulting prejudice from logical conclusions and variations in the conditions. These variations are far less in the sea battle compared to the land battle, and each unit — ship — becomes always a target of attack.

With regard to the airplane, conditions here are very similar to that being obtained via the navy rather than the army. That is, rather than a group of objects, each enemy plane in the air is a target of attack, and the following rule applies:

Modifying the hypothesis.

Even when deviating from the main subject, the policy of this logic is certainly interesting and very precise, and it leads to a somewhat unpredictable conclusion. If the initial hypothesis is modified to the conditions of long-range artillery, assuming that the artillery bombardment is concentrated on a certain region secured by the enemy, and assuming that this region is not affected by the number of enemy force, then following the previously shown equations

$$\left.\begin{aligned}-\frac{db}{dt} &= b \times Nr \\ -\frac{dr}{dt} &= r \times Mb\end{aligned}\right\} \times \text{(Constant)} \qquad \begin{aligned}-M\frac{db}{dt} &= Mb \cdot Nr \\ -N\frac{dr}{dt} &= Nr \cdot Mb\end{aligned}$$

(Note: In this case, the ratio of loss is considered to be proportional to one's own number of men.)

Therefore,

$$M\frac{db}{dt} = N\frac{dr}{dt}$$

The loss ratio is not affected by the number of fighting men, but is directly affected by the value of the weapons. Under these conditions, the fighting power is proportionate to the number of men, and there is no direct advantage of concentration, but the advantage of rapid fire is relatively great; therefore, these conditions become close to those of the ancient wars.

(Note: In this case, the value of the weapons is not different by each unit and remains the same; therefore, each army does not need to be converted to units.)

Therefore, similar conditions become:

$$\frac{db}{dt} = \frac{dr}{dt}$$

And from equations (3) and (4):

$$\frac{db}{dt} = -Nr \times \text{(Constant)} \qquad \frac{dr}{dt} = -Mb \times \text{(Constant)}$$

Thus: $Nr = Mb$ \quad (6)

In other words, the following definition can be declared: When a war is fought by individual versus individual (unit versus unit), then the fighting strength is proportionate to the square of the value of the weapons per unit for each individual multiplied by the number of men. The previous equation (5) applies to the case where a war is fought group versus group.

Unexpected result.

It goes without saying that for the superior side in terms of the number of men to achieve a greater concentration effect, it must approach the enemy as closely as possible, or it must enter a clear shooting range as quickly as possible.

In an extreme case, let's assume army A with 100 men equipped with machine guns is fighting army B with 1,200 men equipped with rifles. We assume both armies are spread across a certain front line and are at a long range. We also assume that the loss ratio of army B against army A is 16. If war could go on under such conditions, then army B would be destroyed. But if army B makes an attack and closes up to a distance where each man and each gunner becomes an individual target, then the scene will change and the above equations and conditions will apply.

For example, even if army B loses half its men in order to capture new positions, army B still wins the battle with a remaining force of 600 men. This is because the total fighting strength on both sides is army B $600^2 \times 1$ versus army A $100^2 \times 6$.

It should be noted, however, with such weapons as machine guns that carry a high kill ratio, one cannot totally rule out that under certain conditions, such close encounters may not actually occur.

Specific historical examples.

Most authorities agree that on a battlefield, concentration is the most important issue. In fact, it is well-recognized that in the modern warfare, both strategically and tactically, concentration is one of the factors that must be managed. The theory of concentration is explained appropriately by the remarkable outcome of major historical battles in which attacks on opposing forces have been documented.

One example is Napoleon's defeat of the Austrian army near Verona in North Italy during the campaign of Italy. Before two flanks of the Austrian army joined ranks, he dealt with them separately (Note: The battle of Castiglion, August 5, 1796). Another well-known example is the defeat of Moreau army and Jourdan army at the Danube shore by Archduke Charles in 1796.

Regardless of the extent of differences in conditions involved in large-area battlefields where military tactics unfolded, in essence, these examples correspond to the previous hypothesis and the rules derived from it. That is, the fighting strength of any given force is represented by the square of the number of men.

Nelson's memo and Battle Plan.

To confuse the enemy's advance force and to effectively prevent the enemy from joining the battle, the attack plan called for an allocation of force so that a small number of ships were assigned to block the advance of the advance fleet. In short, fighting on a small scale regardless of other forces is clearly a losing battle. On this subject, Nelson's memo includes the following (Note: 12 days prior to the Trafalgar naval battle on October 21, 1805). Before the start of the battle, Nelson estimated that there would be 40 ships in his fleet and 46 in the France-Spain coalition. These numbers were in reality much higher than the actual numbers of ships that finally engaged in the battle (Note: 27 versus 37), but here let's study Nelson's memo not the actual battle.

Nelson divides the British navy into 2 main ranks of 16 ships each and a small rank of 8 ships. The predefined plan of attack, which was going to unfold as soon as the enemy fleet was detected at the front, is shown concisely as follows: One of the main ranks divides the enemy fleet in two. Another main rank attacks the 12 ships from behind. The small rank engages with 3 to 4 ships from the center of the enemy fleet. It must block the enemy front from aiding their embattled center or rear to the greatest degree possible. In a word, the goal is to prevent the advance force in the enemy coalition from joining the main battle. The plan can be illustrated as in the following figure.

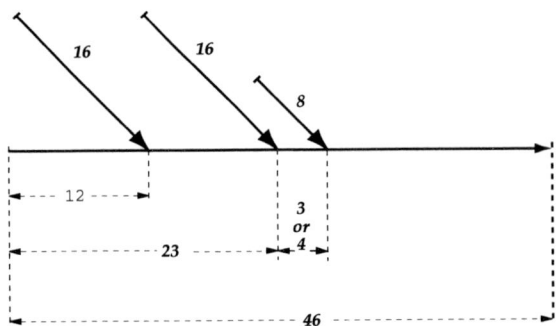

Analyzing Nelson's tactics.

Studying the numbers from the previous fleet formation is very insightful. The total number of ships planned by Nelson to surround half of the joint enemy force, that is 23 ships, were 32. According to the N Square Law, this definitely brings about a superiority of 2 to 1 in terms of fighting strength (Note: 32^2 vs. 23^2, or 1.9 vs. 1). Even if the loss inflicted by the other 8 ships is not taken into account, and the fighting with the other half of the coalition force continues, the fighting continues only under similar conditions. In fact, the advance fleet in the coalition incurs certain losses when it encounters the small British flotilla. This tactic realizes the aggressive strength and the best result that can be derived from the British fighting strength. These circumstances can be calculated as follows (Note: based on an arbitrary n^2 unit):

British fighting strength: $32^2 + 8^2 = 1{,}088$
Coalition fighting strength: $23^2 + 23^2 = 1{,}058$

British force advantage: $= 30$

That is, the number of ships surviving in the British force is the square root of $\sqrt{30}$, or approximately five and a half ships (assuming the battle continues to the end).

For comparison, if the battle were fought under conditions that the commander of French forces, Villeneuve, described excellently as "conventional" (Note: fighting in parallel with enemy), then the outcome would be:

$$
\begin{array}{ll}
\text{Fighting strength coalition:} & 46^2 = 2{,}116 \\
\text{Fighting strength British force:} & 40^2 = 1{,}600 \\
\hline
\text{Enemy force advantage:} & = 516
\end{array}
$$

That is, even if the British force was totally destroyed, the survivors of the coalition would be equal to the square root of $\sqrt{516}$, or approximately 23 ships. This explains the importance of a right stratagem in leadership. If the conventional stratagem was adopted in the actual battle, it would be very doubtful if the exalted British naval spirit or their superiority in gunnery could have been saved from destructive attacks. The actual force on the day of battle was 27 ships on the British side against 33 ships on the coalition side.

This was a far worse ratio than what Nelson predicted in his memo (Note: 46^2 vs. 40^2 is approximately 1.32 vs. 1, and 33^2 vs. 27^2 is approximately 1.49 vs. 1). In the actual naval battle, the British force attacked the coalition with 2 flotillas rather than 3 as indicated in the memo; however, the tactics of concentration was observed. In reality, since there was almost no wind, removing the advance force of the enemy from the battle with 2 flotillas was quite sufficient. But when analyzing the memo, it includes far more important facts than those in the actual events.

That is, in this analysis, first, the expression of dividing the enemy into two equal parts — or according to the N^2 Law, to a ratio that minimizes the loss to one's own forces — is particularly important. Second, other important facts are finding a force capable of dealing with each half of the enemy force on an equal footing, the selection of a ratio that is the closest integer value that corresponds to the theory of the square root of 2, and directing the remaining 8 ships to the front half of the coalition to wear down and prevent the enemy force in an attempt to bring success to the main battle plan.

On a fair evaluation, rather than a random coincidence (see Note), even though Nelson probably did not know about the n^2 Law, this case must have been based on enough conviction on his part in estimating the value of his own tactics.

(Note: As experiments show, this is considered to be a case where the conclusion is reached at an arrangement that is logically proved positive, but the coincidence is just too remarkable.)

2.1.3 Two basic models for competition

There is a special room in the Museum of Industrial Technology in Coventry where Lanchester-related books and private documents are on display. These items span such varied topics as aeronautics, economy, industry, the theory of relativity, fiscal policies, and military strategy. This display shows Lanchester's breath of interests and that he was not merely an engineer.

The real gem in Lanchester's quantitative analysis of battles is his unique insight that even though the number of forces on both sides may be equal, their fighting strengths depend on how they engage in a battle. Let's look at his equation one more time. Assuming that army A and army B are engaged in a battle:

The number of forces in army A: b. The efficiency of weapons per unit: M
The number of forces in army B: r. The efficiency of weapons per unit: N

The battle can be largely fought in two ways: One model is a duel model where swords, spears, bows and arrows, or at most, rifles are used in single man-to-man combats, and the other model is a group-to-group model where machine guns and artillery are used in large- and wide-scale fighting.

In the case of single combats, the fighting strengths of opposing forces are only equal if the products of the number of forces and the efficiency of the weapons per unit are equal. Or, expressed mathematically:

$$Mb = Nr \quad \begin{pmatrix} \text{Lanchester does not directly show this equation,} \\ \text{but as noted previously, we can obtain this} \\ \text{equation (6) by summarizing his views.} \end{pmatrix}$$

In other words, the fighting strength of a force is proportional to the number of force multiplied by the efficiency of the weapons per unit. That is, the fighting strength and the amount of attack against an enemy can be defined as follows:

Single combat:
(Fighting strength) = (Weapon efficiency) × (Force) (2.1)

Naturally, to win against the enemy; i.e., to increase one's fighting strength, when forces are equal, one must increase the weapon efficiency, and if the weapon efficiencies are equal, then the force must be increased.

During the Japanese civil wars, Nobunaga was a general who increased his forces' weapon efficiency by forming rifle troops and won a victory (in the battle of Nagashino against Katsuyori Takeda), and Hideyoshi Toyotomi was a general who won by superiority of the number of his forces. For example, in the battle of Yamazaki, Hideyoshi massed 40,000 men against Mitsuhide Akechi's force of 17,000 men. Losses on Hideyoshi's side were 3,300 men and on Mitsuhide's side were 3,000 men, roughly equal numbers (*The History of Japanese Battles* by Mitsutoshi Takayanagi and Akira Suzuki, Gakugeishorin Publications, 1968).

$$Mb^2 = Nr^2$$

On the other hand, in "group-to-group combat," the fighting strength of a force is proportional to the square of the number of forces multiplied by the efficiency of the weapons. That is, the fighting strength and the amount of attack against an enemy can be defined as follows:

Group-to-group combat:
(Fighting strength) = (Weapon efficiency) × (Force)²   (2.2)

As described above, in single combat, the force and weapon efficiency work equally toward the fighting strength; however, in group-to-group combat, the force has a far greater influence on the fighting strength. In other words, to win in such a combat, it is more important to increase the concentration of force than to increase the weapon efficiency.

Conversely, with the weapon efficiencies being equal, the enemy's force must be divided. Nelson's tactics simply followed this rule. Lanchester himself emphasized group-to-group combat and presented "the Law of N^2" as a phenomenological model and a certainty model. The battle and competition of opposing forces can be divided into two basic models: the single combat, which is an accumulation of duels, and the wide-area, total group-to-group combat.

Lanchester divided the opposing forces in each basic model into two elements and studied them quantitatively: the fighting strength (the efficiency of weapons) and volume of attack (force). Currently, what is commonly known as the first law of Lanchester, Lanchester's Linear Law, refers to the analysis of the single combat, and the second law of Lanchester, Lanchester's Square Law, refers to the analysis of the group-to-group combat.

2.1.4 Contributions of the U.S. Navy OR research team

These two laws were not presented in such a sequence until the Second World War (1940s). Theodore von Kármán (1881-1963) a disciple of German Prantdtl who came to the U.S. invited by California Engineering University in 1930 and acted as the head of research at the Gugenheim Aeronautics Research Center, and as chairman at National Advisory Committee for Aeronautics (NACA), the forerunner of NASA as well as NATO's Advisory Committee for Aeronautics Research and Development, writes about Lanchester as follows:

> ... I still remember; I visited him in the summer of 1912 at the fifth international mathematical conference in England. We met at Cambridge and then he took me on a tour of various places. He drove me in his car at a frightening speed on narrow English roads. This was my first experience in a car, so I was somewhat nervous to discuss aeronautics at such a high speed, but he was completely oblivious. He was very versatile and full of creativity. For example, during World War I, he published his theory of tactics; however, a few years ago, when a read in Operational Analysis, one of the first military science books in America, I was surprised to see that it started with Lanchester's Theory. ("Aerodynamics," Kármán Th., von, Cornell University Press, 1954).

What surprised Kármán is the OR classic, *Methods of Operations Research*, Morse and Kimball, The MIT Press, 1950. And here, the prestigious title of Father of OR is bestowed on Lanchester. Philip M. Morse (1903 –) graduated from Princeton University and became a physics professor at MIT (1930 – 1967), the head of the Computing Center (1956 – 1968), and the head of the OR Center (1958-1970). His book, *Library Effectiveness: A Systems Approach* (1968) received the Lanchester Award ($1,000) from the American OR Society. He also attended the OR Joint International Conference in Japan in 1975.

George E. Kimball (1906 – 1967) was a professor of chemistry at Columbia University and after retirement became vice chairman at Arthur D. Little, Inc., one of the few mathematical based consulting firms in America.

During World War II, American scientists were also drafted. Morse acted as an investigator for the Navy Weapons Organization Evaluation Team and Kimball acted as a deputy for the Navy Operations Group (Strategy Research Team). Specially, in 1942, when the U.S. OR team was formed in response to the formation of transport convoys to deal with U boats, various research projects were conducted by Bernard O. Koopman (1900 –), the professor of mathematics at Columbia University, Arthur A. Brown, and others. This lead to the development of the Lanchester Law and the establishment of Lanchester's Strategic Equations.

Brown continued his activities at the OR Group, which became part of the Defense Department after World War II, and in 1952, moved to Arthur D. Little, Inc. Koopman also after retiring from Columbia University (1927 –1968) followed Kimball to the same company. He visited Japan for the OR Joint International Conference with Morse in 1975, and published *Air-Terminal Queues under Time-Dependent Conditions*.

2.2 Lanchester's Linear Law

2.2.1 Single combats and the ratio of forces in duels

Let's consider the ratio of forces and men in the case of single combat, which is an accumulation of duels. Let's assume that army m and army n clash and the efficiency and performance of their weapons are mutually equal.

For example, m is 3 and n is 2; m_1 battles n_1, m_2 battles n_2, and n_3 is left without an opposing force to fight. The following diagram shows these relationships.

The case of duel (single combat)

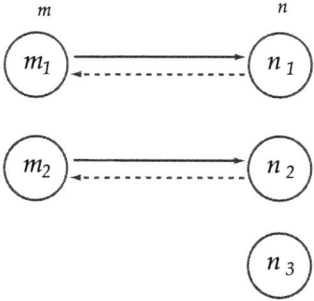

The force ratio $\dfrac{1}{1} \times 2 : \dfrac{1}{1} \times 3 = 2 : 3$

Even in the Genpei era, where swords, spears, and bows and arrows were used, or in the Japanese civil wars era, where Tanegashima rifles were used, after hand-to-hand combat, to kill off an enemy, one must cut the enemy's throat with a dagger. But in this case, the side who won the duel himself sustained extensive injuries and was in no shape to face another enemy, fresh and with full strength. The same situation applies to combative sports such as Sumo, Judo, and boxing, where fighting parties are of equal strength.

That is, the fighting strength of army m in terms of a force that corresponds one-to-one equals 2 units, and the fighting strength of army n in terms of a force that corresponds one-to-one equals 3 units.

Since these forces clash, then, $\dfrac{1}{1} \times 2 : \dfrac{1}{1} \times 3$, and the ratio of fighting strength is 2:3, which is equal to the number of forces (men) army m and army n have committed.

Thus, in the case of single combat, which is an accumulation of duels, if the efficiency of weapons is equal on both sides, then the side with the greater number of men, which has a free force (without opposition), will win, or have the advantage. The famous Prussian strategist, Karl von Clausewitz (1780 – 1831), also writes if there are no differences in the weapons, troops formation, and various techniques, no matter how capable a general may be, it is very difficult to beat an enemy twice in size (Karl von Clausewitz, *The Theory of War*).

With the start of World War I, Lanchester became very interested in the application of airplanes, to which he had been contributing, in the war. In the first month of the war, airplanes were used in aerial reconnaissance (men were flown for direct ground observation). Next, their missions included the observation of artillery targets. This was first accomplished using different colors of light for a signal, and later, wireless communication was employed.

Aerial photography was also tried; other attempts included the observation of the situation of one's own infantry on the ground, and gathering of information on the possibility of any counterattacks by the enemy. These actions lead to a natural willingness to interfere with the enemy's information gathering activities, which in turn lead to aerial combats, and escalated the drive for dominance of the sky.

There are numerous aerial battle movies that are based on this period. Among them are such classics as "Wings," staring Gary Cooper, "Hell's Angles," directed by Howard Hughes. More recent movies include "Blue Max ," "Telemark's Fortress ," 1976, "The Great Air Force Strategy," and "Sky Ace," directed by S. Benjamin Feez , featuring such British airplanes as the S.E.5a, among others. All these fighter planes had multiple wings. The fighter plane loved above all by the legendary Red Baron of Germany, Captain Manfred von Richtoven, was the Foker Dr. 1, a 3-wing craft.

As shown in the data chart, the speed of these fighter planes on either side (friends and foes) was less than that of today's bullet trains, and in the beginning, only rifles and pistols were used, and they had to make close, visual contacts with the enemy before shooting effectively. Such encounters were therefore very idyllic and resembled duels. Soon after, machine guns were installed, which lead to accidents and crashes by hitting one's own propeller with the machine gun. A year after the start of WWI, beginning with Germany's Foker fighter plane, synchronized devices were used to guide the bullets through the propellers without smashing them. This brought severe and huge losses to the British fighter planes. The average survival time of young pilots sent to the front after a little more than 10 hours of training was only about 12 days.

In 1916, entering the second year of the war, a new method called "circus" was developed, mainly by Germans, which was based on a special flying formation. In this formation, a commander is selected, who in turn selects his own pilot, and then forms a special company. This company can then be flown dynamically, and whenever needed on an order from the higher command, to any part of the front to skillfully gain air supremacy. It was obvious that a squadron of fighter planes was superior to a single aircraft, but in real numbers, it did not mean that the smaller squadrons were more likely to be shot down and defeated. This was where the "veteran" came to the fore.

Among these veteran sky fighters, Germany's Boelcke, Richthoven, and Immelmann; France's Guynemer and Fonck; Britain's Mannok and Ball are also famous. They were able to perform some very complex aerial acts and maneuvers, such as tailspins and surprise attacks from behind, to compensate any numeric inferiority, and increase the winning advantage through superior skills and techniques even though the efficiency of the weapons were equal.

Lanchester's efficiency of the weapons was limited directly to measurable efficiency of the weapons (for example, the number of shots per unit of time), but specially in single combats, skills and the participation of veterans cannot be ignored. As a result, the efficiency of the weapons can be measured from the amount of losses sustained by both sides; therefore, skills and experience can be factored into the efficiency of the weapons.

2.2.2 Differential equations in single combats and duels

Let's assume army m and army n enter a combat, and Let's assume the efficiency of the weapons and skills for army m to be b, and for army n to be a. The survival rates of both armies at any given time can be represented as follows:

$$\begin{cases} \dfrac{1}{1} \cdot \dfrac{dm}{dt} = -a \\ \dfrac{1}{1} \cdot \dfrac{dn}{dt} = -b \end{cases} \text{...that is,} \quad \begin{cases} \dfrac{dm}{dt} = -a & (2.1) \\ \dfrac{dn}{dt} = -b & (2.2) \end{cases}$$

a and b are arbitrary

These equations are similar to that of the rate of depreciation (continuous fixed depreciation) as discussed in Chapter 1. Because mutual depreciation rates depend on the efficiency of the weapons, the survival rates are represented as a system of equations.

To study the ratio of survival rates, let army m be the reference, then

$$\dfrac{\dfrac{1}{1} \cdot \dfrac{dn}{dt}}{\dfrac{1}{1} \cdot \dfrac{dm}{dt}} = \dfrac{-b}{-a} \qquad \dfrac{\dfrac{dn}{dt}}{\dfrac{dm}{dt}} = \dfrac{b}{a}$$

The time unit is common to both armies and can be reduced from the denominator and the numerator. Let E represent the ratio of the efficiencies of the weapons and skills for two armies, or $\dfrac{b}{a} = E$, then

British S.E. 5a   Fokker Dr. 1

Data chart of Germany's main fighter planes

Name	Fokker E3	Fokker D3	Albatros D.5a	Fokker Dr.1	Fokker D.7
Number of Crew	1	1	1	1	1
Engine	Uberursel	Mercedes	Mercedes	Uberursel	Mercedes/BMW
Horse Power	100	160	180	110	185/220
Total wingspan (m)	9.52	9.40	9.05	7.19	8.90
Total length (m)	7.20	6.95	7.33	5.77	7.00
Main wing surface area (m^2)	16.0	22.17	21.2	18.66	20.5
Total weight (Kg)	610	905	937	586	850
Maximum speed (Km/hr)	140	169	187	165	200/217
Number of machine guns	1~2	2	2	2	2

Data chart of England's main fighter planes

Name	Avro (504k)	F.E.2b	F.E.8	Pup	Camel	S.E.5a	Bristol F2.b
Number of Crew	2	2	1	1	1	1	2
Engine	Rhone 120	Beardmore	Gnome	La Rhone	Clerget	Wolseley	R.R. Falcon
Horse Power	120	120	100	80	130	200/220	275
Total wingspan (m)	10.97	14.55	9.60	8.08	8.53	8.15	11.96
Total length (m)	8.97	9.83	7.70	5.89	5.72	6.42	7.87
Main wing surface area (m^2)	30.0	46.0	24.0	23.5	21.4	23.0	37.6
Total weight (Kg)	830	1,346	611	556	659	956	1,261
Maximum speed (Km/hr)	144	130	151	179	182	205/212	192
Number of machine guns	1~2	1~2	1	1	2	2	2~3

$$\frac{dn}{dm} = E, \quad dn = E\,dm, \quad \int dn = E\int dm, \quad n + C_1 = E(m + C_2)$$

$$n = Em + (EC_2 - C_1)$$

Inside the ( ) is the calculation of constants and itself a constant, C.

$$n = Em + C, \quad \therefore C = n - Em$$

Here, when t=0, forces committed by armies m and n are m_0 and n_0 (initial condition). Substituting:

$$n = Em + n_0 - Em_0, \quad Em_0 - Em = n_0 - n$$

$$\therefore n_0 - n = E(m_0 - m) \quad (2.3)$$

This is Lanchester's Linear Law as arranged by Kimball and Koopman. E, the ratio of the efficiencies of the weapons, is called the Exchange Rate.

Also, the force unit is represented in men or tanks for ground forces, ships for sea forces, and planes for air forces. It is analogous to individual athletes in sporting events. Here, let a+b=K (constant), then:

$$\begin{cases} \dfrac{dm}{dt} = -a = -\dfrac{a}{K}K = -\dfrac{a}{a+b}K = -\dfrac{1}{1+\dfrac{b}{a}}K = -\dfrac{1}{1+E}K \\[2em] \dfrac{dn}{dt} = -b = -\dfrac{b}{K}K = -\dfrac{b}{a+b}K = -\dfrac{\dfrac{b}{a}}{1+\dfrac{b}{a}}K = -\dfrac{E}{1+E}K \end{cases}$$

The time variable unit change is arbitrary. Let $Kt = T$.

Differentiating both sides with respect to t: $\dfrac{dT}{dt} = K$ and $dt = \dfrac{1}{K}dT$;

thus:

$$\begin{cases} \dfrac{dm}{dt} = \dfrac{dm}{\frac{1}{K}dT} = K\dfrac{dm}{dT} \\ \dfrac{dn}{dt} = \dfrac{dn}{\frac{1}{K}dT} = K\dfrac{dn}{dT} \end{cases} \therefore \begin{cases} \dfrac{dm}{dT} = -\dfrac{1}{1+E} & (2.4) \\ \dfrac{dn}{dT} = -\dfrac{E}{1+E} & (2.5) \end{cases}$$

Let $a + b = K$, $T = Kt$, and $\dfrac{b}{a} = E$

To solve differential equations (2.1) and (2.2), since they mutually don't include the other party's variable, each can be easily solved, as in the case of continuous fixed-sum depreciation, using the quadrature method

$$\begin{cases} \dfrac{dm}{dt} = -a \\ \dfrac{dn}{dt} = -b \end{cases} \begin{cases} dm = -adt \\ dn = -bdt \end{cases} \begin{cases} \int dm = -a\int dt \\ \int dn = -b\int dt \end{cases} \begin{cases} m = -at + C_1 \\ n = -bt + C_2 \end{cases}$$

For the initial conditions (t=0) m_0 and n_0, then $C_1 = m_0$ and $C_2 = n_0$

$$\begin{cases} m = m_0 - at & (2.6) \\ n = n_0 - bt & (2.7) \end{cases}$$

Similarly, let $\begin{array}{c} a+b=K \\ T=Kt \\ \dfrac{b}{a}=E \end{array}$, then $\begin{cases} m = m_0 - \dfrac{1}{1+E}T \\ n = n_0 - \dfrac{E}{1+E}T \end{cases}$

This equation is linear with respect to t. For example, if a = b = 100, m_0 = 1000, and n_0 = 500, then army m wins (t=5).
This can be graphed as follows:

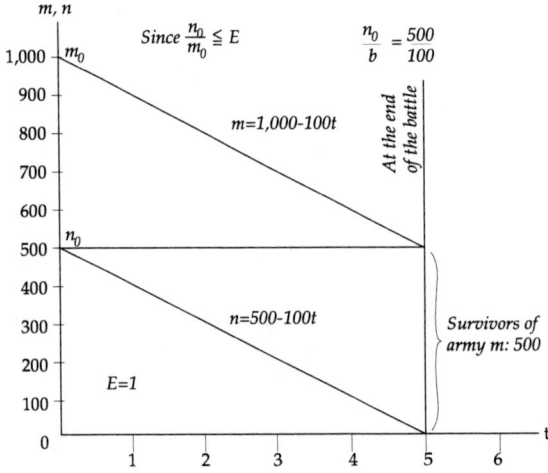

At the battle s end; that is, starting with t=0 and until the number of survivors m or n is 0 (total destruction), we have

$\begin{cases} 0 = m_0 - at \\ 0 = n_0 - bt, \end{cases} \begin{cases} at = m_0 \\ bt = n_0, \end{cases} \therefore \begin{cases} t = \dfrac{m_0}{a} \\ t = \dfrac{n_0}{b} \end{cases}$

Of these, the smallest one is the upper limit of t. thus

$$\frac{m_0}{a} \leq \frac{n_0}{b}, \quad \frac{b}{a} \leq \frac{n_0}{m_0}, \quad E \leq \frac{n_0}{m_0}, \quad 0 \leq t \leq \frac{m_0}{a} \quad (2.8)$$

$$\frac{n_0}{b} \leq \frac{m_0}{a}, \quad \frac{n_0}{m_0} \leq \frac{b}{a}, \quad \frac{n_0}{m_0} \leq E, \quad 0 \leq t \leq \frac{n_0}{b} \quad (2.9)$$

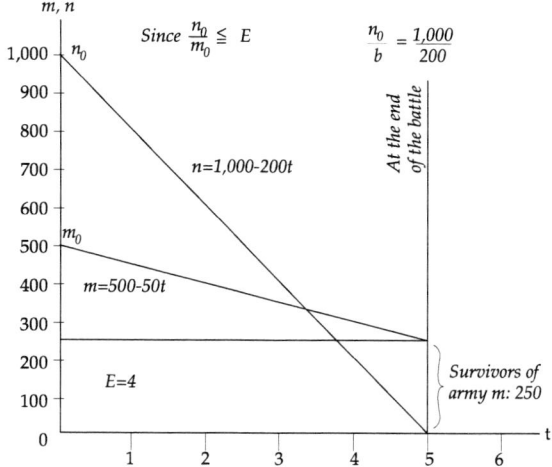

Army m may be inferior to army n in force, but superior in the efficiency of the weapons. Let the efficiency of the weapons (a) for army n be equal to 50, the efficiency of the weapons (b) for army m be equal to 200, and let the initial force (t=0) for army m (m_0) be equal to 500 and for army n (n_0) be equal to 1000. In this scenario, army m wins (t=5), as shown in the previous graph.

2.2.3 Conditions to win a single combat

Winning in a combat means to maintain a positive number of surviving force and reducing the enemy's survivors to zero. This does not mean to wipe out the enemy. Reducing the enemy's force to zero means some could flee or surrender.

Let army m be the friend and army n be the foe. According to Lanchester's Linear Law, the conditions to win are as follows:

$$n_0 - n = E(m_0 - m)$$
$$\downarrow \qquad \downarrow$$
$$0 \qquad +$$
$$n_0 = Em_0 - Em$$
$$\therefore \quad Em = Em_0 - n_0$$

Because $E>0$, then $Em>0$, and winning conditions can be expressed as:

$$Em_0 > n_0$$

$$\begin{cases} m_0 > \dfrac{n_0}{E} & (2.10) \\[2mm] E > \dfrac{n_0}{m_0} & (2.11) \end{cases}$$

In equation (2-10), if $E=1$, then when $m_0 > n_0$, army m is going to win. In equation (2-11), if $m_0 = n_0$ or $m_0 < n_0$, then E must be greater than $\dfrac{n_0}{m_0}$ for army m to win. For example, in the case of $m_0 = 3$ and $n_0 = 2$, E must be greater than 1.5.

In summary, to win in a single combat, either the force or the efficiency of the weapons must be superior. The choice between these two conditions depends on each situation, neither choice being preferred over the other. However, as in sporting events, where the number of participants remains equal, to win, the efficiency (skills and techniques) must be enhanced.

Also, when one's force is clearly inferior in number, not only must the efficiency be increased, but one must strive to concentrate its available forces, while giving the enemy the opposite impression. This strategy is called feint operation (diversionary tactics).

Summary

Lanchester's Linear Law applies to a single combat. If the combat is between two armies m and n, initial forces at t = 0 are m_0 and n_0, the number of survivors at any given time are m and n, the efficiencies of weapons are b and a, and the Exchange Rate is $E = \dfrac{b}{a}$, then:

Differential equations:
$$\begin{cases} \dfrac{dm}{dt} = -a \\ \dfrac{dn}{dt} = -b \end{cases} \quad \text{Let } a+b = K, \text{ and } T = Kt$$

$$\begin{cases} \dfrac{dm}{dT} = -\dfrac{1}{1+E} \\ \dfrac{dn}{dT} = -\dfrac{1}{1+E} \end{cases}$$

Particular solutions:
$$\begin{cases} m = m_0 - at \\ n = n_0 - bt \end{cases} \quad \text{Let } a+b = K, \text{ and } T = Kt$$

$$\begin{cases} m = m_0 - \dfrac{1}{1+E}T \\ n = n_0 - \dfrac{E}{1+E}T \end{cases}$$

Time range:
$$\begin{cases} E \le \dfrac{n_0}{m_0} & \text{if } 0 \le t \le \dfrac{m_0}{a} \qquad 0 \le T \le (1+E)m_0 \\ \dfrac{n_0}{m_0} \le E & \text{if } 0 \le t \le \dfrac{n_0}{b} \qquad 0 \le T \le \left(1+\dfrac{1}{E}\right)n_0 \end{cases}$$

Lanchester's Linear Equation: $n_0 - n = E(m_0 - m)$

Winning conditions:
$$\begin{cases} m_0 > \dfrac{n_0}{E} \\ E > \dfrac{n_0}{m_0} \end{cases} \text{m army as reference} \qquad \begin{cases} n_0 > Em_0 \\ E < \dfrac{n_0}{m_0} \end{cases} \text{n army as reference}$$

Calculating efficiencies of weapons and skills, a and b After the lapse of time T (t=0 at the start of the battle). Integrating from 0 to T:

$$\dfrac{dm}{dt} = -a, \quad dm = -a\,dt, \quad \int_0^T dm = -a\int_0^T dt, \quad [m]_0^T = -a[t]_0^T,$$

$$m_T - m_0 = -aT$$

$$\therefore a = \dfrac{m_0 - m_T}{T}, \quad \text{and similarly } b = \dfrac{n_0 - n_T}{T}$$

This is losses sustained by the enemy after the lapse of time T, divided by time T (normally in days).

If army m wins and army n is destroyed, then T will be the lapsed time until the end of the battle, $n_T = 0$, $b = \dfrac{n_0}{T}$.

2.3 Lanchester's N-Squared Law

2.3.1 The ratio of forces in group-to-group combat or total war

Let's assume that army m and army n enter a group-to-group combat with equal efficiencies of weapons and skills, or E=1. Let's also assume that army m consists of 2 units and army n of 3 units. The corresponding relations are shown in the following diagram.

Total war (group – to – group combat)

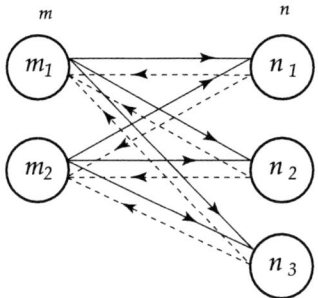

$$\text{Ratio of forces } \frac{1}{3} \times 2 : \frac{1}{2} \times 3 = 2^2 : 3^2$$

In contrast to the single combat, m_1 must face n_1, n_2, and n_3 ; on the other hand, n_1 must face m_1 and m_2. As in soccer, rugby, or football, other than individual skills, the 'stamina' of the whole team determines the outcome. In a trench war, for example, extreme care must be taken to avoid surprise attacks by individual enemy soldiers, which could come from anywhere. This is even more important with the introduction of machine guns, artillery, and missiles.

Forces must be distributed uniformly (in equal strength) against all enemy forces, and that's how we derive the ratio of forces as shown in this diagram. In other words, in group-to-group combat, forces are (mutually) discounted by those committed by the enemy. Therefore, the volume of attack and losses is an amount equal to the enemy forces discounted by one's own forces.

In this case, the ratio of forces for armies m and n is shown to be:

— that is a ratio of $2^2 : 3^2$ the square of forces committed by armies m and n. This ratio is not only valid at the start of the battle but also at any given time during the battle with respect to the number of survivors, or $\frac{1}{n}m : \frac{1}{m}n = \frac{m^2}{mn} : \frac{n^2}{mn} = m^2 : n^2$.

Lanchester introduced this as the N-Squared law in his 1916 book.

2.3.2 Differential equations in group-to-group combat or total war

Let's assume armies m and n enter into combat and their efficiencies of weapons and skills are b and a. The number of survivors for both armies can be represented in the following system of differential equations:

$$\begin{cases} \dfrac{1}{n} \cdot \dfrac{dm}{dt} = -a \\ \dfrac{1}{m} \cdot \dfrac{dn}{dt} = -b \end{cases}, \quad \begin{cases} \dfrac{dm}{dt} = -an \quad (2.12) \\ \dfrac{dn}{dt} = -bm \quad (2.13) \end{cases}$$

where a and b are arbitrary constants

Here, looking at the ratio of the number of survivals at any given time, and considering m as the reference:

$$\frac{\frac{1}{m} \cdot \frac{dn}{dt}}{\frac{1}{n} \cdot \frac{dm}{dt}} = \frac{-b}{-a} \qquad \frac{n \cdot \frac{dn}{dt}}{m \cdot \frac{dm}{dt}} = \frac{b}{a}$$

After reductions and substituting E for b/a

$$\frac{ndn}{mdm} = E, \quad ndn = Emdm, \quad \int ndn = E \int mdm,$$

$$\frac{1}{2}n^2 + C_1 = E\left(\frac{1}{2}m^2 + C_2\right) \quad \text{thus,} \quad n^2 = Em^2 + (2EC_2 - 2C_1)$$

Substituting C for the content inside the parentheses (also a constant)

$$n^2 = Em^2 + C, \quad \therefore C = n^2 - Em^2$$

When t=0, m= m_0 and n= n_0 (initial conditions).

Substituting $C = n_0^2 - Em_0^2$

$$n^2 = Em^2 + n_0^2 - Em_0^2, \quad Em_0^2 - Em^2 = n_0^2 - n^2,$$

$$\therefore \quad n_0^2 - n^2 = E(m_0^2 - m^2) \qquad (2.14)$$

This is called Lanchester's Square Law as arranged by Kimball, Koopman, and the U.S. Navy Tactical Operations Research team. Sometimes, it is also referred to as the Napoleon Law.

Furthermore, let a+b=K (constant), then:

$$\begin{cases} \dfrac{dm}{dt} = -an = -\dfrac{a}{K}Kn = -\dfrac{a}{a+b}Kn = -\dfrac{1}{1+\dfrac{b}{a}}Kn = -\dfrac{K}{1+E}n \\ \\ \dfrac{dn}{dt} = -bm = -\dfrac{b}{K}Kn = -\dfrac{b}{a+b}Km = -\dfrac{\dfrac{b}{a}}{1+\dfrac{b}{a}}Km = -\dfrac{KE}{1+E}m \end{cases}$$

Let T = Kt; after taking differential of both sides with respect to t, since $\dfrac{dT}{dt} = K, \quad dt = \dfrac{1}{K}dT$ then:

$$\begin{cases} \dfrac{dm}{dt} = \dfrac{dm}{\dfrac{1}{K}dT} = K\dfrac{dm}{dT} \\ \dfrac{dn}{dt} = \dfrac{dn}{\dfrac{1}{K}dT} = K\dfrac{dn}{dT} \end{cases} \therefore \begin{cases} \dfrac{dm}{dT} = -\dfrac{1}{1+E}n & (2.15) \\ \dfrac{dn}{dT} = -\dfrac{E}{1+E}m & (2.16) \end{cases}$$

Here, $a + b = K$, $T = Kt$, and $\dfrac{b}{a} = E$

Solving equations (2.12) and (2.13) is complex (in contrast to those of the Lanchester's Linear Law) because they both include the other party's variable (survivors m and n). Therefore, let's first arrange the equations to remove the other party's variable. Again,

$$\begin{cases} \dfrac{dm}{dt} = -an & (2.12) \\ \dfrac{dn}{dt} = -bm & (2.13) \end{cases}$$

Differentiating (2.12) with respect to t again: $\dfrac{d^2m}{dt^2} = -a\dfrac{dn}{dt}$

And from equation 2.13

$$\dfrac{d^2m}{dt^2} = -a(-bm) = abm \therefore \dfrac{d^2m}{dt^2} - abm = 0 \quad (2.17)$$

This is generally presented as $\dfrac{d^2m}{dt^2} + p\dfrac{dm}{dt} + qm = 0$, that is, $m'' - pm' + qm = 0$, which is linear with respect to m, m', and m'' and its coefficients are constants, and thus is called a homogeneous linear second-order ordinary differential equation with constant coefficients. Their general solutions are represented as cofactor m_c and n_c.

To find these cofactors, one solution of $\dfrac{d^2m}{dt^2} - p\dfrac{dm}{dt} + qm = 0$ is assumed to be $m = e^{\lambda t}$ (where λ is an arbitrary constant).

Thus we get $\dfrac{dm}{dt} = \lambda e^{\lambda t}$, $\dfrac{d^2m}{dt^2} = \lambda^2 e^{\lambda t}$.

By substituting these in our original equation, we obtain:

$$\lambda^2 e^{\lambda t} + p(\lambda e^{\lambda t}) + q(e^{\lambda t}) = 0$$

$$\{\lambda^2 + p\lambda + q\}e^{\lambda t} = 0$$

Because $e^{\lambda t} \ne 0$, $\{\ \} = 0$. This is called the characteristic equation, or the secular equation of the original equation. Because the original differential equation is of the second order, this also becomes an equation of the second order. The root discriminant $D = p^2 - 4q$ in the case of (2-17) because p = 0 and q = -ab, D = 4ab > 0 (a,b > 0), and the characteristic equation has two distinctive real roots.

These characteristic roots, λ (eigen value), are:

$$\lambda = \dfrac{-p \pm \sqrt{D}}{2} = \pm\dfrac{\sqrt{4ab}}{2} = \pm\sqrt{ab} \quad \therefore \lambda_1 = \sqrt{ab},\ \lambda_2 = -\sqrt{ab}$$

Also, in relation to the roots and coefficient of the equation of the second order we have:

$$\lambda_1 + \lambda_2 = -p, \quad \sqrt{ab} + \left(-\sqrt{ab}\right) = 0$$

$$\lambda_1 \cdot \lambda_2 = q, \quad \left(\sqrt{ab}\right)\left(-\sqrt{ab}\right) = -ab$$

The original equation $\dfrac{d^2m}{dt^2} + p\dfrac{dm}{dt} + qm = 0$ will look as follows:

$$\dfrac{d^2m}{dt^2} - (\lambda_1 + \lambda_2)\dfrac{dm}{dt} + (\lambda_1 \cdot \lambda_2)m = 0 \qquad (2.18)$$

We first arrange this equation in the following manner:
$$\frac{d^2m}{dt^2} - \lambda_2 \frac{dm}{dt} = \lambda_1\left(\frac{dm}{dt} - \lambda_2 m\right)$$

Let $\left(\dfrac{dm}{dt} - \lambda_2 m\right) = u$, and differentiate both sides with respect to t

$$\frac{d^2m}{dt^2} - \lambda_2 \frac{dm}{dt} = \frac{du}{dt} \qquad \therefore \frac{du}{dt} = \lambda_1 u$$

Separating variables:

$$\frac{1}{u}du = \lambda_1 dt \qquad \int \frac{1}{u}du = \lambda_1 \int dt$$

$$\log u = \lambda_1 t + C_1 \qquad \therefore u = C_1 e^{\lambda_1 t}$$

This is called the elementary or fundamental solution.

$$\therefore \frac{dm}{dt} - \lambda_2 m = C_1 e^{\lambda_1 t} \qquad (2.19)$$

On the other hand, rearranging (2.18)

$$\frac{d^2m}{dt^2} - \lambda_1 \frac{dm}{dt} = \lambda_2\left(\frac{dm}{dt} - \lambda_1 m\right)$$

We substitute $\left(\dfrac{dm}{dt} - \lambda_1 m\right) = v$

and differentiate both sides with respect to t

$$\frac{d^2m}{dt^2} - \lambda_1 \frac{dm}{dt} = \frac{dv}{dt} \qquad \therefore \frac{dv}{dt} = \lambda_2 v$$

Separating variables:

$$\frac{1}{v}dv = \lambda_2 dt \qquad \int \frac{1}{v}dv = \lambda_2 \int dt$$

$$\log v = \lambda_2 t + C_2 \qquad \therefore v = C_2 e^{\lambda_2 t}$$

$$\therefore \frac{dm}{dt} - \lambda_1 m = C_2 e^{\lambda_2 t} \qquad (2.20)$$

By removing $\dfrac{dm}{dt}$ from (2.19) and (2.20), that is, by subtracting both sides

$$(\lambda_1 - \lambda_2)m = C_1 e^{\lambda_1 t} - C_2 e^{\lambda_2 t}$$

$$\therefore m = \dfrac{C_1}{(\lambda_1 - \lambda_2)} e^{\lambda_1 t} - \dfrac{C_2}{(\lambda_1 - \lambda_2)} e^{\lambda_2 t}$$

Substituting the above coefficients with new constants, C_1 and C_2, such that: $\dfrac{C_1}{(\lambda_1 - \lambda_2)} = C_1$ and $-\dfrac{C_2}{(\lambda_1 - \lambda_2)} = C_2$ with respect to the general solution (cofactor) for the homogeneous linear second-order differential equation with constant coefficients, after substituting characteristic roots of the equations with λ_1 and λ_2, as a linear combination of the elementary solution, we get:

$$m_c = C_1 e^{\lambda_1 t} + C_2 e^{\lambda_2 t} \qquad (2.21)$$

Since $\lambda_1 = \sqrt{ab},$ and $\lambda_2 = -\sqrt{ab}$
the general solution for m is :

$$m = C_1 e^{(\sqrt{ab})t} + C_2 e^{(-\sqrt{ab})t} \quad (2.22)$$

Next, to find the general solution for n, we utilize the differential operator D, $\left(\dfrac{d}{dt}\right)$

$$\begin{cases} Dm = -an & (2.23) \\ Dn = -bm & (2.24) \end{cases}$$

Differential operator $\begin{cases} Dm + an = 0 & \times b \\ bm + Dn = 0 & \times D \end{cases}$

$$\therefore \begin{cases} bDm + abn = 0 \\ bDm + D^2n = 0 \end{cases} \quad \text{Removing term } m \quad \therefore D^2n - abn = 0$$

This means that $\dfrac{d^2n}{dt^2} - abn = 0$, and as we did before, by introducing the differential operator D, we obtain:

$$\{D^2 - ab\}n = 0 \quad \text{or, after factoring}$$

$$\{(D - \sqrt{ab})(D + \sqrt{ab})\}n = 0$$

The characteristic differential equation $h^2 - ab = 0$ where D is substituted by an arbitrary constant h is identical to the case for m, and characteristic roots are represented as 2 different real roots in the following manner:

$$h_1 = \sqrt{ab}, \quad h_2 = -\sqrt{ab} \quad \therefore \{(D - h_1)(D - h_2)\}n = 0$$

Here, substituting $(D - h_2)n = w$

Thus $(D - h_1)w = 0, \quad Dw - h_1 w = 0$

This is none other than a homogeneous linear first-order differential equation with constant coefficients. Hence:

$$\dfrac{dw}{dt} = h_1 w, \quad \dfrac{1}{w} dw = h_1 dt, \quad \int \dfrac{1}{w} dw = h_1 \int dt, \quad \log w = h_1 t + C_3$$

$$\therefore w = C_3 e^{h_1 t} \quad \therefore (D - h_2)n = C_3 e^{h_1 t}$$

Next, substituting $(D - h_1)n = x$,
Therefore,

$$(D - h_2)x = 0, \quad Dx - h_2 x = 0$$

$$\dfrac{dx}{dt} = h_2 x, \quad \dfrac{1}{x} dx = h_2 dt, \quad \int \dfrac{1}{x} dx = h_2 \int dt, \quad \log x = h_2 t + C_4$$

$$\therefore x = C_4 e^{h_2 t} \quad \therefore (D - h_1)n = C_4 e^{h_2 t}$$

Thus:
$$\begin{cases} Dn - h_2 n = C_3 e^{h_1 t} \\ Dn - h_1 n = C_4 e^{h_2 t} \end{cases}$$

Removing Dn from both expressions: $(h_1 - h_2)n = C_3 e^{h_1 t} - C_4 e^{h_2 t}$

$$\therefore n = \frac{C_3}{h_1 - h_2} e^{h_1 t} - \frac{C_4}{h_1 - h_2} e^{h_2 t}$$

Again, Substituting the above coefficients with new constants, C_3 and C_4, we obtain:

$$n_c = C_3 e^{h_1 t} + C_4 e^{h_2 t}$$

$$\therefore n = C_3 e^{(\sqrt{ab})t} + C_4 e^{(-\sqrt{ab})t}$$

And the general solutions for m and n are

$$\begin{cases} m = C_1 e^{(\sqrt{ab})t} + C_2 e^{(-\sqrt{ab})t} & (2.22) \\ n = C_3 e^{(\sqrt{ab})t} + C_4 e^{(-\sqrt{ab})t} & (2.25) \end{cases}$$

Since at $t = 0$, $m = m_0$, and $n = n_0$, let's find the particular solutions with proper arbitrary constants C_1, C_2, C_3 and C_4. Since there are 4 constants, there must also be 4 equations. Differentiating (2.22) and (2.25) with respect to t:

$$Dm = \frac{dm}{dt} = C_1 \sqrt{ab} e^{(\sqrt{ab})t} - C_2 \sqrt{ab} e^{(-\sqrt{ab})t} = -an \quad (2.26)$$

$$Dn = \frac{dn}{dt} = C_3 \sqrt{ab} e^{(\sqrt{ab})t} - C_4 \sqrt{ab} e^{(-\sqrt{ab})t} = -bm \quad (2.27)$$

Considering the initial conditions, including original equations (2.12) and (2.13), $m_0 = C_1 + C_2$ and $n_0 = C_3 + C_4$

$$[Dm]_{t=0} = \left[\frac{dm}{dt}\right]_{t=0} = C_1 \sqrt{ab} - C_2 \sqrt{ab} = -an_0,$$

$$[Dn]_{t=0} = \left[\frac{dn}{dt}\right]_{t=0} = C_3 \sqrt{ab} - C_4 \sqrt{ab} = -bm_0$$

Therefore,

$$\begin{cases} C_1 + C_2 = m_0 \\ \sqrt{ab}(C_1 - C_2) = -an_0 \end{cases} \qquad \begin{cases} C_3 + C_4 = n_0 \\ \sqrt{ab}(C_3 - C_4) = -bm_0 \end{cases}$$

However, $C_2 = m_0 - C_1$ $\qquad\qquad C_4 = n_0 - C_3$

$$\sqrt{ab}\{C_1 - (m_0 - C_1)\} = -an_0 \qquad \sqrt{ab}\{C_3 - (n_0 - C_3)\} = -bm_0$$

$$\sqrt{ab}(2C_1 - m_0) = -an_0 \qquad\qquad \sqrt{ab}(2C_3 - n_0) = -bm_0$$

$$2\sqrt{ab}\,C_1 = \sqrt{ab}\,m_0 - an_0$$

$$\therefore C_1 = \frac{1}{2}\left(m_0 - \sqrt{\frac{a}{b}}n_0\right)$$

$$\therefore C_2 = m_0 - \frac{1}{2}\left(m_0 - \sqrt{\frac{a}{b}}n_0\right)$$

$$= m_0 - \frac{1}{2}m_0 + \frac{1}{2}\sqrt{\frac{a}{b}}n_0 = \frac{1}{2}\left(m_0 + \sqrt{\frac{a}{b}}n_0\right)$$

$$2\sqrt{ab}\,C_3 = \sqrt{ab}\,n_0 - bm_0$$

$$\therefore C_3 = \frac{1}{2}\left(n_0 - \sqrt{\frac{b}{a}}m_0\right) = -\frac{1}{2}\left(\sqrt{\frac{b}{a}}m_0 - n_0\right)$$

$$\therefore C_4 = n_0 - \frac{1}{2}\left(n_0 - \sqrt{\frac{b}{a}}m_0\right) = n_0 - \frac{1}{2}n_0 + \frac{1}{2}\sqrt{\frac{b}{a}}m_0$$

$$= \frac{1}{2}\left(n_0 + \sqrt{\frac{b}{a}}m_0\right) = \frac{1}{2}\left(\sqrt{\frac{b}{a}}m_0 + n_0\right)$$

However, from (2.25) and (2.26) we have:

$$C_1\sqrt{ab}e^{(\sqrt{ab})t} - C_2\sqrt{ab}e^{(-\sqrt{ab})t} = -a\{C_3 e^{(\sqrt{ab})t} + C_4 e^{(-\sqrt{ab})t}\}$$

$$= -C_3 a e^{(\sqrt{ab})t} - C_4 a e^{(-\sqrt{ab})t}$$

$$C_1 = \sqrt{ab} = -C_3 a, \qquad -C_2\sqrt{ab} = -C_4 a$$

$$-\frac{\sqrt{ab}}{a}C_1 = C_3, \qquad C_2 = \frac{a}{\sqrt{ab}}C_4$$

$$\therefore -\sqrt{\frac{b}{a}}C_1 = C_3, \qquad \therefore C_2 = \sqrt{\frac{a}{b}}C_4$$

Particular solutions for the initial conditions (t=0) of m_0 and n_0 are:

$$m = \frac{1}{2}\left\{\left(m_0 - \sqrt{\frac{a}{b}}n_0\right)e^{(\sqrt{ab})t} + \left(m_0 + \sqrt{\frac{a}{b}}n_0\right)e^{(-\sqrt{ab})t}\right\} \qquad (2.28)$$

$$n = \frac{1}{2}\left\{-\left(\sqrt{\frac{b}{a}}m_0 - n_0\right)e^{(\sqrt{ab})t} + \left(\sqrt{\frac{b}{a}}m_0 + n_0\right)e^{(-\sqrt{ab})t}\right\} \qquad (2.29)$$

Modifying both equations, we obtain:

$$m = \frac{1}{2}\left\{m_0 e^{(\sqrt{ab})t} + m_0 e^{(-\sqrt{ab})t} - \sqrt{\frac{a}{b}}n_0 e^{(\sqrt{ab})t} + \sqrt{\frac{a}{b}}n_0 e^{(-\sqrt{ab})t}\right\}$$

$$= m_0\left\{\frac{e^{(\sqrt{ab})t} + e^{(-\sqrt{ab})t}}{2}\right\} - \sqrt{\frac{a}{b}}n_0\left\{\frac{e^{(\sqrt{ab})t} - e^{(-\sqrt{ab})t}}{2}\right\}$$

$$n = \frac{1}{2}\left\{n_0 e^{(\sqrt{ab})t} + n_0 e^{(-\sqrt{ab})t} - \sqrt{\frac{b}{a}}m_0 e^{(\sqrt{ab})t} + \sqrt{\frac{b}{a}}m_0 e^{(-\sqrt{ab})t}\right\}$$

$$= n_0\left\{\frac{e^{(\sqrt{ab})t} + e^{(-\sqrt{ab})t}}{2}\right\} - \sqrt{\frac{b}{a}}m_0\left\{\frac{e^{(\sqrt{ab})t} - e^{(-\sqrt{ab})t}}{2}\right\}$$

Both equations include hyperbolic sine and cosine in their terms

$$\begin{cases} m = m_0 \cosh\{e^{(\sqrt{ab})t}\} - \sqrt{\dfrac{a}{b}} n_0 \sinh\{e^{(\sqrt{ab})t}\} \\ n = n_0 \cosh\{e^{(\sqrt{ab})t}\} - \sqrt{\dfrac{b}{a}} m_0 \sinh\{e^{(\sqrt{ab})t}\} \end{cases}$$

Since the unit of time is arbitrary, let $(\sqrt{ab})t = \tau$

$$\begin{cases} m = m_0 \cosh\tau - \sqrt{\dfrac{a}{b}} n_0 \sinh\tau \\ n = n_0 \cosh\tau - \sqrt{\dfrac{b}{a}} m_0 \sinh\tau \end{cases}$$

This is a hyperbola representing a catenary curve of power cable.

Particular solutions (2.28) and (2.29) are defined for all real values of t; however, in practice, $0 \leq t$, and mutual forces m and n are $m \geq 0$ and $n \geq 0$; thus:

$$m = \dfrac{1}{2}\left\{\left(m_0 - \sqrt{\dfrac{a}{b}}n_0\right)e^{(\sqrt{ab})t} + \left(m_0 - \sqrt{\dfrac{a}{b}}n_0\right)e^{(-\sqrt{ab})t}\right\} \geq 0$$

$$\therefore \left(m_0 - \sqrt{\dfrac{a}{b}}n_0\right)e^{(\sqrt{ab})t} + \left(m_0 + \sqrt{\dfrac{a}{b}}n_0\right)e^{(-\sqrt{ab})t} \geq 0$$

$$\therefore \left(m_0 + \sqrt{\dfrac{a}{b}}n_0\right)e^{(-\sqrt{ab})t} \geq -\left(m_0 - \sqrt{\dfrac{a}{b}}n_0\right)e^{(-\sqrt{ab})t}$$

Here, $\left(m_0 - \sqrt{\dfrac{a}{b}}n_0\right) < 0$ and $m_0 < \sqrt{\dfrac{a}{b}}n_0$

$$\frac{\sqrt{\frac{a}{b}}n_0 + m_0}{\sqrt{\frac{a}{b}}n_0 - m_0} \geq \frac{e^{(\sqrt{ab})t}}{e^{(-\sqrt{ab})t}}$$

$$\therefore \quad e^{2(\sqrt{ab})t} \leq \frac{\sqrt{\frac{a}{b}}n_0 + m_0}{\sqrt{\frac{a}{b}}n_0 - m_0}$$

$$2(\sqrt{ab})t \leq \log \frac{\sqrt{\frac{a}{b}}n_0 + m_0}{\sqrt{\frac{a}{b}}n_0 - m_0}$$

Definition range for *t* is:

$$\therefore \; 0 \leq t \leq \frac{1}{2\sqrt{ab}} \log \frac{\sqrt{\frac{a}{b}}n_0 + m_0}{\sqrt{\frac{a}{b}}n_0 - m_0} \qquad (2.30)$$

However, $m_0 < \sqrt{\frac{a}{b}}n_0$ Also, from (2.28),

$$n = \frac{1}{2}\left\{\left(\sqrt{\frac{b}{a}}m_0 - n_0\right)e^{(\sqrt{ab})t} + \left(\sqrt{\frac{b}{a}}m_0 + n_0\right)e^{(-\sqrt{ab})t}\right\} \geq 0$$

$$\therefore \; -\left(\sqrt{\frac{b}{a}}m_0 - n_0\right)e^{(\sqrt{ab})t} + \left(\sqrt{\frac{b}{a}}m_0 + n_0\right)e^{(-\sqrt{ab})t} \geq 0$$

$$\left(\sqrt{\frac{b}{a}}m_0 + n_0\right)e^{(-\sqrt{ab})t} \geq \left(\sqrt{\frac{b}{a}}m_0 - n_0\right)e^{(\sqrt{ab})t}$$

Here, $\left(\sqrt{\dfrac{b}{a}}m_0 - n_0\right) > 0$ thus: $n_0 < \sqrt{\dfrac{b}{a}}m_0$

$$\dfrac{\sqrt{\dfrac{b}{a}}m_0 + n_0}{\sqrt{\dfrac{b}{a}}m_0 - n_0} \geq \dfrac{e^{(\sqrt{ab})t}}{e^{(-\sqrt{ab})t}}$$

$$\therefore\ e^{2(\sqrt{ab})t} \leq \dfrac{\sqrt{\dfrac{b}{a}}m_0 + n_0}{\sqrt{\dfrac{b}{a}}m_0 - n_0}$$

$$\therefore\ 2(\sqrt{ab})t \leq \log\dfrac{\sqrt{\dfrac{b}{a}}m_0 + n_0}{\sqrt{\dfrac{b}{a}}m_0 - n_0}$$

Definition range for t is:

$$\therefore\ 0 \leq t \leq \dfrac{1}{2\sqrt{ab}}\log\dfrac{\sqrt{\dfrac{b}{a}}m_0 + n_0}{\sqrt{\dfrac{b}{a}}m_0 - n_0} \qquad (2.31)$$

However, $n_0 < \sqrt{\dfrac{b}{a}}m_0$

Substituting the above with the E (Exchange Rate) representation

$$E = \dfrac{b}{a},\ a+b = K,\ a = \dfrac{1}{1+E},\ b = \dfrac{KE}{1+E},\ \sqrt{\dfrac{b}{a}} = \sqrt{E}$$

Therefore, again, $\sqrt{\dfrac{a}{b}} = \dfrac{1}{\sqrt{E}}$, $\sqrt{ab} = \dfrac{K\sqrt{E}}{1+E}$

The following system of differential equations:

$$\begin{cases} \dfrac{dm}{dT} = -\dfrac{1}{1+E}n \\ \dfrac{dn}{dT} = -\dfrac{E}{1+E}m \end{cases} \quad (a+b=K, \text{ constant}) \quad (\text{Substitute } T = Kt)$$

With the particular solution:

$$\begin{cases} m = \dfrac{1}{2}\left\{\left(m_0 - \dfrac{n_0}{\sqrt{E}}\right) e^{\left(\dfrac{\sqrt{E}}{1+E}\right)T} + \left(m_0 + \dfrac{n_0}{\sqrt{E}}\right) e^{\left(-\dfrac{\sqrt{E}}{1+E}\right)T}\right\} \\ n = \dfrac{1}{2}\left\{-\left(\sqrt{E}m_0 - n_0\right) e^{\left(\dfrac{\sqrt{E}}{1+E}\right)T} + \left(\sqrt{E}m_0 + n_0\right) e^{\left(-\dfrac{\sqrt{E}}{1+E}\right)T}\right\} \end{cases}$$

And as a hyperbolic function:

$$\begin{cases} m = m_0 \cosh \tau - \dfrac{n_0}{\sqrt{E}} \sinh \tau \\ n = n_0 \cosh \tau - \sqrt{E}m_0 \sinh \tau \end{cases} \quad \left(\tau = \dfrac{\sqrt{E}}{1+E}T = \dfrac{\sqrt{E}}{1+E}Kt\right)$$

Functions definition range: range of value for T

$$\begin{cases} \text{When } \sqrt{E}m_0 < n_0 \quad 0 \leq T \leq \dfrac{1+E}{2\sqrt{E}} \log \dfrac{n_0 + \sqrt{E}m_0}{n_0 - \sqrt{E}m_0} \\ \text{When } n_0 < \sqrt{E}m_0 \quad 0 \leq T \leq \dfrac{1+E}{2\sqrt{E}} \log \dfrac{\sqrt{E}m_0 + n_0}{\sqrt{E}m_0 - n_0} \end{cases}$$

Here, for example, if both a and b are equal to 1 (a = b = 1) and t = 0 (initial condition), then when $m_0 = 1000$ and $n_0 = 500$.

The system of differential equations from (2.12) and (2.13) is:

$$\begin{cases} \dfrac{dm}{dt} = -n \\ \dfrac{dn}{dt} = -m \end{cases} \quad \text{However, } E = \dfrac{b}{a} = 1$$

The resulting particular solutions from (2.28) and (2.29) are:

$$\begin{cases} m = \dfrac{1}{2}\{(1000-500)e^t + (1000+500)e^{-t}\} \\ \quad = \dfrac{1}{2}(500e^t + 1500e^{-t}) = 250(3e^{-t} + e^t) \\ n = \dfrac{1}{2}\{-(1000-500)e^t + (1000+500)e^{-t}\} \\ \quad = \dfrac{1}{2}(-500e^t + 1500e^{-t}) = 250(3e^{-t} - e^t) \end{cases}$$

The range of t (from equation 2.31) because $n_0 < m_0$ is:

$$0 \geq t \geq \dfrac{1}{2}\log\dfrac{1000+500}{1000-500} = \dfrac{\log 3}{2} = 0.549306145$$

At the upper limit of time variable, t, $\dfrac{\log 3}{2} = 0.5493$, and army n will be totally destroyed (n=0); therefore, according to Lanchester's Square Law, $n_0^2 - n^2 = E(m_0^2 - m^2)$, the number of army m survivors, m, is given by $500^2 = 1000^2 - m^2$ or $m^2 = 1000^2 - 500^2$, so that $m = \sqrt{750,00} = 866.0254$. This is exactly the same result when calculating the particular solution $t = \dfrac{\log 3}{2} = 0.5493$ as shown below:

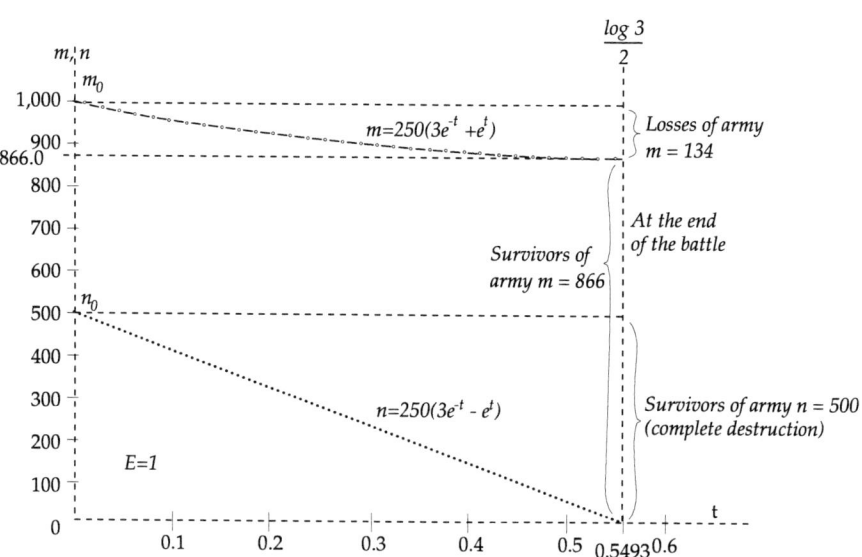

- Conversely, army m is inferior to army n in numbers, but let's consider the case where army m compensates with better efficiency.

Let's assume $a=1, b=5, m_0 = 500$, $n_0 = 1000$ and at time t=0.

System of differential equations from (2.12) and (2.13) is:

$$\begin{cases} \dfrac{dm}{dt} = -n \\ \dfrac{dn}{dt} = -5m \end{cases} \quad \text{However,} \quad E = \dfrac{b}{a} = 5$$

The particular solution from (2.28) and (2.29) is:

$$m = \frac{1}{2}\left\{\left(500 - \sqrt{\frac{1}{5}} \cdot 1000\right)e^{\sqrt{5}t} + \left(500 + \sqrt{\frac{1}{5}} \cdot 1000\right)e^{-\sqrt{5}t}\right\}$$

$$= \left(52.7864 e^{\sqrt{5}t} + 947.2136 e^{-\sqrt{5}t}\right)$$

$$= 473.6068^{-\sqrt{5}t} + 26.3932^{\sqrt{5}t}$$

$$n = \frac{1}{2}\left\{-\left(\sqrt{5} \cdot 500 - 1000\right)e^{\sqrt{5}t} + \left(\sqrt{5} \cdot 500 + 1000\right)e^{-\sqrt{5}t}\right\}$$

$$= \frac{1}{2}\left(-118.0340 e^{\sqrt{5}t} + 2118.0340 e^{-\sqrt{5}t}\right)$$

$$= 1059.0170 e^{-\sqrt{5}t} - 59.0170 e^{\sqrt{5}t}$$

$n_0 < \sqrt{\frac{b}{a}} m_0$, That is $1000 < \sqrt{5} \cdot 500$, $1000 < 1118.0340$

The range of t (from equation 2.31) since $n_0 > m_0$:

$$0 \le t \le \frac{1}{2\sqrt{5}} \log \frac{\sqrt{5} \cdot 500 + 1000}{\sqrt{5} \cdot 500 - 1000} = \frac{1}{2\sqrt{5}} \log 17.9443$$

$$= 0.64561341$$

Based on the upper limit of t, 0.6456, when army n is totally destroyed (n=0), the number of army m survivors, m = 223.6068, which is what we get from Lanchester's Square Law, $Em^2 = Em_0^2 - n_0^2$, or

$5m^2 = 5 \times 500^2 - 1000^2 = 250{,}000$, $m = \sqrt{50{,}000} = 223.6068$

as shown graphically on the following page:

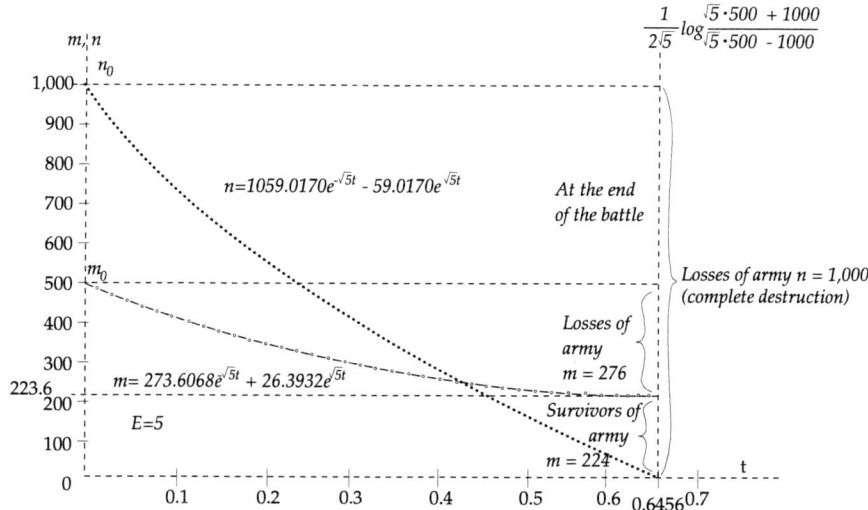

It seems that the Japanese navy was also aware of Lanchester's Square Law and solutions to the above system of differential equations. Mr. Yoshio Takeuchi, a director at Daido Life, writes as follows:

"The law of superiority of numbers is based on what the Japanese Navy called 'the N^2 Law,' which means the fighting strength is proportional to the square of the number of force."

The author studied the solution of this model in its most complex form using differentiation and integration during his math course at the Navy Academy. I am told that the solution was kept a top secret. Keeping a solution to a mathematical problem so secret was, no doubt, an expression of inferiority on the part of the Japanese Navy toward the U.S. Navy. (*Management Guide*, May 1978, *Military Strategies in Business* (5), College of Industry Efficiency).

2.3.3 Winning: Conditions for victory in a total war

Winning in a battle, in a word, means maintaining one's surviving number of forces as a positive value, while reducing the number of the enemy's survivors to zero. This does not mean killing or destroying all the enemy's forces. Some may flee or surrender.

Let army m be the friend and army n the foe. According to Lanchester's Square Law, the winning conditions can be presented as follows:

$$n_0^2 - n^2 = E(m_0^2 - m^2)$$
$$\downarrow \qquad\qquad \downarrow$$
$$0 \qquad\qquad +$$
$$n_0^2 = Em_0^2 - Em^2$$
$$\therefore \quad Em^2 = Em_0^2 - n_0^2$$

Since the exchange rate $E > 0$, then $Em^2 > 0$;
Therefore, the winning conditions are:

$$Em_0^2 > n_0^2$$

$$\begin{cases} m_0^2 > \dfrac{n_0^2}{E} \qquad m_0 > \dfrac{n_0}{\sqrt{E}} \qquad (2.32) \\[2ex] E > \left(\dfrac{n_0}{m_0}\right)^2 \qquad \sqrt{E} > \dfrac{n_0}{m_0} \qquad (2.33) \end{cases}$$

In the first equation, (2.32), if $E = 1$, then similar to the Lanchester's Linear Law, $m_0 > n_0$, and the only condition to win is to commit more forces.

In the next equation, (2.33), if the number of one's own forces are equal or less than those of the enemy's, then to win, E must be equal or greater than the square of $\frac{n_0}{m_0}$. For example, when $m_0 = 2$ and $n_0 = 3$, then $E > \left(\frac{3}{2}\right)^2 = 1.5^2 = 2.25$, which spells a greater burden compared to a single combat case.

In a single battle, one could either increase the number of forces committed or increase the efficiency of fighting; however, in a total war, increasing the concentration of one's own forces, or dispersing the enemy's forces in order to relatively increase one's own forces are far more important than enhancing the efficiency of fighting, E. In general, enhancing the efficiency of fighting, E, is not so simple; even more so, when it must be greater than the square of the ratio of forces.

To the contrary, when $E = 1$, and the ratio of forces is 101:100, even though the difference in the forces is only 1 unit, the difference in a total war is the square of this ratio, $101^2 : 100^2 = 10,201 : 10,000$, – an advantage of 201 units.

The stronger side with the greater forces naturally has the advantage of turning the battle into a total war and achieving a quick and decisive victory. On the other hand, the weaker side with fewer forces, would do better if, rather than enhancing its efficiency of the weapons, it could avoid a total war and at the same time divide the enemy forces and create a break-up in its concentration.

Koopman writes [1] the following on the optimum solution for dividing and dispersing the enemy: Army n is maneuvered by army m. Within a certain period of time after the start of the battle, a part of army n becomes separated from army n. Let's reperesent the ratio of separation $0 < \theta < 1$.

[1] A quantitative aspect of combat, B. O. Koopman, OEMsr-1007, Applied Mathematics panel, Note 6, AMG-Columbia, August 1943, AMP-900-M2, Microfilmed. Published in *Lanchester Readings 1914 – 1998* by Lanchester Press, Sunnyvale, CA 94086.

The initial forces, n_0, will then be reduced by θn_0, or will be equal to $(1-\theta)n_0$. Let the exchange rate E be equal to 1, then, from (2.32), the winning condition for army m is:

$$m_0^2 > \{(1-\theta)n_0\}^2 \quad \therefore m_0^2 > (1-2\theta+\theta^2)n_0^2$$

First, after army m wins, from Lanchester's Square Law, the number of survivors $m_{(1)}$ can be represented as follows:

$$m_{(1)}^2 = m_0^2 - \{(1-\theta)n_0\}^2 = m_0^2 - (1-\theta)^2 n_0^2 = m_0^2 - (1-2\theta+\theta^2)n_0^2$$

Next, in a similar manner, the winning condition for the surviving army m – after fighting the split army n, θn_0 – is $m_{(1)}^2 > \theta^2 n_0^2$.

From the above two equations

$$m_0^2 - (1-2\theta+\theta^2)n_0^2 > \theta^2 n_0^2$$
$$\therefore m_0^2 > (1-2\theta+2\theta^2)n_0^2 > (1-2\theta+\theta^2)n_0^2$$

That is, $m_0^2 > (1-2\theta+2\theta^2)n_0^2$ is the final condition for winning.

Also, the final number of survivors in army m, $m_{(2)}$ – after battling the split army n, θn_0 – is:

$$m_{(2)}^2 = m_{(1)}^2 - (\theta n_0)^2 = m_0^2 - (1-2\theta+\theta^2)n_0^2 - \theta^2 n_0^2 = m_0^2 - (1-2\theta+2\theta^2)n_0^2$$

Here, should army m divide and disperse army n, even if $m_0 \leq n_0$, for army m having a chance to defeat army n, $m_0^2 > (1-2\theta+2\theta^2)n_0^2$.

In dividing army n, for army m the optimum value of θ creates the greatest number of $m_{(2)}$. From the above equations, since m_0 and n_0 are considered constants, $(1-2\theta+2\theta^2)$ must then be minimized. In mathematical terms, for testing the minimum condition, it is necessary to set to zero the first-order differentiation by θ, and further, the number with the second-order differentiation by θ is greater than zero.

$$\frac{d}{d\theta}(1-2\theta+2\theta^2) = 4\theta-2, \quad 4\theta-2=0 \quad \therefore \theta = \frac{1}{2}$$

$$\frac{d^2}{d\theta^2}(1-2\theta+2\theta^2) = 4 > 0$$

Hence, if army m splits the initial forces of army n into two equal numbers, army m should have the best chance of defeating army n with less forces. Army m's level of forces, from the final winning condition, after substituting $\theta = 1/2$ is:

$$m_0^2 > \left\{1 - 2\times\frac{1}{2} + 2\times\left(\frac{1}{2}\right)^2\right\}n_0^2 \quad m_0^2 > \frac{1}{2}n_0^2$$

$$\therefore \quad m_0 > \frac{1}{\sqrt{2}}n_0 \quad m_0 > 0.7071 n_0$$

That is, if army m fights army n with 71% of army n's initial forces, it can still win if it initially succeeds in dividing army n in two. This is what Lanchester refers to as the 'Nelson Tactics.'

Summary

Lanchester's Square Law applies to group-to-group combats, or total wars. If army m and army n engage in a battle, and the initial conditions at the start of the battle (t=0) are m_0 representing the number of men in army m and n_0 representing the number of men in army n, then if the number of survivors in army m and n at any given time are represented as m and n, and the efficiencies of the weapons and skills for army m and n are b and a, and the ratio $E = \frac{b}{a}$ represents the exchange rate, then:

System of differential equations:

$$\begin{cases} \dfrac{dm}{dt} = -an \\ \dfrac{dn}{dt} = -bm \end{cases} \quad \text{Let } a+b = K, \text{ and } T = Kt$$

$$\begin{cases} \dfrac{dm}{dT} = -\dfrac{1}{1+E} n \\ \dfrac{dn}{dT} = -\dfrac{E}{1+E} m \end{cases}$$

Particular solutions:

$$\begin{cases} m = \dfrac{1}{2}\left\{\left(m_0 - \sqrt{\dfrac{a}{b}} n_0\right) e^{(\sqrt{ab})t} + \left(m_0 + \sqrt{\dfrac{a}{b}} n_0\right) e^{(-\sqrt{ab})t}\right\} \\ n = \dfrac{1}{2}\left\{-\left(\sqrt{\dfrac{b}{a}} m_0 - n_0\right) e^{(\sqrt{ab})t} + \left(\sqrt{\dfrac{b}{a}} m_0 + n_0\right) e^{(-\sqrt{ab})t}\right\} \end{cases}$$

Expressing in terms of the exchange rate, E:

$$\begin{cases} m = \dfrac{1}{2}\left\{\left(m_0 - \dfrac{n_0}{\sqrt{E}}\right) e^{\left(\dfrac{\sqrt{E}}{1+E}\right)T} + \left(m_0 + \dfrac{n_0}{\sqrt{E}}\right) e^{\left(-\dfrac{\sqrt{E}}{1+E}\right)T}\right\} \\ n = \dfrac{1}{2}\left\{-\left(\sqrt{E} m_0 - n_0\right) e^{\left(\dfrac{\sqrt{E}}{1+E}\right)T} + \left(\sqrt{E} m_0 + n_0\right) e^{\left(-\dfrac{\sqrt{E}}{1+E}\right)T}\right\} \end{cases}$$

As hyperbolic functions:

$$\begin{cases} m = m_0 \cosh \tau - \sqrt{\dfrac{a}{b}} n_0 \sinh \tau \\ n = n_0 \cosh \tau - \sqrt{\dfrac{b}{a}} m_0 \sinh \tau \end{cases} \quad \tau = (\sqrt{ab})t$$

Expressing in terms of the exchange rate, E:

$$\begin{cases} m = m_0 \cosh \tau - \dfrac{n_0}{\sqrt{E}} \sinh \tau \\ n = n_0 \cosh \tau - \sqrt{E} m_0 \sinh \tau \end{cases} \left(\tau = \dfrac{\sqrt{E}}{1+E} T = \dfrac{\sqrt{E}}{1+E} Kt \right)$$

Time range:

if $m_0 < \sqrt{\dfrac{a}{b}} n_0$, $\quad 0 \leq t \leq \dfrac{1}{2\sqrt{ab}} \log \dfrac{\sqrt{a/b} n_0 + m_0}{\sqrt{a/b} n_0 - m_0}$

if $n_0 < \sqrt{\dfrac{b}{a}} m_0$, $\quad 0 \leq t \leq \dfrac{1}{2\sqrt{ab}} \log \dfrac{\sqrt{b/a} m_0 + n_0}{\sqrt{b/a} m_0 - n_0}$

Expressing in terms of the exchange rate, E:

When $\sqrt{E} m_0 < n_0$, $\quad 0 \leq T \leq \dfrac{1+E}{2\sqrt{E}} \log \dfrac{n_0 + \sqrt{E} m_0}{n_0 - \sqrt{E} m_0}$

When $n_0 < \sqrt{E} m_0$, $\quad 0 \leq T \leq \dfrac{1+E}{2\sqrt{E}} \log \dfrac{\sqrt{E} m_0 + n_0}{\sqrt{E} m_0 - n_0}$

Lanchester's Square Law: $n_0^2 - n^2 = E(m_0^2 - m^2)$
Winning condition:

Army m reference $\begin{cases} m_0^2 > \dfrac{n_0^2}{E} \\ E > \left(\dfrac{n_0}{m_0} \right)^2 \end{cases}$ or $\quad m_0 > \dfrac{n_0}{\sqrt{E}}$
$\sqrt{E} > \dfrac{n_0}{m_0}$

Army n reference $\begin{cases} n_0^2 > Em_0^2 \\ E < \left(\dfrac{n_0}{m_0}\right)^2 \end{cases}$ or $\begin{matrix} n_0 > \sqrt{E}m_0 \\ \sqrt{E} < \dfrac{n_0}{m_0} \end{matrix}$

Dividing the condition for winning:

When E = 1, if the initial forces are at least 71% of the enemy's, the optimum tactics requires an equal division of the enemy's forces, (assuming the efficiencies of the weapons and skills are a and b).

Let T, an arbitrary amount of time, lapse after the start of the battle from (t=0), then:

$$\frac{dm}{dt} = -an, \quad dm = -andt, \quad \int_0^T dm = -a\int_0^T ndt$$

$$[m]_0^T = -a\int_0^T ndt, \quad m_T - m_0 = -a\int_0^T ndt$$

Here, after substituting $\int_0^T ndt \approx \sum_{t=0}^{T} n_t$ as an approximation for a relatively short interval, then:

$$m_T - m_0 \approx -a\sum_{t=0}^{T} n_t \quad \therefore a = \frac{m_0 - m_T}{\sum_{t=0}^{T} n_t} \quad \text{and} \quad b = \frac{n_0 - n_T}{\sum_{t=0}^{T} m_t}$$

This represents the enemy's losses up to the lapsed time of T, divided by the cumulative number of survivors of the opposing side up to time T.

These must be 'read' from the actual battle records. Specially, to estimate the enemy's efficiency of the weapons and skills, one must first estimate the accumulated number of the enemy's surviving forces. Obviously, if army m wins and army n is totally destroyed, then $n_T = 0$.

2.3.4 Pacific War examples

Lanchester's Law belongs to the so-called phenomenological model. Therefore, it is necessary to confirm the extent to which a fact can be explained. If something is too detached from the fact, it cannot be convincing to anyone. Chikio Hayashi (Head of Mathematical Statistics Research at the Ministry of Education and Chairman of Japan Quantitative Behavioral Science Society) writes about the Lanchester Model as follows:

"The ideas here should be viewed more as mathematical operation of concepts than analysis of data based on measurements. The way data apply here, rather than the issue of verification, they are represented in expressions of conceptual inference, and from this viewpoint, interpreting a mathematical model is appropriate. They belong to the same category of the mathematical model in the theoretical economy – and to some extent, quantitative economy, which also inherits similar traits. When viewed as data analysis, which is an operating view, there are many criticisms and indecisive issues – this approach is not well accepted by quantitative standards, which target clear-cut issues. But it can be approved by a qualitative thought experience that takes a general view that is macro in nature and conceptual."

It is well known that Richardson's military expansion equations also belong to the same format (Chikio Hayashi, 4. *Mathematical Model of Social Conflicts*. An Annual Report of Social Psychology, Issue 12, Conflict and Strife, Keiso Publications, 1971, pp. 68 – 69).

However, when dealing with real problems, we just cannot treat them as complex and strange. Certain thought organization is required to approach the problem. First, try to express the problem in the simplest form. If not possible, then try and make it complex but to the least degree. This is the principle of mathematical expression of phenomena.

Demand forecast is a good example of this. Specially, in the case of a single battle, which cannot be repeated, it is impossible to pursue perfection, considering available records. This is more appropriate where the defeated side is concerned.

Regardless of such complexities, in the battles of the Pacific between theUnited States and Japanese Imperial Navies, including those of Guam and Saipan, Lanchester's Square Law was verfied elegantly in the real world.

In June 1944, the United States began its landing operation on Saipan, Tenian, Rota, Guam, and other Mariana islands to secure airfields for its B29 bombers in order to attack the Japanese mainland. In the battle for Guam that began in June 15, there were 60,000 U.S. marines attacking and 18,500 Japanese defending. The U.S. casualties for a fighting period of 20 days were initially estimated at 8,000 (that is, 52,000 survivors).

Therefore, according to Lanchester's Square Law, based on the time range (2.31) and the winning condition, the exchange rate E, viewed from the U.S. side, and the efficiencies of the weapons and skills for the Japanese and U.S. forces, a and b, can be expressed as follows:

$$\sqrt{ab} = \frac{1}{2t} \log \frac{\sqrt{\frac{b}{a}} m_0 + n_0}{\sqrt{\frac{b}{a}} m_0 - n_0} = \sqrt{C}$$

$$\frac{b}{a} = E = \frac{n_0^2}{m_0^2 - m^2}$$

Here, let m_0=8,000, n_0=18,500, m=52,000, and t=20; assuming a=1,

We obtain:

$$E = \frac{18,500^2}{60,000^2 - 52,000^2} = 0.381975446429$$

$$ab = C = \left(\frac{1}{2\times 20}\log\frac{60{,}000\sqrt{E}+18{,}500}{60{,}000\sqrt{E}-18{,}500}\right)^2$$

$$= \left(\frac{1}{40}\log\frac{60{,}000\times\sqrt{0.38197544}+18{,}500}{60{,}000\times\sqrt{0.38197545}-18{,}500}\right)^2$$

$$= \left(\frac{1}{40}\log\frac{55{,}582.4973}{18{,}582.4973}\right)^2$$

$$= \left(\frac{1}{40}\log 2.99112097\right)^2 = \left(\frac{1}{40}1.09564822\right)^2$$

$$= (0.023739121)^2 = 0.000750278142$$

Since $ab = C$ and $\dfrac{b}{a} = E$, then $b = aE$ and $a^2 E = C$;

Hence $a = \sqrt{\dfrac{C}{E}}$, and $b = \sqrt{CE}$

$$a = \sqrt{\frac{0.00075028}{0.38197545}} = \sqrt{0.00196421} = 0.04431935$$

$$b = \sqrt{0.00075028 \times 0.38197545} = \sqrt{0.00028659} = 0.01692891$$

In other words, $E = \dfrac{b}{a} = \dfrac{0.01692891}{0.04431935} = 0.38197545$

The exchange rate E, can be represented as the ratio of losses sustained by the two armies as follows:

$$(E) = \frac{\text{(Number of Japanese soldiers killed by U.S. soldiers per unit of time)}}{\text{(Number of U.S. soldiers killed by Japanese soldiers per unit of time)}}$$

Here, the assumption is that the unit of time is day, 10,000 U.S. soldiers kill 169 Japanese soldiers and 10,000 Japanese soldiers kill 443 U.S. soldiers. That is, the exchange rate E, viewed from the Japanese side was 0.04431935/0.01692891 = 2.6180; in other words, the U.S. marines had already factored in a very fierce resistance by Japanese defending forces.

From the above, particular solutions (2.28) and (2.29) can be illustrated as follows. The graph is shown in dotted lines.

(U.S. marines) $\quad m = 15{,}033.3705 e^{0.0273912 1t} + 44{,}966.6296 e^{-0.0273912 1t}$

(Japanese defense) $n = -9{,}291.2487 e^{0.0273912 1t} + 27{,}791.2487 e^{-0.0273912 1t}$

However, the actual fighting continued for 22 days between June 15 and July 7. The U.S. casualties were higher also, 8,800 killed or injured (51,200 survivors); both the fighting period and the casualties were 10% above the initial estimates. As a result, the final calculations for the efficiencies of the weapons and skills for the Japanese and the U.S. forces, a and b, are as follows:

$$E = \frac{18{,}500^2}{60{,}000^2 - 51{,}200^2} = 0.349748610202$$

$$C = \left(\frac{1}{2 \times 22} \log \frac{60{,}000 \times \sqrt{0.34974861} + 18{,}500}{60{,}000 \times \sqrt{0.34974861} - 18{,}500} \right)^2$$

$$= (0.02628243)^2 = 0.000690766143$$

U.S. forces and Japanese forces at Guam June 15 through July 7, 1942.

$$a = \sqrt{\frac{0.00069077}{0.34974861}} = \sqrt{0.00197504} = 0.04444138$$

$$b = \sqrt{0.00069077 \times 0.34974861} = \sqrt{0.00024159} = 0.01554331$$

As seen from these equations, the Japanese efficiency of counterattack (a) was close to what was predicted. However, the U.S. efficiency of attack (b) was somewhat lower. In other words, this also tells us about the disparate nature of the counterattack by the Japanese defenders.

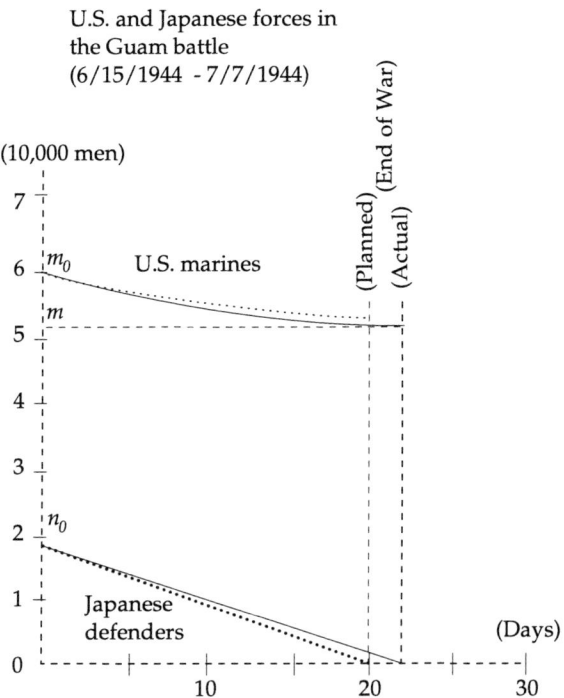

The actual results are shown in solid lines; the particular solutions are as follows:

(U.S. marines) $\quad m = 14{,}359.0277 e^{0.02628243 t} + 45{,}640.9716 e^{-0.02628243 t}$

(Japanese defenders) $\quad n = -8{,}491.8637 e^{0.02628243 t} + 26{,}991.8638 e^{-0.02628243 t}$

The mainland attack by the U.S. was commenced by a squadron of 45 B29 bombers against the Yahata Industrial site in North Kyushu, flying from the Chengtu base in China on June 15, the starting date for the battle of Guam. Poor results out of the U.S.-Soviet negotiations on the use of the Siberian base lead to the landing of marine forces on the Mariana islands 3 months ahead of schedule. The B29 bombing of the Japanese mainland began in earnest in late November 1944.

Against this onslaught, for the Japanese forces, Iwo Jima, a small island at the southern tip of the Ogasawara islands, between the Mariana islands and the Japanese mainland, became a crucial base for intercepting B29 bombers and the bombing of the Mariana islands. On the other hand, for the U.S. forces, Iwo Jima became a focal point not only for removing an obstacle for the B29 bombing missions, but also as a base for B29 escort fighters and a foothold for the eventual Japanese mainland invasion.

After 74 days of continuous bombing of Iwo Jima by B24s, which began in December 1944, and 3 days of non-stop artillery fire by 6 battle ships and 5 destroyers, on February 19, 1945, the 4th and 5th marine divisions began landing, which were followed later by the 3rd division. During the first landing operation, 54,000 U.S. marines were met with 22,000 Japanese defenders.

As a result, the initial 5-day plan was extended to more than a month of battle, and on March 26, after 35 days of fighting, other than 2,000 captives, the remaining Japanese forces were completely destroyed. American casualties also numbered more than 20,000 men, exceeding those of the Japanese defenders.

With respect to an attack schedule of 5 days, modifying the time range (2.23), and assuming that the Japanese army's efficiency of weapons and skills $a = 1$, then $b = E$, $\sqrt{b} = \sqrt{C} = \sqrt{E}$, hence:

$$t_{MAX} = \frac{1}{2\sqrt{E}} \log \frac{\sqrt{E}m_0 + n_0}{\sqrt{E}m_0 - n_0}, \quad \therefore e^{2t\sqrt{E}} \frac{\sqrt{E}m_0 + n_0}{\sqrt{E}m_0 - n_0} = 0$$

Here, $m_0 = 54{,}000$, $n_0 = 22{,}000$, $t = 5$, and let E be an unkown value, solving the polynomial equation:

$$e^{2 \times 5\sqrt{E}} - \frac{54{,}000\sqrt{E} + 22{,}000}{54{,}000\sqrt{E} - 22{,}000} = 0, \quad \sqrt{E} = 0.419833079385 = \sqrt{C}$$

$$\therefore \quad E = 0.176259814545 = C = ab$$

Furthermore, assuming that at the end of the fighting, where all Japanese defenders are destroyed, American casualties are equal to Japanese casualties; we have $E = \dfrac{b}{a}$ and:

$$E = \dfrac{22,000^2}{54,000^2 - (54,000 - 22,000)^2} = \dfrac{22,000^2}{54,000^2 - 32,000^2} = 0.25581395$$

Thus:
The Japanese defense efficiency of weapons and skills is:

$$a = \sqrt{\dfrac{0.17625981}{0.25581395}} = \sqrt{0.68901564} = 0.83006966$$

And the U.S. marine efficiency of weapons and skills is:

$$b = \sqrt{0.17625981 \times 0.25581395} = \sqrt{0.04508972} = 0.21234340$$

Similarly, from the American perspective, from one extreme to another, considering total casualties from 54,000 (0 survivors) to 0 (54,000 survivors).

$0.16598080 < E < 484,000,000$
$1.03049938 > a > 0.00001908$
$0.17104311 < b < 9236.32774632$

Since $ab = C$, then a and b are inversely proportional; that is, one side increases when the other side decreases.

Also, when $E=1$ and $a = b = \sqrt{C} = 0.41983308$, the number of American survivors $m = \sqrt{54,000^2 - 22,000^2} = 49,315$, and the amount of losses is $54,000 - 49,315$, or $4,785$; therefore, the amount of losses cannot be kept under approximately 9%.

Assuming various values for a and b, compared to values $a = 0.044$ and $b = 0.016$, as seen in the battle for Guam, they are detached from reality. This misperception is caused by the initial assumption of 5 days for the duration of the fighting.

After the Pacific War, research of the surviving war records revealed the following numbers:

Japanese defense efficiency of weapons and skills, a = 0.054

U.S. marine efficiency of weapons and skills, b = 0.011

Therefore, (the exchange rate from the U.S. marine side) E = 0.2037

(Kazuo Tada, *Easy OR*, Nikkagiren, 1970, p. 22.)

Comparing this to the battle for Guam, the Japanese defense efficiency of weapons is high; on the other hand, whereas that of the U.S. marines is low. From the Japanese defense viewpoint, E is approximately equal to 5, which is an indicator of the severity and fierceness of defense put up by the Japanese forces and the battle in general.

Mr. Tada's quote is based on J.H. Engels, *A Verification of Lanchester Laws*, Operations Research, Vol 2, 1954, pp. 163 – 171. To estimate the U.S. forces efficiency of weapons b, Engel assumes that all the 21,500 Japanese defenders (n) were eliminated during the fighting period of 35 days (T). The accumulated American forces $\sum_{t=0}^{T} m_t$ are calculated to be 2,037,000 men.

Then he calculates b as follows:

$$b = \frac{n_0 - n_T}{\sum_{t=0}^{T} m_t} = \frac{n_0 - n_T}{\sum_{t=0}^{36} m_t} = \frac{21,500 - 0}{2,037,000} = 0.011$$

Next, to estimate the Japanese defense efficiency of weapons a, since the American forces were reinforced twice, letting p be the increment, and making minor modifications to the differential equations, then integrating from the starting time (t=0) to T

$$\frac{dm}{dt} = -an + p, \quad \int_0^T dm = -a\int_0^T n\,dt + \int_0^T p\,dt,$$

As mentioned in the Summary, the American defense efficiency of the weapons a can be approximated as follows:

$$m_T - m_0 = -a\sum_{t=0}^{T} n_t + \sum_{t=0}^{T} p_t \quad \therefore \quad a = \frac{\left(m_0 + \sum_{t=0}^{T} p_t\right) - m_T}{\sum_{t=0}^{T} n_t}$$

Engel first estimated that the total U.S. forces $(m_0) = 54{,}000$, additional forces $(p_3) = 6{,}000$, and $(p_6) = 13{,}000$, and the total number $= 19{,}000$. Regarding the number of American survivors m_T, the fighting period was not considered to be 36 days, but 28 days, starting on February 19, 1945 and lasting through March 18, the day that brought Iojima under full control of the U.S. forces; therefore, when T=28, the number of American survivors $(m_{28}) = 52{,}735$ the accumulated number of Japanese forces $\left(\sum_{t=0}^{T} n_t\right)$ is estimated to be 372,500 men. Then b is figured as follows:

$$a = \frac{(54{,}000 + 19{,}000) - 52{,}735}{372{,}500} = 0.054$$

Obviously, there are no remaining records of the decimated Japanese forces; we only know the initial number of Japanese forces. Based on available Japanese and American records, let's look at the number of Japanese and American survivors. The number of U.S. marines at the start of the landing was $m_{(1)0} = 54{,}400$, the number of Japanese defenders was $n_0 = 22{,}000$; American forces were increased to $m_{(2)0} = 56{,}000$ on the 3rd day of the battle, and further to $m_{(3)0} = 66{,}000$ on the 6th day of the battle. From (2.28) and (2.29), we get the following equations in the period starting on the 1st day of the battle and ending on the 3rd, which are represented as dotted lines in the figure below (1).

(U.S. marines) $m = 2{,}627.8848 e^{0.02437211 t} + 51{,}372.1152 e^{-0.02437211 t}$

(Japanese defenders) $n = -1{,}186.0576 e^{0.02437211 t} + 23{,}186.0576 e^{-0.02437211 t}$

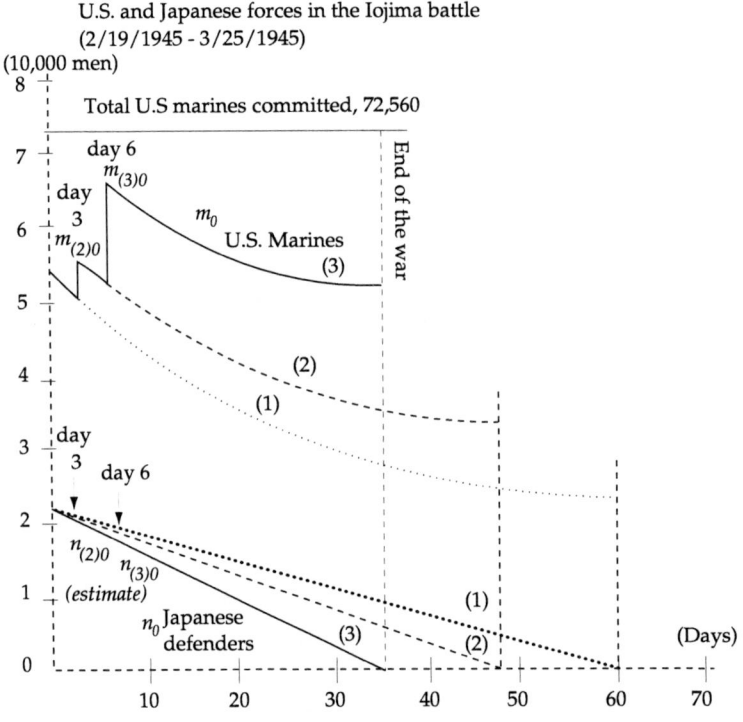

The surviving forces on day 3 of the battle (t=3) are m = 50,577 and n = 20,275 (estimates). That is, losses on the U.S. side are 3,423 men and on the Japanese side, 1,725 men (estimates).

At the end of the battle, from (2.31) we have:

$$t = \frac{1}{2\sqrt{0.054 \times 0.011}} \log \frac{\sqrt{\frac{0.011}{0.054}} \times 54,000 + 22,000}{\sqrt{\frac{0.011}{0.054}} \times 54,000 - 22,000} \approx 61$$

$$m = \sqrt{\frac{0.2037 \times 54,000^2 - 22,000^2}{0.2037}} \approx 23,238$$

On day 61, surviving marine forces are 23,238 men and losses are 30,762 men, both exceeding the 30,000 level.

On the 3rd day, marine forces increase to $m_{(2)0} = 56,000$, but because of the initial surviving forces of $m = 50,577$, the actual reinforcement is 5,422 men. Here, the battle continued between the surviving marine forces of $m_{(2)0} = 56,000$ and the surviving Japanese defenders of $n_{(2)0} = 20,275$.

From (2.28) and (2.29), the surviving forces are shown as follows,

(U.S. marines) $\quad m = 2,627.8848 e^{0.0243721 1t} + 51,372.1152 e^{-0.0243721 1t}$

(Japanese defenders) $n = -1,186.0576 e^{0.0243721 1t} + 23,186.0576 e^{-0.0243721 1t}$

as represented as dashed lines in the figure (2).

At the end of the battle, from (2.31) we have:

$$t = \frac{1}{2\sqrt{0.054 \times 0.011}} \log \frac{\sqrt{\frac{0.011}{0.054}} \times 56,000 + 20,275}{\sqrt{\frac{0.011}{0.054}} \times 56,000 - 20,275} \approx 45$$

$$m = \sqrt{\frac{0.2037 \times 56,000^2 - 20,275^2}{0.2037}} \approx 33,436$$

On day 45, 48 days after the landing, the surviving marine forces are 33,436 men and losses are 22,564 men. The accumulated losses from the start of the battle are 25,987, exceeding the 26,000 level, and far beyond those of the Japanese defenders.

Furthermore, after 3 days, that is, on day 6 of the landing, the American side adds the 3rd division and brings the total force to $m_{(3)0} = 66,000$.

At this time, the number of survivors from the previous battles, after substituting t=3 in the above 2 equations, are m=52,862 and n=18,480 (estimates); therefore, the actual American reinforcement is 13,138 men, and the accumulated number of marines committed from the start of the battle is 54,000 + 5,423 + 13,138 = 72,560 (approximately).

Again, the battle continues between the surviving marine forces of $m_{(3)0} = 66,000$ and the surviving Japanese defenders of $n_{(3)0} = 18,480$. From (2.28) and (2.29), the surviving forces are shown as follows:

(U.S. marines) $\quad m = 12,527.4232 e^{0.02437211 t} + 53,472.5768 e^{-0.02437211 t}$

(Japanese defenders) $\quad n = -5,654.0704 e^{0.02437211 t} + 24,134.0704 e^{-0.02437211 t}$

represented as solid lines in the figure (3).

And at the end of the battle, from (2.31) we have:

$$t = \frac{1}{2\sqrt{0.054 \times 0.011}} \log \frac{\sqrt{\frac{0.011}{0.054}} \times 66,000 + 18,480}{\sqrt{\frac{0.011}{0.054}} \times 66,000 - 18,480} \approx 30$$

$$m = \sqrt{\frac{0.2037 \times 66,000^2 - 18,480^2}{0.2037}} \approx 51,764$$

On day 30, 36 days after the landing, the surviving marine forces are 51,764 men and losses are 14,236 men, and the accumulated losses from the start of the battle is 3,423 + 3,138 + 14,236 = 20,800 (approximately). Considering the number of captured Japanese defenders was 2,000, the losses are greater on the American side.

In the battle of Iwo Jima, to defeat a Japanese defending force of 22,000 men, Americans committed 72,560 men, suffered losses of 20,800 men, and succeeded in taking total control of the island 36 days after the landing.

Consequently, the surviving number of American forces, based on the remaining war records, verifies Lanchester's Square Law.

2.4 Lanchester Law Based on the Theory of Probability

2.4.1 Why the probability approach is required

Both of Lanchester's Laws, regardless of how battles are fought, postulate that a battle continues based on the initial forces of m_0 and n_0. As a result, the principles are quite simple; if E=1, the inferior side (with less men) always loses. This is why Lanchester's Law is sometimes disdainfully referred to as a simple "Law of Quantity."

However, even though the total fighting strength may be inferior, as proven in the case of Nelson's naval battle or Napoleon's defeat of the Austrian army, certain tactics could still bring a victory. That is, regardless of the threat, Lanchester Laws come to play in actual battlefields where two opposing forces clash. Among the Imagawa's 25,000-men army, there were only 2,000 men in Yoshimoto's Okehazam's headquarters, and there were a total of 3,000 men in Nobunaga's army, when they launched a sudden attack.

Also, in the naval battle of Midway, the ratio of Japanese to American war ships was 4 to 1, but the Japanese joint fleet did not catch the movements of the American fleet in time, and the first task force of such aircraft carriers as Hiryu and Toranoko came under heavy fire. This rendered efforts of the main forces, such as the Yamato battleship, waiting in the rear, ineffective and forced them to retreat.

As an actual problem, even if the initial forces of the army m is m_0, the commander in chief of army m does not necessarily commit all the forces to the fighting. This is the same for the opposing army n. Even though the ratio of forces may be 5 units to 3, if the 5-unit army commits 1 unit and the 3-unit army commits 3 units, the latter 3-unit army is going to win the battle. Of course, the 5-unit army may not be willingly committing 1 unit, this could be just a ploy; its real intention may be a later surprise attack from behind with its remaining forces. Army n, aware of this ruse, may actually try to disperse army m by starting a campaign of deception, and then actually attack army m's headquarters.

This is akin to a game of chance, or dealing cards in a win or lose gamble; no matter how superior or inferior one side may be, the chances of winning is not always zero. Therefore, to reflect such differences in the way a battle is fought, the analysis of Lanchester's Laws based on the theory of probability becomes necessary.

First, in the case of Lanchester's Linear Law, in the case of the differential equations (2.1) and (2.2), we have:

$$\frac{dm}{dt} = -a \quad (2.1) \text{ where } a \text{ is } n \text{ army weapon efficiency and skill}$$

$$\frac{dn}{dt} = -b \quad (2.2) \text{ where } b \text{ is } m \text{ army weapon efficiency and skill}$$

Substituting E for the exchange rate; since the unit of time variable is an arbitrary constant, we have:

$$E = \frac{b}{a}, \quad a+b = K, \quad a = \frac{K}{1+E}, \quad b = \frac{KE}{1+E},$$

$$T = Kt \quad \therefore \quad dt = \frac{1}{K}dT$$

$$\frac{dm}{\frac{1}{K}dT} = -\frac{K}{1+E} \qquad \frac{dm}{dT} = -\frac{1}{1+E} \qquad (2.4)$$

$$\therefore$$

$$\frac{dm}{\frac{1}{K}dT} = -\frac{KE}{1+E} \qquad \frac{dn}{dT} = -\frac{E}{1+E} \qquad (2.5)$$

That is, in single combats, per each single duel, on the average, army m loses $\frac{1}{1+E}$ units and army n loses $\frac{E}{1+E}$ units.

In other words, the average rate of loss per each battle is $\frac{1}{1+E}$ for army m and $\frac{E}{1+E}$ for army n.

If the survivors of both armies are represented as m and n, the number of loses as α and β, and the initial forces as m_0 and n_0, then $\alpha = m_0 - m$ and $\beta = n_0 - n$. Winning in this case means reducing the number of enemy s survivors to 0 ($\alpha = m_0$, $\beta = n_0$) while maintaining a positive number of it's own s surviving forces. Therefore, the surviving range for army m is m_0, or from m_0 to 1, and the surviving range for army n is n_0, or from n_0 to 1, and the total should be ($m_0 + n_0$). However, as long as both sides are fighting, one side is eventualy reduced to 0 – an increasing range – and the added range of both survivors becomes $2 \leq m + n \leq m_0 + n_0 + 1$.

Conversely, from the perspective of losses, the range of α is 0, or 1, 2, ..., $m_0 - 1$, m_0 and the range of β is 0, or 1, 2, ..., $n_0 - 1$, n_0 and the total should be ($m_0 + n_0$). However, as long as both sides are fighting, one side sustains a total loss; therefore the range of both losses combined becomes $0 \leq \alpha + \beta \leq m_0 + n_0 - 1$.

Since the average loss rate for army m is $\frac{1}{1+E}$, then the average survivor rate is $\left(1 - \frac{1}{1+E}\right) = \frac{E}{1+E}$. Similarly, the average survivor rate for army n is $\frac{1}{1+E}$. If losses are considered 'with characteristics,' then survivors are 'without characteristics.' In the theory of probability, this allows the application of binominal distribution.

2.4.2 Binominal distribution

A coin is tossed 60 times, and at each toss the record of tail or head is taken. Since each toss is not affected by the previous one, the total of a certain number of tosses can be an abstract sample of an indefinite number of tosses. This abstract sampling also applies when all 60 coins are tossed simultaneously because head or tail for each coin is independent of the others. When there is no effect from the previous condition or when the condition for each event or person is independent of the others, the sampling is referred to as non-related or independent.

Because tossing 100 times or a toss of 100 coins is not easy, let's try 4 times or toss 4 coins at once. Head is shown in white and tail in black circles. There is a total of 16 combinations as shown in the following table:

	1st time / 1st coin	2nd time / 2nd coin	3rd time / 3rd coin	4th time / 4th coin	Occurrence probability
1)	●	●	●	●	1/16
2)	●	●	●	○	"
3)	●	●	○	●	"
4)	●	●	○	○	"
5)	●	○	●	●	"
6)	●	○	●	○	"
7)	●	○	○	●	"
8)	●	○	○	○	"
9)	○	●	●	●	"
10)	○	●	●	○	"
11)	○	●	○	●	"
12)	○	●	○	○	"
13)	○	○	●	●	"
14)	○	○	●	○	"
15)	○	○	○	●	"
16)	○	○	○	○	"

Generally, when the the number of conditions is k (2 in this case: head and tail), and the number of trials is n (4 in this case), the total possible combinations will be k^n (or $2^4 = 16$ in this case).

When a die is tossed twice or 2 dice are tossed simultaneously, then the total possible combinations will be $6^2 = 36$. There is no order of times in tossing a coin, but as seen in the table, rows 8), 12), 14), and 15) are all head 3 times and tail 1 time. These groups, or combinations can be summarized in the following table:

(Combination)	Number of heads ○	Number of tails ●	(Same group)	Occurrence probability
●●●●	0 -	4	1)	1/16
○●●●	1 -	3	2) 3) 5) 9)	4/16
○○●●	2 -	2	4) 6) 7) 10) 11) 13)	6/16
○○○●	3 -	1	8) 12) 14) 15)	4/16
○○○○	4 -	0	16)	1/16

In the case of tossing a coin, we use a bag containing a large and equal number of round white and black stones (used in the game of Go); after mixing them well, we draw 4 stones, and from 5 combinations of black and white, we record the matching combination. The 4 stones are returned to the bag, and the same course is repeated. Counting the number of combinations, this is called "restore sampling."

As the number of times (repeating times) increases, the ratio of the number of repeats against the total number of repeats will approach the occurrence probability. I mentioned a large number of stones; however, since each time 4 samples (stones) are drawn, at least a total of 8 stones, 4 black and 4 white, must be in the bag. This collection of stones is a collection prior to the drawing of the samples and therefore is a super set, and the ratio of the number of black and white stones against this population ratio is 1/2.

Let's assume the head is 'with characterstic,' and the tail 'without characterstic,' and their probabilities are p and q, respectively. In the case of a coin, $p = \dfrac{1}{2}$ and $q = \dfrac{1}{2} = 1 - p$. Also, in the case of a die, if the sides with an odd number of dots are 'with characterstics,' and the sides with an even number of dots are 'without characterstics,' then the results will match those of a coin. And if the side with one dot is 'with characterstic,' and the other sides are 'without characteristics,' then $p = \dfrac{1}{6}$ and $q = \dfrac{5}{6} - 1 - p$. The occurrence probability of the previous 5 combinations can be shown as follows:

(Combination)	Occurrence probability	Number of white circles		Number of black circles
●●●●	$q \cdot q \cdot q \cdot q = q^4$	0	-	4
○●●●	$4 \cdot p \cdot q \cdot q \cdot q = 4pq^3$	1	-	3
○○●●	$6 \cdot p \cdot p \cdot q \cdot q = 6p^2q^2$	2	-	2
○○○●	$4 \cdot p \cdot p \cdot p \cdot q = 4p^3q$	3	-	1
○○○○	$p \cdot p \cdot p \cdot p = p^4$	4	-	0

When the numbers of white circles 'with characteristics,' x, which vary from 0, when there are no heads, to the number of samples, are all added, the sum of all probabilities becomes 1. This can be shown as follows:

$$\sum_{x=0}^{4} P(x) = q^4 + 4pq^3 + 6p^2q^2 + 4p^3q + p^4 = 1$$

The right side is equal to the expansion of $(p+q)^4$, and based on the initial premise, p+q=1, and the coefficient of each expanded term is the combination of white circles of x items and black circles of (4-x) items; therefore, in general, when the number of samples is n, this can be shown as follows:

$$\sum_{x=0}^{n} P(x) = (p+q)^n = 1$$

$$= \binom{n}{0} p^0 q^n + \binom{n}{1} p^1 q^{n-1} + \ldots\ldots$$

$$\ldots\ldots \binom{n}{x} p^x q^{n-x} + \ldots\ldots$$

$$\cdots\cdots\cdots\cdots + \binom{n}{n-1}p^{n-1}q^1 + \binom{n}{n}p^n q^0$$

(Generally) $P(x) = \binom{n}{x}p^x q^{n-x}$, $\binom{n}{x} = \dfrac{n!}{x!(n-x)!}$ (Combination)

When x varies as 1, 2, ..., n, the probability of each x item included in those 'with characteristics' among n samples is obtained. In other words, during n times of trial, the probability distribution of x times of occurrence of certain phenomena can be calculated; hence, this is called 'binominal distribution' and is generally represented as $B(x;\ n,\ p)$:

$$\sum_{x=0}^{n} B(x;n,p) = \sum_{x=0}^{n} \binom{n}{x} p^x q^{n-x} = (p+q)^n = 1$$

Each probability of the binominal distribution comes from the fact that it is each term in the expanded binominal $(p+q)^n$ of the sum of ratios of those 'with characteristics' and those 'without characteristics.'

Note: The definition of $\sum_{x=0}^{n}$ which is the sum of terms as the x variable runs from 0 to n. The definition of $n!$ is the factorial as a product of terms $n! = n(n-1)(n-2)\ldots 3\cdot 2\cdot 1$, and by definition $0! = 1$.

Next, let's consider the average of the binominal distribution, m. Let's go back to the coin tossing, and let the number of coins be n, the number of heads of those 'with characteristics,' x, varies from 0 to n; therefore, the average of the binominal distribution, μ, can be shown as the sum product of the head or tail condition and the probability. This is called 'expected value':

$$\mu = \sum_{x=0}^{n} x \binom{n}{x} p^x q^{n-x}$$

When x=0, the first term becomes 0 and can be removed, we obtain:

$$\mu = \sum_{x=0}^{n} x \binom{n}{x} p^x q^{n-x} = \sum_{x=1}^{n} x \binom{n}{x} p^x q^{n-x}$$

The expression can be further rearranged according to the following relationship:

$$x\binom{n}{x} = x\frac{n!}{x!(n-x)!} = n\frac{(n-1)}{(x-1)!\{(n-1)-(x-1)\}!} = n\binom{n-1}{x-1}$$

$$\therefore \quad \mu = np \sum_{x=1}^{n} x \binom{n-1}{x-1} p^{x-1} q^{n-x}$$

$x - 1 = y$ then $n - x = n - (y+1) = (n-1) - y$

$$\mu = np \sum_{y=0}^{n-1} x \binom{n-1}{y} p^y q^{(n-1)-y} = np(p+q)^{n-1}$$

$$\therefore \mu = np \qquad (p+q = 1)$$

Note: The expected value of the probability variable x is shown as E(x). For example, (x) for a die ranges from 1 to 6, but the expected value for each side, which is the average for the side, can be shown in the following manner, since the probability for each side is 1/6.

$$E(x) = 1 \times \frac{1}{6} + 2 \times \frac{1}{6} + 3 \times \frac{1}{6} + 4 \times \frac{1}{6} + 5 \times \frac{1}{6} + 6 \times \frac{1}{6}$$

$$= \frac{1}{6}(1+2+3+4+5+6) = \frac{21}{6} = 3.5$$

2.4.3 The case of Lanchester's Linear Law

When the binominal distribution is applied, the general term $P(\alpha, \beta)$ of the occurrence of losses for 2 armies based on the system of identities in the combination $\binom{r}{k} = \binom{r}{r-k}$ can be shown as follows:

Viewed from army m:

$$P(a, \beta) = P\left(\alpha; \alpha + \beta, \frac{1}{1+E}\right)$$

$$= \binom{\alpha+\beta}{\alpha}\left(\frac{1}{1+E}\right)^{\alpha}\left(\frac{E}{1+E}\right)^{(\alpha+\beta)-\alpha} = \binom{\alpha+\beta}{\alpha}\left(\frac{1}{1+E}\right)^{\alpha}\left(\frac{E}{1+E}\right)^{\beta}$$

Viewed from army n:

$$P(a, \beta) = P\left(\beta; \alpha + \beta, \frac{E}{1+E}\right)$$

$$= \binom{\alpha+\beta}{\beta}\left(\frac{E}{1+E}\right)^{\beta}\left(\frac{1}{1+E}\right)^{(\alpha+\beta)-\beta} = \binom{\alpha+\beta}{\alpha}\left(\frac{1}{1+E}\right)^{\alpha}\left(\frac{E}{1+E}\right)^{\beta}$$

Viewed from both armies, we have:

$$P(\alpha, \beta) = \binom{\alpha+\beta}{\alpha}\frac{E^{\beta}}{(1+E)^{\alpha+\beta}} = \frac{(\alpha+\beta)!}{\alpha!\,\beta!} \cdot \frac{E^{\beta}}{(1+E)^{\alpha+\beta}}$$

The possible range of sum of losses for both armies from the start of the battle is: $0 \leq \alpha + \beta \leq m_0 + n_0 - 1$.

From the loss standpoint, army m or n wins the battle when the upper limit is met, or $\alpha + \beta = m_0 + n_0 - 1$; in the case of army m, the losses of army n, $\beta = n_0$, and $0 \leq \alpha \leq m_0 - 1$; in the case of army n, the losses of army m, $\alpha = m_0$, and $0 \leq \beta \leq n_0 - 1$; the winning probability of armies m and n according to losses (survivors) of each army, as the general term of the binominal distribution is:

For army m

$$P\left(\alpha; m_0+n_0-1, \frac{1}{1+E}\right) = \binom{m_0+n_0-1}{\alpha}\left(\frac{1}{1+E}\right)^{\alpha}\left(\frac{E}{1+E}\right)^{(m_0+n_0-1)-\alpha}$$

And for army n

$$P\left(\beta; m_0+n_0-1, \frac{E}{1+E}\right) = \binom{m_0+n_0-1}{\beta}\left(\frac{E}{1+E}\right)^{\beta}\left(\frac{1}{1+E}\right)^{(m_0+n_0-1)-\beta}$$

Furthermore, by representing the winning probability of army m as $\sum P_m$ and that of army n as $\sum P_n$, we have:

Winning probability of army m

$$\sum P_m = \sum_{\alpha=0}^{m_0-1}\binom{m_0+n_0-1}{\alpha}\left(\frac{1}{1+E}\right)^{\alpha}\left(\frac{E}{1+E}\right)^{(m_0+n_0-1)-\alpha} \quad (2.34)$$

Winning probability of army n

$$\sum P_n = \sum_{\beta=0}^{n_0-1}\binom{m_0+n_0-1}{\beta}\left(\frac{1}{1+E}\right)^{(m_0+n_0-1)-\beta}\left(\frac{E}{1+E}\right)^{\beta} \quad (2.35)$$

Based on the range condition of $\alpha+\beta$, since $m_0+\beta \le m_0+n_0-1$ $\alpha \le (m_0+n_0-1)-\beta$, and $\beta \le (m_0+n_0-1)-\alpha$, then, by rewriting $\sum P_n$:

$$\sum P_n = \sum_{\beta=m_0}^{m_0+n_0-1}\binom{m_0+n_0-1}{\beta}\left(\frac{1}{1+E}\right)^{\alpha}\left(\frac{E}{1+E}\right)^{(m_0+n_0-1)-\alpha}$$

Also, since $\binom{r}{k} = \binom{r}{r-k}$, then $\binom{m_0+n_0-1}{\beta} = \binom{m_0+n_0-1}{\alpha}$; hence:

$$\sum P_n = \sum_{a=m_0}^{m_0+n_0-1} \binom{m_0+n_0-1}{a} \left(\frac{1}{1+E}\right)^a \left(\frac{E}{1+E}\right)^{(m_0+n_0-1)}$$

The sum of winning chances of two armies is the sum of all probabilities of the binominal distribution, 1.

$$\sum P_m + \sum P_n = \sum_{a=0}^{m_0+n_0-1} \binom{m_0+n_0-1}{a} \left(\frac{1}{1+E}\right)^a \left(\frac{E}{1+E}\right)^{(m_0+n_0-1)-a}$$

$$= \left(\frac{1}{1+E} + \frac{E}{1+E}\right)^{m_0+n_0-1} = 1 \qquad (2.36)$$

In other words, the winning chance of each army is the partial sum of binomial distribution of winning chances for both armies.

Note: The partial sum of the binominal distribution is used in 3-point evaluation with regard to the OR method in the civic engineering and construction, as well as time scheduling in PERT-CPM. The computation of the partial sum of the binominal distribution becomes complicated once the overall range (n) increases, but it can be handled by a computer once it is represented as the incomplete beta function ratio $I_p(\gamma, \delta)$:

Lower probability

$$\sum_{x=0}^{k-1} \binom{n}{x} p^x (1-p)^{n-x} = 1 - I_p(k, n-k+1) = I_{1-p}(n-k+1, k)$$

Upper probability

$$\sum_{x=k}^{n} \binom{n}{x} p^x (1-p)^{n-x} = I_p(k, n-k+1) = 1 - I_{1-p}(n-k+1, k)$$

Here, if $m_0 = 5$, $n_0 = 3$, $E = 1$, then $m_0 + n_0 - 1 = 7$

and $\dfrac{1}{1+E} = \dfrac{E}{1+E} = 0.5$; therefore,

Winning probability of army m is: $\sum P_m = I_{0.5}(3, 5) = 0.77343750$

Winning probability of army n is: $\sum P_n = I_{0.5}(5, 3) = 0.22656250$

Again, winning probability for each army according to the losses (survivors) of each army must be calculated separately.

Here, in (2.34), $\left(\dfrac{E}{1+E}\right)^{n_0}$ is a constant; therefore it can be factored out:

$$\Sigma P_m = \sum_{\alpha=0}^{m_0-1} \binom{m_0+n_0-1}{\alpha} \left(\dfrac{1}{1+E}\right)^{\alpha} \left(\dfrac{E}{1+E}\right)^{(m_0+n_0-1)-\alpha}$$

$$= \left(\dfrac{E}{1+E}\right)^{n_0} \left[\sum_{\alpha=0}^{m_0-1} \binom{m_0+n_0-1}{\alpha} \left(\dfrac{1}{1+E}\right)^{\alpha} \left(\dfrac{E}{1+E}\right)^{m_0-1-\alpha}\right]$$

$$= \left(\dfrac{E}{1+E}\right)^{n_0} \left[\sum_{\alpha=0}^{m_0-1} \binom{m_0+n_0-1}{\alpha} \left(\dfrac{1}{1+E}\right)^{\alpha} \left(\dfrac{1}{1+E}\right)^{m_0-1-\alpha}\right.$$

$$\left.\left(\dfrac{1+E}{1}\right)^{m_0-1-\alpha} \left(\dfrac{E}{1+E}\right)^{m_0-1-\alpha}\right]$$

$$= \left(\dfrac{E}{1+E}\right)^{n_0} \left[\sum_{\alpha=0}^{m_0-1} \binom{m_0+n_0-1}{\alpha} \left(\dfrac{1}{1+E}\right)^{m_0-1} E^{m_0-1-\alpha}\right]$$

Since $\left(\dfrac{1}{1+E}\right)^{m_0-1}$ is also a constant, then:

$$= \left(\dfrac{E}{1+E}\right)^{n_0} \left(\dfrac{1}{1+E}\right)^{m_0-1} \left[\sum_{\alpha=0}^{m_0-1} \binom{m_0+n_0-1}{\alpha} E^{m_0-1-\alpha}\right]$$

In addition, from the system of identity of binominal coefficients, we have:

$$\binom{r+s+1}{k} = \sum_{x=0}^{k} \binom{r+x}{x}\binom{s-x}{k-x}$$

Here, if $r = n_0 - 1$, $s = m_0 - 1$, $k = \alpha$, then:

$$\binom{m_0 + n_0 - 1}{\alpha} = \sum_{x=0}^{\alpha} \binom{(n_0 - 1) + x}{x}\binom{(m_0 - 1) + x}{\alpha - x}$$

Rearranging the contents inside the brackets [ ]

$$\Sigma P_m = \left(\frac{E}{1+E}\right)^{n_0} \left(\frac{1}{1+E}\right)^{m_0-1} \left[\binom{m_0+n_0-1}{0} E^{(m_0-1)}\right.$$

$$+ \binom{m_0+n_0-1}{1} E^{(m_0-1)-1}$$

$$\vdots$$

$$+ \binom{m_0+n_0-1}{\alpha} E^{(m_0-1)-\alpha}$$

$$\vdots$$

$$+ \binom{m_0+n_0-1}{(m_0-1)-1} E^{(m_0-1)-\{(m_0-1)-1\}}$$

$$\left. + \binom{m_0+n_0-1}{(m_0-1)} E^{(m_0-1)-(m_0-1)}\right]$$

$$\Sigma P_m = \left(\frac{E}{1+E}\right)^{n_0} \left(\frac{1}{1+E}\right)^{m_0-1} \left[\binom{n_0-1}{0}\binom{m_0-1}{0} E^{(m_0-1)}\right.$$

$$+ \binom{n_0-1}{0}\binom{m_0-1}{1} E^{(m_0-1)-1} + \binom{(n_0-1)+1}{1}\binom{(m_0-1)-1}{0} E^{(m_0-1)-1}$$

$$+ \cdots$$

$$+ \binom{n_0-1}{0}\binom{m_0-1}{\alpha} E^{(m_0-1)-\alpha} + \binom{(n_0-1)+1}{1}\binom{(m_0-1)-1}{\alpha-1} E^{(m_0-1)-\alpha} + \cdots$$

$$+ \binom{n_0-1}{0}\binom{m_0-1}{(m_0-1)-1} E^1 + \binom{(n_0-1)+1}{1}\binom{(m_0-1)-1}{\{(m_0-1)-1\}-1} E^1 + \cdots$$

$$+ \binom{n_0-1}{0}\binom{m_0-1}{m_0-1} E^0 + \binom{(n_0-1)+1}{1}\binom{(m_0-1)-1}{(m_0-1)-1} E^0 + \cdots$$

$$\cdots + \binom{(n_0-1)+\alpha}{\alpha}\binom{(m_0-1)-\alpha}{0} E^{(m_0-1)-\alpha}$$

$$\cdots$$

$$\cdots + \begin{Bmatrix}(n_0-1)+\alpha \\ \alpha\end{Bmatrix}\begin{pmatrix}(m_0-1)-\alpha \\ \{(m_0-1)-1\}-\alpha\end{pmatrix}E^1 + \cdots + \begin{Bmatrix}(n_0-1)+\{(m_0-1)-1\} \\ (m_0-1)-1\end{Bmatrix}\begin{pmatrix}(m_0-1)-\{(m_0-1)-1\} \\ (m_0-1)-1-\{(m_0-1)-1\}\end{pmatrix}E^1$$

$$\cdots + \begin{Bmatrix}(n_0-1)+\alpha \\ \alpha\end{Bmatrix}\begin{pmatrix}(m_0-1)-\alpha \\ (m_0-1)-\alpha\end{pmatrix}E^0 + \cdots + \begin{Bmatrix}(n_0-1)+\{(m_0-1)-1\} \\ (m_0-1)-1\end{Bmatrix}\begin{pmatrix}(m_0-1)-\{(m_0-1)-1\} \\ (m_0-1)-1-\{(m_0-1)-1\}\end{pmatrix}E^0$$

$$+ \begin{Bmatrix}(n_0-1)+(m_0-1) \\ (m_0-1)\end{Bmatrix}\begin{pmatrix}(m_0-1)-(m_0-1) \\ (m_0-1)-(m_0-1)\end{pmatrix}E^0\Bigg]$$

Rearranging the contents inside the brackets [   ],

$$\Sigma P_m = \left(\frac{E}{1+E}\right)^{n_0}\left(\frac{1}{1+E}\right)^{m_0-1}\Bigg[\begin{pmatrix}n_0-1 \\ 0\end{pmatrix}\Bigg\{\begin{pmatrix}m_0-1 \\ 0\end{pmatrix}E^{(m_0-1)} + \begin{pmatrix}m_0-1 \\ 1\end{pmatrix}E^{(m_0-1)-1} + \cdots\cdots$$

$$\cdots\cdots + \begin{pmatrix}m_0-1 \\ \alpha\end{pmatrix}E^{(m_0-1)-\alpha} + \cdots + \begin{pmatrix}m_0-1 \\ (m_0-1)-1\end{pmatrix}E^1 + \begin{pmatrix}m_0-1 \\ m_0-1\end{pmatrix}E^0\Bigg\}$$

$$+ \begin{pmatrix}(n_0-1)+1 \\ 1\end{pmatrix}\begin{pmatrix}m_0-2 \\ 0\end{pmatrix}E^{(m_0-2)}, \ldots + \begin{pmatrix}m_0-2 \\ \alpha-1\end{pmatrix}E^{(m_0-2)-(\alpha-1)} + \cdots + \begin{pmatrix}m_0-2 \\ (m_0-2)-1\end{pmatrix}E^1 + \begin{pmatrix}m_0-2 \\ m_0-2\end{pmatrix}E^0\Bigg\} + \cdots$$

$$\Sigma P_m = \left(\frac{E}{1+E}\right)^{n_0}\left(\frac{1}{1+E}\right)^{m_0-1}\left[\binom{(n_0-1)+0}{0}\binom{(n_0-1)+1}{1}(1+E)^{m_0-1} + \binom{(n_0-1)+\{(m_0-1)-1\}}{(m_0-1)-1}(1+E)^{(m_0-1)-1} + \cdots\cdots \right.$$

$$\cdots + \binom{(n_0-1)+\alpha}{\alpha}(1+E)^{(m_0-1)-\alpha} + \cdots + \binom{(n_0-1)+(m_0-1)}{m_0-1}(1+E)^0 \Bigg]$$

$$= \left(\frac{E}{1+E}\right)^{n_0}\left[\binom{(n_0-1)+0}{0}\binom{(n_0-1)+1}{1}(1+E)^{-1} + \cdots + \binom{(n_0-1)+\alpha}{\alpha}(1+E)^{-\alpha} + \cdots\cdots\right.$$

$$\cdots + \binom{(n_0-1)+\{(m_0-1)-1\}}{(m_0-1)-1}(1+E)^{-(m_0-1)-1]} + \binom{(n_0-1)+(m_0-1)}{m_0-1}(1+E)^{-(m_0-1)} \Bigg]$$

Also, since $(1+E)^s = \sum_{x=0}^{s}\binom{s}{x}E^{s-x}$

$$= \left(\frac{E}{1+E}\right)^{n_0}\left[\binom{(n_0-1)+0}{0}\left(\frac{1}{1+E}\right)^0 + \binom{(n_0-1)+1}{1}\left(\frac{1}{1+E}\right)^1 + \cdots + \binom{(n_0-1)+\alpha}{\alpha}\left(\frac{1}{1+E}\right)^\alpha + \cdots\right.$$

$$+ \binom{(n_0-1)+\{(m_0-1)-1\}}{(m_0-1)-1}\left(\frac{1}{1}\right)\binom{1}{0}E^1 + \binom{1}{1}E^0\Bigg\}$$

$$+ \binom{(n_0-1)+(m_0-1)}{(m_0-1)}\Bigg\{\binom{0}{0}E^0\Bigg\}$$

$$+ \binom{(n_0-1)+\alpha}{\alpha}\Bigg\{\binom{(m_0-1)-\alpha}{0}E^{(m_0-1)-\alpha} + \text{L} + \binom{(m_0-1)-\alpha}{\{(m_0-1)-\alpha\}-1}E^1 + \binom{(m_0-1)-\alpha}{(m_0-1)-\alpha}E^0\Bigg\} + \cdots$$

$$\cdots + \binom{(n_0-1)+\{(m_0-1)-1\}}{(m_0-1)-1}\left(\frac{1}{1+E}\right)^{(m_0-1)-1}\left(\frac{E}{1+E}\right)^{n_0} + \binom{(n_0-1)+(m_0-1)}{(m_0-1)}\left(\frac{1}{1+E}\right)^{(m_0-1)}$$

$$= \left(\frac{E}{1+E}\right)^{n_0}\left[\sum_{\alpha=0}^{m_0-1}\binom{\alpha+n_0-1}{\alpha}\left(\frac{1}{1+E}\right)^{\alpha}\right]$$

$$= \sum_{\alpha=0}^{m_0-1}\binom{\alpha+n_0-1}{\alpha}\left(\frac{1}{1+E}\right)^{\alpha}\left(\frac{E}{1+E}\right)^{n_0}$$

Winning probability of army m :

$$\Sigma P_m = \sum_{\alpha=0}^{m_0-1}\binom{m_0+n_0-1}{\alpha}\left(\frac{1}{1+E}\right)^{(m_0+n_0-1)-\alpha}\left(\frac{E}{1+E}\right)^{\alpha}$$

$$= \sum_{\alpha=0}^{m_0-1}\binom{\alpha+n_0-1}{\alpha}\left(\frac{1}{1+E}\right)^{\alpha}\left(\frac{E}{1+E}\right)^{n_0} = \sum_{\alpha=0}^{m_0-1}\frac{(\alpha+n_0-1)!}{\alpha!(n_0-1)!}\cdot\frac{E^{n_0}}{(1+E)^{\alpha+n_0}}$$

Similarly from equation 2.35, the winning probability of army n :

$$\Sigma P_n = \sum_{\beta=0}^{n_0-1}\binom{m_0+n_0-1}{\beta}\left(\frac{1}{1+E}\right)^{(m_0+n_0-1)-\beta}\left(\frac{E}{1+E}\right)^{\beta}$$

$$= \sum_{\beta=0}^{n_0-1}\binom{\beta+m_0-1}{\beta}\left(\frac{1}{1+E}\right)^{m_0}\left(\frac{E}{1+E}\right)^{\beta} = \sum_{\beta=0}^{n_0-1}\frac{(\beta+m_0-1)!}{\beta!(m_0-1)!}\cdot\frac{E^{\beta}}{(1+E)^{\beta+m_0}}$$

Accordingly, the general term of winning probability per each loss (survival) unit for both armies can be shown as follows:

In the case of army m:

$$P(\alpha, n_0) = \binom{\alpha + n_0 - 1}{\alpha} \left(\frac{1}{1+E}\right)^\alpha \left(\frac{E}{1+E}\right)^{n_0} = \frac{(\alpha + n_0 - 1)!}{\alpha!(n_0 - 1)!} \cdot \frac{E^{n_0}}{(1+E)^{\alpha+n_0}}$$

In the case of army n:

$$P(m_0, \beta) = \binom{\beta + m_0 - 1}{\beta} \left(\frac{1}{1+E}\right)^{m_0} \left(\frac{E}{1+E}\right)^\beta = \frac{(\beta + m_0 - 1)!}{\beta!(m_0 - 1)!} \cdot \frac{E^\beta}{(1+E)^{\beta+m_0}}$$

Note that:

$$\binom{\alpha + n_0 - 1}{\alpha} =_{n_0 + \alpha - 1} C_\alpha =_{n_0} H_\alpha, \quad \binom{\beta + n_0 - 1}{\beta} =_{m_0 + \beta - 1} C_\beta =_{m_0} H_\beta$$

Each is of a $n_0(m_0)$ kind, and means the number of combinations allowing repetition, taking as many as $\alpha(\beta)$; in other words, it means a multiple combination.

Generally, this is shown in the following chart, which includes the probability $P(\alpha, \beta)$ per each loss (survival) unit for both fighting armies. However, since this is impossible, $P(m_0, n_0) = 0$.

The thick lines a, b, and c respond to the state of the time variable T (=Kt). For example, T=2 against line a and T=n_0+1 against line b. In the case of line b, the intersection of horizontal and vertical parts of the thick line indicate the end of the battle, and the intersection of the slanted parts indicate that the battle has not ended and is still in progress.

Line c indicates $T \geq m_0 + n_0$ after all the possible battles have ended. Of course, the sum of all probabilities for all intersections along any arbitrary single thick line is equal to 1.

$P(\alpha, \beta)$ During Battle

		0	1	2
$m_0 - m = \alpha$	m	m_0	$m_0 - 1$	$m_0 - 2$
$n_0 - n = \beta$	n			
0	n_0	$P(0,0)$ $\dfrac{0!}{0!0!}\left(\dfrac{1}{1+E}\right)^0\left(\dfrac{E}{1+E}\right)^0 = 1$	$P(1,0)$ $\dfrac{1!}{1!0!}\left(\dfrac{1}{1+E}\right)^1\left(\dfrac{E}{1+E}\right)^0 = \dfrac{1}{1+E}$	$P(2,0)$ $\dfrac{2!}{2!0!}\left(\dfrac{1}{1+E}\right)^2\left(\dfrac{E}{1+E}\right)^0 = \left(\dfrac{1}{1+E}\right)^2$ **a**
1	$n_0 - 1$	$P(0,1)$ $\dfrac{1!}{1!0!}\left(\dfrac{1}{1+E}\right)^0\left(\dfrac{E}{1+E}\right)^1 = \dfrac{E}{1+E}$	$P(1,1)$ $\dfrac{2!}{1!1!}\left(\dfrac{1}{1+E}\right)^1\left(\dfrac{E}{1+E}\right)^1 = 2\dfrac{E}{(1+E)^2}$	$P(2,1)$ $\dfrac{3!}{2!1!}\left(\dfrac{1}{1+E}\right)^2\left(\dfrac{E}{1+E}\right)^1 = 3\dfrac{E}{(1+E)^3}$
2	$n_0 - 2$	$P(0,2)$ $\dfrac{2!}{0!2!}\left(\dfrac{1}{1+E}\right)^0\left(\dfrac{E}{1+E}\right)^2 = \left(\dfrac{E}{1+E}\right)^2$	$P(1,2)$ $\dfrac{3!}{1!2!}\left(\dfrac{1}{1+E}\right)^1\left(\dfrac{E}{1+E}\right)^2 = 3\dfrac{E^2}{(1+E)^3}$	$P(2,2)$ $\dfrac{4!}{2!2!}\left(\dfrac{1}{1+E}\right)^2\left(\dfrac{E}{1+E}\right)^2 = 6\dfrac{E^2}{(1+E)^4}$
(β)	(n)	$P(0,\beta)$ $\dfrac{\beta!}{0!\beta!}\left(\dfrac{1}{1+E}\right)^0\left(\dfrac{E}{1+E}\right)^\beta = \left(\dfrac{E}{1+E}\right)^\beta$		
$n_0 - 1$	1	$P(0, n_0-1)$ $\dfrac{(n_0-1)!}{0!(n_0-1)!}\left(\dfrac{1}{1+E}\right)^0\left(\dfrac{E}{1+E}\right)^{n_0-1}$	$P(1, n_0-1)$ $\dfrac{n_0!}{1!(n_0-1)!}\left(\dfrac{1}{1+E}\right)^1\left(\dfrac{E}{1+E}\right)^{n_0-1}$	$P(2, n_0-1)$ $\dfrac{(n_0+1)!}{2!(n_0-1)!}\left(\dfrac{1}{1+E}\right)^2\left(\dfrac{E}{1+E}\right)^{n_0-1}$ **b**
n_0	0	$P(0, n_0)$ $\dfrac{(n_0-1)!}{0!(n_0-1)!}\left(\dfrac{1}{1+E}\right)^0\left(\dfrac{E}{1+E}\right)^{n_0}$	$P(1, n_0)$ $\dfrac{n_0!}{1!(n_0-1)!}\left(\dfrac{1}{1+E}\right)^1\left(\dfrac{E}{1+E}\right)^{n_0}$	$P(2, n_0)$ $\dfrac{(n_0+1)!}{2!(n_0-1)!}\left(\dfrac{1}{1+E}\right)^2\left(\dfrac{E}{1+E}\right)^{n_0}$ **c**

$P(\alpha, n_0)$
Army m wins
n destroyed

			Army n wins m destroyed $P(m_0, \beta)$
(a)		$m_0 - 1$	m_0
(m)		1	0
$P(\alpha, 0)$ $\dfrac{\alpha!}{\alpha!0!}\left(\dfrac{1}{1+E}\right)^\alpha\left(\dfrac{E}{1+E}\right)^0 = \left(\dfrac{1}{1+E}\right)^\alpha$		$P(m_0-1, 0)$ $\left(\dfrac{1}{1+E}\right)^{m_0-1}$	**b** $P(m_0, 0)$ $\left(\dfrac{1}{1+E}\right)^{m_0}$ **c**
		$P(m_0-1, 1)$ $\dfrac{m_0!}{(m_0-1)!1!}\left(\dfrac{1}{1+E}\right)^{m_0-1}\left(\dfrac{E}{1+E}\right)^1$	$P(m_0, 1)$ $\dfrac{m_0!}{(m_0-1)!1!}\left(\dfrac{1}{1+E}\right)^{m_0}\left(\dfrac{E}{1+E}\right)^1$
		$P(m_0-1, 2)$ $\dfrac{(m_0+1)!}{(m_0-1)!2!}\left(\dfrac{1}{1+E}\right)^{m_0-1}\left(\dfrac{E}{1+E}\right)^2$	$P(m_0, 2)$ $\dfrac{(m_0+1)!}{(m_0-1)!2!}\left(\dfrac{1}{1+E}\right)^{m_0}\left(\dfrac{E}{1+E}\right)^2$
$P(\alpha, \beta)$ $\dfrac{(\alpha+\beta)!}{\alpha!\beta!}\left(\dfrac{1}{1+E}\right)^\alpha\left(\dfrac{E}{1+E}\right)^\beta$			$P(m_0, \beta)$ $\dfrac{(m_0-1+\beta)!}{(m_0-1)!\beta!}\left(\dfrac{1}{1+E}\right)^{m_0}\left(\dfrac{E}{1+E}\right)^\beta$
		$P(m_0-1, n_0-1)$ $\dfrac{(m_0-n_0-2)!}{(m_0-1)!(n_0-1)!}\left(\dfrac{1}{1+E}\right)^{m_0-1}\left(\dfrac{E}{1+E}\right)^{n_0-1}$	$P(m_0, n_0-1)$ $\dfrac{(m_0-n_0-2)!}{(m_0-1)!(n_0-1)!}\left(\dfrac{1}{1+E}\right)^{m_0}\left(\dfrac{E}{1+E}\right)^{n_0-1}$
$P(\alpha, n_0)$ $\dfrac{(\alpha+n_0-1)!}{\alpha!(n_0-1)!}\left(\dfrac{1}{1+E}\right)^\alpha\left(\dfrac{E}{1+E}\right)^{n_0}$		$P(m_0-1, n_0)$ $\dfrac{(m_0-n_0-2)!}{(m_0-1)!(n_0-1)!}\left(\dfrac{1}{1+E}\right)^{m_0-1}\left(\dfrac{E}{1+E}\right)^{n_0}$	$P(m_0, n_0)$ 0

$5-m=\alpha$ $3-n=\beta$		0	1	2
	m n	5	4	3
0	3	$P(0,0)$ $\dfrac{0!}{0!0!}\cdot\dfrac{1^0}{2^0}=1$	$P(1,0)$ $\dfrac{1!}{1!0!}\cdot\dfrac{1^0}{2^1}=\dfrac{1}{2}$	$P(2,0)$ $\dfrac{2!}{2!0!}\cdot\dfrac{1^0}{2^2}=\dfrac{2}{8}$
1	2	$P(0,1)$ $\dfrac{1!}{0!1!}\cdot\dfrac{1^1}{2^1}=\dfrac{1}{2}$	$P(1,1)$ $\dfrac{2!}{1!1!}\cdot\dfrac{1^1}{2^2}=\dfrac{2}{4}$	$P(2,1)$ $\dfrac{3!}{2!1!}\cdot\dfrac{1^1}{2^3}=\dfrac{6}{16}$
2	1	$P(0,2)$ $\dfrac{2!}{0!2!}\cdot\dfrac{1^2}{2^2}=\dfrac{2}{8}$	$P(1,2)$ $\dfrac{3!}{1!2!}\cdot\dfrac{1^2}{2^3}=\dfrac{6}{16}$	$P(2,2)$ $\dfrac{4!}{2!2!}\cdot\dfrac{1^2}{2^4}=\dfrac{24}{64}$
$P(\alpha,3)$ m wins n losses	0	$P(0,3)$ $\dfrac{2!}{0!2!}\cdot\dfrac{1^3}{2^3}=\dfrac{2}{16}$	$P(1,3)$ $\dfrac{3!}{1!2!}\cdot\dfrac{1^3}{2^4}=\dfrac{6}{32}$	$P(2,3)$ $\dfrac{4!}{2!2!}\cdot\dfrac{1^3}{2^5}=\dfrac{24}{128}$

As an example, let $m_0 = 5$, $n_0 = 3$, and E=1. The chart for $P(\alpha, \beta)$, $P(\alpha, 3)$, and $P(5, \beta)$ is shown above.

The sum of probabilities according to variations of the time variable T (=Kt) is equal to 1.

$T = 0$ $P(0,0) = 1$

1 $P(0,1)+(1,0) = \dfrac{1}{2}+\dfrac{1}{2} = 1$

2 $P(0,2)+P(1,1)+P(2,0) = \dfrac{2}{8}+\dfrac{2}{4}+\dfrac{2}{8} = 1$

3 $P(0,3)+P(1,2)+P(2,1)+P(3,0) = \dfrac{2}{16}+\dfrac{6}{16}+\dfrac{6}{16}+\dfrac{6}{48} = 1$

			m looses n wins
	3	4	$P(5, \beta)$ 5
	2	1	0
	$P(3,0)$ $\dfrac{3!}{3!0!} \cdot \dfrac{1^0}{2^3} = \dfrac{6}{48}$	$P(4,0)$ $\dfrac{4!}{4!0!} \cdot \dfrac{1^0}{2^3} = \dfrac{24}{384}$	$P(5,0)$ $\dfrac{4!}{4!0!} \cdot \dfrac{1^0}{2^5} = \dfrac{24}{768}$
	$P(3,1)$ $\dfrac{4!}{3!1!} \cdot \dfrac{1^1}{2^4} = \dfrac{24}{96}$	$P(4,1)$ $\dfrac{5!}{4!1!} \cdot \dfrac{1^1}{2^5} = \dfrac{120}{768}$	$P(5,1)$ $\dfrac{5!}{4!1!} \cdot \dfrac{1^1}{2^6} = \dfrac{120}{1,536}$
	$P(3,2)$ $\dfrac{5!}{3!2!} \cdot \dfrac{1^2}{2^5} = \dfrac{120}{384}$	$P(4,2)$ $\dfrac{6!}{4!2!} \cdot \dfrac{1^2}{2^6} = \dfrac{720}{3,072}$	$P(5,2)$ $\dfrac{6!}{4!2!} \cdot \dfrac{1^2}{2^6} = \dfrac{720}{6,144}$
	$P(3,3)$ $\dfrac{5!}{3!2!} \cdot \dfrac{1^3}{2^6} = \dfrac{120}{768}$	$P(4,3)$ $\dfrac{6!}{4!2!} \cdot \dfrac{1^3}{2^7} = \dfrac{720}{6,144}$	$P(5,3)$ 0

4 $P(0,3) + P(1,3) + P(2,2) + P(3,1) + P4,0) = \dfrac{2}{16} + \dfrac{6}{32} + \dfrac{24}{64} + \dfrac{24}{96} + \dfrac{24}{384} = 1$

5 $P(0,3) + P(1,3) + P(2,3) + P(3,2) + P(4,1) + P(5,0)$

$$= \dfrac{2}{16} + \dfrac{6}{32} + \dfrac{24}{128} + \dfrac{120}{384} + \dfrac{120}{768} + \dfrac{24}{768} = 1$$

6 $P(0,3) + P(1,3) + P(2,3) + P(3,3) + P(4,2) + P(5,1) + P(5,0)$

$$= \dfrac{2}{16} + \dfrac{6}{32} + \dfrac{24}{128} + \dfrac{120}{768} + \dfrac{720}{3072} + \dfrac{120}{1536} + \dfrac{24}{768} = 1$$

7 $\underline{P(0,3) + P(1,3) + P(2,3) + P(3,3) + P(4,3)} + \underline{P(5,2) + P(5,1) + P(5,0)}$

   (Winning probability of army m)   (Winning probability of army n)

$$= \underbrace{\dfrac{2}{16} + \dfrac{6}{32} + \dfrac{24}{128} + \dfrac{120}{768} + \dfrac{720}{6144}}_{\dfrac{4752}{6144} = \dfrac{99}{128}} + \underbrace{\dfrac{720}{6144} + \dfrac{120}{1536} + \dfrac{24}{768}}_{\dfrac{1392}{6144} = \dfrac{29}{128}} = 1$$

Based on the upper limit of the sum of both army's losses with $\alpha + \beta = m_0 + n_0 - 1$, when T is greater than 7, all are the same; therefore, we chose (7+). The number of survivors for both armies as time passes is the sum product of the number of survivors that correlate with the number of losses and the probability per each loss unit; that is, the expected value.

Expected value for army m survivors:

$$E(m)_T = \sum_{\alpha=0}^{m_0-1}(m_0 - \alpha)P(\alpha,\beta) \quad \text{Note that } \beta = T - \alpha \leq n_0$$

Expected value for army n survivors:

$$E(n)_T = \sum_{\beta=0}^{n_0-1}(n_0 - \alpha)P(\alpha,\beta) \quad \text{Note that } \alpha = T - \beta \leq m_0$$

For example, if T = 2 during the fighting, then:

$$E(m)_{T=2} = 5P(0,2) + 4P(1,1) + 3P(2,0)$$

$$= 5 \times \frac{2}{8} + 4 \times \frac{2}{4} + 3 \times \frac{2}{8} = \frac{5}{4} + \frac{8}{4} + \frac{3}{4} = \frac{16}{4} = 4$$

$$E(n)_{T=2} = 3P(2,0) + 2P(1,1) + 1P(0,2)$$

$$= 3 \times \frac{2}{8} + 2 \times \frac{2}{4} + 1 \times \frac{2}{8} = \frac{3}{4} + \frac{4}{4} + \frac{1}{4} = \frac{8}{4} = 2$$

If T = 4, including when the fighting is in progress, then:

$$E(m)_{T=4} = 5P(0,3) + 4P(1,3) + 3P(2,2) + 2P(3,1) + 1P(4,0)$$

$$= 5 \times \frac{2}{16} + 4 \times \frac{6}{32} + 3 \times \frac{24}{64} + 2 \times \frac{24}{96} + 1 \times \frac{24}{384} = \frac{49}{16} = 3.0625$$

$$E(n)_{T=4} = 3P(4,0) + 2P(3,1) + 1P(2,2) + 0P(1,3) + 0P(0,3)$$

$$= 3 \times \frac{24}{384} + 2 \times \frac{24}{96} + 1 \times \frac{24}{64} = \frac{17}{16} = 1.0625$$

Furthermore, the expected value for survivors when one side wins can be obtained from (2.37) and (2.38).

Expected value for survivors when army m wins   (2.39)

$$E(m) = \sum_{\alpha=0}^{m_0-1}(m_0 - \alpha)P(\alpha,n_0) = \sum_{\alpha=0}^{m_0-1}(m_0 - \alpha)\frac{(\alpha+n_0-1)!}{\alpha!(n_0-1)!} \cdot \frac{E^{n_0}}{(1+E)^{\alpha+n_0}}$$

Expected value for survivors when army n wins   (2.40)

$$E(n) = \sum_{\beta=0}^{n_0-1}(n_0 - \beta)P(m_0,\beta) = \sum_{\beta=0}^{n_0-1}(n_0 - \beta)\frac{(\beta+m_0-1)!}{\beta!(m_0-1)!} \cdot \frac{E^{\beta}}{(1+E)^{\beta+m_0}}$$

And arranging when $m_0 = 5$, $n_0 = 3$, and $E = 1$, then:

[Army m wins. Army n is destroyed]

Loss α	Survivors m	Winning probability $P(\alpha,n_0)$	Expected value for survivors $(m_0 - \alpha)P(\alpha,n_0)$
0	5	$P(0,3) = \dfrac{2}{16} = \dfrac{16}{128}$	$5 \times \dfrac{16}{128} = \dfrac{80}{128} = 0.6250$
1	4	$P(1,3) = \dfrac{6}{32} = \dfrac{24}{128}$	$4 \times \dfrac{24}{128} = \dfrac{96}{128} = 0.7500$
2	3	$P(2,3) = \dfrac{24}{128}$	$3 \times \dfrac{24}{128} = \dfrac{72}{128} = 0.5625$
3	2	$P(3,3) = \dfrac{120}{768} = \dfrac{20}{128}$	$2 \times \dfrac{20}{128} = \dfrac{40}{128} = 0.3125$
4	1	$P(4,3) = \dfrac{720}{6,144} = \dfrac{15}{128}$	$1 \times \dfrac{15}{128} = \dfrac{15}{128} = 0.1172$

(Winning probability for army m) $\Sigma P_m = 0.7734 = \dfrac{99}{128}$

(Expected value for survivors) $E(m) = 2.3672$

[Army n wins. Army m is destroyed]

Loss	Survivors	Winning probability	Expected value for survivors
β	n	$P(m_0, \beta)$	$(n_0 - \beta)P(m_0, \beta)$
0	3	$P(5,0) = \dfrac{24}{768} = \dfrac{4}{128}$	$3 \times \dfrac{4}{128} = \dfrac{12}{128} = 0.0938$
1	2	$P(5,1) = \dfrac{120}{1{,}536} = \dfrac{10}{128}$	$2 \times \dfrac{10}{128} = \dfrac{20}{128} = 0.1563$
2	1	$P(5,2) = \dfrac{720}{6{,}144} = \dfrac{15}{128}$	$1 \times \dfrac{15}{128} = \dfrac{15}{128} = 0.1172$

(Winning probability for army n) $\Sigma P_n = 0.2266 = \dfrac{29}{128}$

(Expected value for survivors) $E(n) = 0.3672$

Note: In Morse & Kimball, *The Methods of Operations Research* (p. 68), $E(m) = 3.061$ and $E(n) = 1.621$. These are erroneous.

That is, the winning probability for army n is 22.66%, or one out of 4 times, and even after winning, the expected value for survivors is 0.3672, which is quite low.

When Lanchester's Linear Law is analyzed based on principles of certainty, and when E = 1, the army with less force would be defeated; however, based on the theory of probability, an inferior army still has a chance to win, and other than enhancing the efficiency of the weapons and skills, it is more advantageous to fight a battle in the way of a single combat.

Regarding the number of survivors, let's compare armies m and n with respect to the theory of probability and Lanchester's Linear Law when $m_0 = 5$, $n_0 = 3$, and $E = 1$.

In Lanchester's Linear Law, the number of survivors are shown as special solutions. From (2.4), (2.5), (2.6) and (2.7), we have:

$$m = m_0 - at \quad \text{survivors of army } m = m_0 - \frac{1}{1+E}T$$

$$n = n_0 - bt \quad \text{survivors of army } n = n_0 - \frac{E}{1+E}T$$

Lanchester's Linear Law.

Particular solutions according to Lanchester's Linear Laws, with $m = 5 - t$, or $m = 5 - T/2$, and $n = 3 - t$, or $n = 3 - T/2$

t	0	0.5	1	1.5	2	2.5	3	3.5
T=2t	0	1	2	3	4	5	6	7+
Survivors of army m (Theory of probability)	5.0	$\frac{9}{2}=4.5$	$\frac{16}{4}=4.0$	$\frac{28}{8}=3.5$	$\frac{49}{16}=3.0625$	$\frac{87}{32}=2.7188$	$\frac{159}{64}=2.4844$	$\frac{303}{128}=2.3672$
(Lanchester's Linear Law)	5.0	4.5	4.0	3.5	3.0	2.5	2.0	2.0
Survivors of army n (Theory of probability)	3.0	$\frac{5}{2}=2.5$	$\frac{8}{4}=2.0$	$\frac{12}{8}=1.5$	$\frac{17}{16}=1.0625$	$\frac{23}{32}=0.7188$	$\frac{31}{64}=0.4844$	$\frac{47}{128}=0.3672$
(Lanchester's Linear Law)	3.0	2.5	2.0	1.5	1.0	0.5	0	0

That is, in the former half of the battle where there are still survivors on both sides, the results for both armies match; however, in the latter half as one army begins to win, the results start to diverge. In Lanchester's Linear Law, the results are based on principles of certainty; however, the theory of probability shows more realism, where based on how the battle is fought, there is still a chance of winning.

Next, based on the theory of probability, let's see what would be the level to which the inferior army should raise its efficiency of the weapons and skills, E, to bring parity to its fighting strength.

According to Lanchester's Linear Law, in this case, to win, at least
$E > \dfrac{n_0}{m_0}$ (or $E > \dfrac{m_0}{n_0}$) With respect to the sum of probabilities of winning
regarding both armies $\left(\sum P_m + \sum P_n\right)$, from (2.36), according to the binominal distribution, each probability of winning is the partial sum of the binominal distribution, as confirmed previously.

$$\sum P_m + \sum P_n = \left(\dfrac{1}{1+E} + \dfrac{E}{1+E}\right)^{m_0+n_0-1} = \left(\dfrac{1}{1+E}\right)^{m_0+n_0-1}(E+1)^{m_0+n_0-1} = 1$$

Note that $\left(\dfrac{1}{1+E}\right)^{m_0+n_0-1}$ is a constant, thus expanding $(E+1)^{m_0+n_0-1}$

$$= \left(\dfrac{1}{1+E}\right)^{m_0+n_0-1}\left[\binom{m_0+n_0-1}{1}E^{m_0+n_0-1} + L + \binom{m_0+n_0-1}{m_0-1}E^{n_0}\right\} m_0 \text{ terms}$$

$$+ \binom{m_0+n_0-1}{m_0}E^{n_0-1} + L + \binom{m_0+n_0-1}{m_0+n_0-1}E^0\right]\right\} n_0 \text{ terms}$$

$$= \left(\dfrac{1}{1+E}\right)^{m_0+n_0-1}\left[\sum\binom{m_0+n_0-1}{\alpha}E^{(m_0+n_0-1)-\alpha} + \sum\binom{m_0+n_0-1}{\beta}E^{\beta}\right]$$

Then, to arrange (2.34) and (2.35),

$$\sum P_m = \sum_{\alpha=0}^{m_0-1}\binom{m_0+n_0-1}{\alpha}\left(\dfrac{1}{1+E}\right)^{\alpha}\left(\dfrac{E}{1+E}\right)^{(m_0+n_0-1)-\alpha}$$

$$= \left(\dfrac{1}{1+E}\right)^{m_0+n_0-1}\left[\sum\binom{m_0+n_0-1}{\alpha}E^{(m_0+n_0-1)-\alpha}\right]$$

$$\sum P_n = \sum_{\beta=0}^{n_0-1}\binom{m_0+n_0-1}{\beta}\left(\dfrac{1}{1+E}\right)^{(m_0+n_0-1)-\beta}\left(\dfrac{E}{1+E}\right)^{\beta}$$

$$= \left(\dfrac{1}{1+E}\right)^{m_0+n_0-1}\left[\sum\binom{m_0+n_0-1}{\beta}E^{\beta}\right]$$

Parity in the fighting strength of both armies means equal probabilities of winning, or:

$$\sum P_m = \sum P_n \quad \therefore \sum_{\alpha=0}^{m_0-1} \binom{m_0+n_0-1}{\alpha} E^{(m_0+n_0-1)-\alpha} = \sum_{\beta=0}^{n_0-1} \binom{m_0+n_0-1}{\beta} E^{\beta}$$

$$\therefore \sum_{\alpha=0}^{m_0-1} \binom{m_0+n_0-1}{\alpha} E^{(m_0+n_0-1)-\alpha} - \sum_{\beta=0}^{n_0-1} \binom{m_0+n_0-1}{\beta} E^{\beta} = 0 \quad (2.41)$$

Finding $(E+1)^{m_0+n_0-1}$ when the power of (m_0+n_0-1) is large, it may be too computationaly intensive and be better handled using a computer.

For example, let's assume army m is inferior; $m_0 = 3$, $n_0 = 5$. In this case, we assume army m is inferior because $E = \dfrac{b}{a}$. If army n is inferior, then E is shown as $\dfrac{1}{E} = \dfrac{a}{b}$, a case we tried to avoid.

Here, $(E+1)^{3+5-1} = (E+1)^7$ is expanded:

$$\sum_{\alpha=0}^{3-1} \binom{7}{\alpha} E^{7-\alpha} = \sum_{\beta=0}^{5-1} \binom{7}{\beta} E^{\beta}$$

$$\therefore E^7 + 7E^6 + 21E^5 = 1 + 7E + 21E^2 + 35E^3 + 35E^4$$

$$\therefore (E^7 + 7E^6 + 21E^5) - (35E^4 + 35E^3 + 21E^2 + 7E + 1) = 0$$

After solving the above polynomial, E = 1.74637688, and according to Lanchester's Linear Law, compared to $E > \dfrac{5}{3} = 1.6667$, this value is somewhat greater.

The winning probabilities and expected values for survivors of armies m and n are calculated as follows on the next page:

Table of results, army m wins, army n is defeated

α	m	Winning probability $P(\alpha, n_o)$		Expected survivors $(m_0 - \alpha)P(\alpha, n_o)$
0	3	$P(0,5)= \dfrac{(0+5-1)!}{0!(5-1)!} \times \dfrac{1.74637688^5}{(1+1.74637688)^{0+5}}$	$= 0.10396549$	$3 \times 0.10396549 = 0.31189646$
1	2	$P(1,5)= \dfrac{(1+5-1)!}{1!(5-1)!} \times \dfrac{1.74637688^5}{(1+1.74637688)^{1+5}}$	$= 0.18927753$	$2 \times 0.18927753 = 0.37855506$
2	1	$P(2,5)= \dfrac{(2+5-1)!}{2!(5-1)!} \times \dfrac{1.74637688^5}{(1+1.74637688)^{2+5}}$	$= 0.20675698$	$1 \times 0.20675698 = 0.20675698$

Winning probability for army m $\sum P_m = 0.5$ Expected value for survivors $E(m) = 0.89720850$

Table of results, army n wins, army m is destroyed

β	n	Winning probability $P(m_0, \beta)$		Expected survivors $(n_o - \beta)P(m_0, \beta)$
0	5	$P(3,0)= \dfrac{(0+3-1)!}{0!(3-1)!} \times \dfrac{1.74637688^0}{(1+1.74637688)^{0+3}}$	$= 0.04827470$	$5 \times 0.04827470 = 0.24137350$
1	4	$P(3,1)= \dfrac{(1+3-1)!}{1!(3-1)!} \times \dfrac{1.74637688^1}{(1+1.74637688)^{1+3}}$	$= 0.09209132$	$4 \times 0.09209132 = 0.36836528$
2	3	$P(3,2)= \dfrac{(2+3-1)!}{2!(3-1)!} \times \dfrac{1.74637688^2}{(1+1.74637688)^{2+3}}$	$= 0.11711878$	$3 \times 0.11711878 = 0.35135634$
3	2	$P(3,3)= \dfrac{(3+3-1)!}{3!(3-1)!} \times \dfrac{1.74637688^3}{(1+1.74637688)^{3+3}}$	$= 0.12412324$	$2 \times 0.12412324 = 0.24824648$
4	1	$P(3,4)= \dfrac{(4+3-1)!}{4!(3-1)!} \times \dfrac{1.74637688^4}{(+1.74637688)^{4+3}}$	$= 0.11839196$	$1 \times 0.11839196 = 0.11839196$

Winning probability for army n $\sum P_n = 0.5$ Expected value for survivors $E(n) = 1.32773356$

In the case of a single battle, the side with fewer initial forces, by enhancing the exchange rate E (1.746 times) and achieving parity, causes a great increase in the expected value for survivors, 2.4435 times ($\frac{0.8972}{0.3672}$).

Let's calculate several examples when the initial forces $m_0 : n_0$ are equal:

	When E=1				The inferior side brings parity to the winning probability (0.5)			
Initial forces	Winning Probability		Expected value for Survivors		Exchange rate for army n	Corresponding value for Survivors		Ratio of values for Survivors
$m_0 : n_0$	ΣP_m	ΣP_n	E(m)	E(n)	E'	E'(m)	E'(n)	E'(n)/E(n)
5 : 3	0.7734	0.2266	2.3672	0.3672	1.7464	1.3277	0.8972	2.4435
10 : 6	0.8491	0.1509	4.3129	0.3129	1.7051	1.9373	1.2714	4.0630
25 : 5	0.9459	0.0540	10.1453	0.1453	1.6817	3.1395	2.0010	13.7697
50 : 30	0.9881	0.0119	20.0370	0.0370	1.6741	4.4910	2.8163	76.1438
100 : 60	0.9993	0.0007	40.0025	0.0025	1.6704	6.4006	3.9653	1,607.6211
200 : 120	0.999997	0.000003	80.00001	0.00001	1.6685	9.1000	5.5874	451,686.7631

As seen here, when initial forces grow in size, the winning probability, expected value for survivors, and exchange rate that has to be enhanced to gain parity or better odds in the winning probability, even when considered from the standpoint of the theory of probability, approach the results predicted by Lanchester's Linear Law.

For example, when $m_0 = 200$, $n_0 = 120$, and $E = 1$, then the success of army m ($\Sigma P_m = 1$), the destruction of army n ($\Sigma P_n = 0$), and the number of survivors for army m ($m = m_0 - n_0$) approaches 200 - 120 = 80. Also, the exchange rate that inferior army n enhances to gain parity $E > \frac{m_0}{n_0}$ approaches 5/3 = 1.6667.

Here, compared to the ratio of exchange rates, which the inferior army enhances to gain parity, the ratio of number of survivors increases dramatically.

Therefore, in single combats, even based on the analysis using the theory of probability, when the initial number of forces grows in size, the winning conditions approach those of Lanchester's Linear Law.

If E = 1, committing more force should lead to victory. If forces are inferior, as long as the exchange rate is not too deviated compared to the ratio of forces, again the battle could be won. That is, depending on the situation, either force could be concentrated or the exchange rate enhanced in order to win the battle.

Summary

Army m and army n are in a combat; if the combat is the accumulation of duels (a single combat), based on an analysis according to the theory of probability, with initial values of m_0 and n_0, and losses of α and β, we have:

Winning probability for army m:

$$\sum P_m = \sum_{\alpha=0}^{m_0-1} P(\alpha, n_0) = \sum_{\alpha=0}^{m_0-1} \frac{(\alpha + n_0 - 1)!}{\alpha!(n_0 - 1)!} \cdot \frac{E^{n_0}}{(1+E)^{\alpha+n_0}}$$

Winning probability for army n:

$$\sum P_n = \sum_{\beta=0}^{n_0-1} P(m_0, \beta) = \sum_{\beta=0}^{n_0-1} \frac{(\beta + m_0 - 1)!}{\beta!(m_0 - 1)!} \cdot \frac{E^{\beta}}{(1+E)^{\beta+m_0}}$$

Note that, $E = \dfrac{b}{a}$ also $\sum P_m + \sum P_n = 1$

Expected value for survivors of army m:

$$E(m) = \sum_{\alpha=0}^{m_0-1}(m_0 - \alpha)P(\alpha, n_0)$$

$$= \sum_{\alpha=0}^{m_0-1}(m_0 - \alpha)\frac{(\alpha + n_0 - 1)!}{\alpha!(n_0 - 1)!} \cdot \frac{E^{n_0}}{(1+E)^{\alpha+n_0}}$$

Expected value for survivors of army n:

$$E(n) = \sum_{\beta=0}^{n_0-1}(n_0 - \beta)P(m_0, \beta)$$

$$= \sum_{\beta=0}^{n_0-1}(n_0 - \beta)\frac{(\beta + m_0 - 1)!}{\beta!(m_0 - 1)!} \cdot \frac{E^{\beta}}{(1+E)^{\beta+m_0}}$$

The exchange rate that the inferior side has to enhance

E is found by expanding $(1+E)^{m_0+n_0-1}$ and solving the resultant polynominal.

$$\sum_{\alpha=0}^{m_0-1}\binom{m_0+n_0-1}{\alpha}E^{(m_0+n_0-1)-\alpha} - \sum_{\beta=0}^{n_0-1}\binom{m_0+n_0-1}{\beta}E^{\beta} = 0$$

Here, when initial values m_0 and n_0 increase, E will approach the winning condition $E > \frac{n_0}{m_0}$ (or $E > \frac{m_0}{n_0}$) according to Lanchester's Linear Law.

2.4.4 Lanchester's Square Law and the exchange rate

To analyze Lanchester's Square Law based on the theory of probability, each combat is considered to be an exchange of volley-firing.

According to differential equations (2.13) and (2.14)

$$\begin{cases} \dfrac{dm}{dt} = -an & (2.12) \ a \text{ is efficiency of the weapons and skills of army } n \\ \dfrac{dn}{dt} = -bm & (2.13) \ b \text{ is efficiency of the weapons and skills of army } m \end{cases}$$

Substituting the exchange rate E; since the unit of the time variable is arbitrary, then:

$$E = \frac{b}{a}, \quad a+b = K, \quad a = \frac{K}{1+E}, \quad b = \frac{KE}{1+E}, \quad \tau = \frac{\sqrt{E}}{1+E} Kt$$

$$\therefore \quad dt = \frac{1+E}{K\sqrt{E}} d\tau$$

Hence:

$$\begin{cases} \dfrac{dm}{\frac{1+E}{K\sqrt{E}} d\tau} = -\dfrac{K}{1+E} n \\ \dfrac{dn}{\frac{1+E}{K\sqrt{E}} d\tau} = -\dfrac{KE}{1+E} m \end{cases} \therefore \begin{cases} \dfrac{dm}{d\tau} = -\dfrac{n}{\sqrt{E}} & (2.42) \\ \dfrac{dn}{d\tau} = -m\sqrt{E} & (2.43) \end{cases}$$

Furthermore, the duration of each instance of volley-firing is short, and losses on both sides during the fighting are not considered to reduce the fighting strength to a great extent. In other words, the existing number of survivors on both sides could be considered constant values.

Thus (2.42) and (2.43), as in the case of single combat, can be expressed as follows:

$$\frac{dm}{d\tau} = -\frac{n}{\sqrt{E}} \qquad \frac{dn}{d\tau} = -m\sqrt{E}$$

$$dm = -\frac{n}{\sqrt{E}} d\tau \qquad dn = -m\sqrt{E}$$

$$\int dm = -\frac{n}{\sqrt{E}} \int d\tau \qquad \int dn = -m\sqrt{E} \int d\tau$$

$$m = -\frac{n}{\sqrt{E}} \tau + C_1 \qquad n = -m\sqrt{E}\tau + C_2$$

When $\tau = 0$, $C_1 = m_0$ and $C_2 = n_0$. Number of losses for armies m and n, $(m_0 - m)$ and $(n_0 - n)$, can be shown as:

$$m_0 - m = \frac{n}{\sqrt{E}} \tau \qquad n_0 - n = m\sqrt{E}\tau \quad \text{(number of losses)}$$

Here, by taking the ratio of number of losses for armies m and n, the average ratio (with respect to men) shot by 1 unit of each opposing army is obtained.

$$\frac{n_0 - n}{m_0 - m} = \frac{m\sqrt{E}\tau}{\frac{n}{\sqrt{E}}\tau} = \frac{\frac{\sqrt{E}}{n}\tau}{\frac{1}{m\sqrt{E}}\tau} \quad \text{in time } \tau$$

(Numerator) ... (Men) shot by 1 unit of army m ... Army n average ratio
(Denominator) ... (Men) shot by 1 unit of army n ... Army m average ratio

Thus, survivors (men not shot) can be represented as follows:
Army m average ratio with respect to men not shot by 1 unit of army n

$$\left(1 - \frac{1}{m\sqrt{E}}\tau\right) \quad \text{in time } \tau$$

Army n average ratio with respect to men not shot by 1 unit of army m

$$\left(1 - \frac{\sqrt{E}}{n}\tau\right) \quad \text{in time } \tau$$

However, for example, when there are 3 men in army n, since some men are skilled shooters and some are not, let's assume the ratios for men not shot with respect to army m are 0.3, 0.8, and 0.9. The probabilities for these 3 men missing their targets are independent of each other, and is equal to 0.3 × 0.8 × 0.9 = 0.216.

The average probability for each man, therefore, is $\sqrt[3]{0.216} = 0.6$. As a result, the probability for each man in army m not to be shot by men in army n can be represented as the average ratio of army m not shot by a unit of army n, raised to the power of the suviving force number in the following manner, $0.6^3 = 0.216$.

In time τ, the probability for each unit (man) in army m or n not to be shot is

$$m: \left(1 - \frac{1}{m\sqrt{E}}\tau\right)^n \qquad n: \left(1 - \frac{\sqrt{E}}{n}\tau\right)^m$$

And the probability to be shot is:

$$m: \left[1 - \left(1 - \frac{1}{m\sqrt{E}}\tau\right)^n\right] \qquad n: \left[1 - \left(1 - \frac{\sqrt{E}}{n}\tau\right)^m\right]$$

Again, as in Lanchester's Linear Law, from the general equation of the binominal distribution, (display of probability is abbreviated).

The probability that among m units of army m, x units are not shot:

$$x = 0,1,2,\text{L L },m$$

$$P_r(x;m) = \binom{m}{x}\left[1 - \frac{1}{m\sqrt{E}}\tau\right]^{nx}\left[1 - \left(1 - \frac{\sqrt{E}}{n}\tau\right)^m\right]^{m-x} \qquad (2.44)$$

The probability that among n units of army n, y units are not shot:

$$y = 0,1,2,......,n$$

$$P_r(y;n) = \binom{n}{y}\left[\left(1-\frac{\sqrt{E}}{n}\tau\right)^m\right]^y\left[1-\left(1-\frac{\sqrt{E}}{n}\tau\right)^m\right]^{n-y} \quad (2.45)$$

Also, from the average of the binominal distribution:

Unit average not shot among army m; $\quad m_{avg} = m\left(1-\frac{1}{m\sqrt{E}}\tau\right)^n$

Unit average not shot among army n; $\quad n_{avg} = n\left(1-\frac{\sqrt{E}}{n}\tau\right)^m$

These naturally do not correspond to particular solutions (2.28) and (2.29) with respect to Lanchester's Square Law. This is because although numbers of survivors m and n of both armies are supposed to decline, we assumed that they are fixed and considered them constants. But if m and n are not too different from the initial values m_0 and n_0, in other words, when the time variable τ is very small, there will be an approximation.

If the number of forces of both armies are very large:

$$\lim_{n\to\infty}\left(1-\frac{1}{m\sqrt{E}}\tau\right)^n = e^{-\frac{n}{m\sqrt{E}}\tau}$$

Since the time unit is arbitrary, if $\quad -\frac{1}{m\sqrt{E}}\tau = \frac{t_1}{n}$

$$\lim_{n\to\infty}\left(1+\frac{t_1}{n}\right)^n = \lim_{n\to\infty}\left[\left(1+\frac{t_1}{n}\right)^{\frac{n}{t_1}}\right]^{t_1} \quad \lim_{n\to\infty}\left[\left(1+\frac{1}{\frac{n}{t_1}}\right)^{\frac{n}{t_1}}\right]^{t_1} = e^{t_1} = e^{-\frac{n}{m\sqrt{E}}\tau}$$

$$\lim_{m\to\infty}\left(1-\frac{\sqrt{E}}{n}\tau\right)^m = e^{-\frac{m\sqrt{E}}{n}\tau}$$

Since the time unit is arbitrary, if $-\frac{\sqrt{E}}{n}\tau = \frac{t_2}{m}$

$$\lim_{m\to\infty}\left(1+\frac{t_2}{m}\right)^m = \lim_{m\to\infty}\left[\left(1+\frac{t_2}{m}\right)^{\frac{m}{t_2}}\right]^{t_2} = \lim_{m\to\infty}\left[\left(1+\frac{1}{\frac{m}{t_2}}\right)^{\frac{m}{t_2}}\right]^{t_2} = e^{t_2} = e^{-\frac{m\sqrt{E}}{n}\tau}$$

Therefore, (2.44) and (2.45) can be represented as follows (display of probability is abbreviated):

The probability that among m_0 units of army m, m units are not shot:

$$P_r(m;m_0) = \binom{m_0}{m}\left(e^{-\frac{n}{m\sqrt{E}}\tau}\right)^m \left(1-e^{-\frac{n}{m\sqrt{E}}\tau}\right)^{m_0-m}$$

And the probability that among n_0 units of army n, n units are not shot

$$P_r(n;n_0) = \binom{n_0}{n}\left(e^{-\frac{m\sqrt{E}}{n}\tau}\right)^n \left(1-e^{-\frac{m\sqrt{E}}{n}\tau}\right)^{n_0-n}$$

First, we assumed that the duration (time) of an instance of fighting is short; thus, considering the accumulation of infinite times, we integrate the above equation with respect to time variable τ (≥ 0).

$$\int_0^\infty P_r\left(m;m_0, e^{-\frac{n}{m\sqrt{E}}\tau}\right)d\tau = \int_0^\infty \binom{m_0}{m}\left(e^{-\frac{n}{m\sqrt{E}}\tau}\right)^m \left(1-e^{-\frac{n}{m\sqrt{E}}\tau}\right)^{m_0-m} d\tau$$

Here, if $e^{-\frac{n}{m\sqrt{E}}\tau} = x$, $-\frac{n}{m\sqrt{E}}\tau = \log x$, $\tau = -\frac{m\sqrt{E}}{n}\log x$

$\therefore \frac{d\tau}{dx} = -\frac{m\sqrt{E}}{n} \cdot \frac{1}{x}$

And when τ varies from 0 to ∞, x simply varies from 1 to 0.

$$= \binom{m_0}{m} \int_1^0 x^m (1-x)^{m_0-m} \frac{d\tau}{dx} \cdot dx$$

$$= \binom{m_0}{m} \int_1^0 x^m (1-x)^{m_0-m} \left(-\frac{m\sqrt{E}}{n} \cdot \frac{1}{x}\right) dx$$

$$= \left(-\frac{m\sqrt{E}}{n}\right)\binom{m_0}{m} \int_1^0 x^{m-1}(1-x)^{m_0-m} dx$$

The integration from 1 to 0 is the same as integration from 0 to 1 if the sign is changed. Hence:

$$= \left(\frac{m\sqrt{E}}{n}\right)\binom{m_0}{m} \int_0^1 x^{m-1}(1-x)^{(m_0-m+1)-1} dx$$

Here, when $r > 0$ and $s > 0$, $\int_0^1 x^{r-1}(1-x)^{s-1} dx$ is called the complete beta function, and is represented as $\beta(r, s)$. Beta functions relate closely to Gamma functions in the following manner:

(Beta function) $\beta(r,s) = \dfrac{\Gamma(r)\Gamma(s)}{\Gamma(r+s)}$

(Gamma function) $\Gamma(r) = \int_0^\infty x^{r-1} e^{-x} dx$

Specially, when r (and s) are integers, $\Gamma(r) = (r-1)!$ Thus:

$$\beta(r,s) = \frac{(r-1)!(s-1)!}{(r+s-1)!}$$

Since $r = m$, $s = m_0 - m + 1$, and they are positive integers, then:

$$= \left(\frac{m\sqrt{E}}{n}\right)\binom{m_0}{m}\beta(m, m_0 - m + 1)$$

$$= \left(\frac{m\sqrt{E}}{n}\right)\binom{m_0}{m}\frac{(m-1)!\{m_0 - m + 1) - 1\}!}{\{m + (m_0 - m + 1) - 1\}!}$$

$$= \left(\frac{m\sqrt{E}}{n}\right)\frac{m_0!}{m!(m_0 - m)!} \cdot \frac{(m-1)!(m_0 - m)!}{m_0!}$$

$$= \frac{\sqrt{E}}{n}$$

$$\therefore \int_0^\infty \Pr\left(m; m_0, e^{-\frac{n}{m\sqrt{E}}\tau}\right) d\tau$$

$$= \int_0^\infty \binom{m_0}{m}\left(e^{-\frac{n}{m\sqrt{E}}\tau}\right)^m \left(1 - e^{-\frac{n}{m\sqrt{E}}\tau}\right)^{m_0 - m} d\tau = \frac{\sqrt{E}}{n}$$

Similarly, in the case of army n, we have:

$$\int_0^\infty \Pr\left(n; n_0, e^{-\frac{m\sqrt{E}}{n}\tau}\right) d\tau$$

$$= \int_0^\infty \binom{n_0}{n}\left(e^{-\frac{m\sqrt{E}}{n}\tau}\right)^n \left(1 - e^{-\frac{m\sqrt{E}}{n}\tau}\right)^{n_0 - n} d\tau = \frac{1}{m\sqrt{E}}$$

Furthermore, when considering infinite time, any time unit may be chosen. Here, we generally assign t for the time unit common to both armies.

$$\begin{cases} \dfrac{1}{\sqrt{E}} \int_0^\infty n \cdot \Pr(m; m_0, e^{-t}) dt = \\[1ex] \dfrac{1}{\sqrt{E}} \int_0^\infty n \binom{m_0}{m} (e^{-t})^m (1 - e^{-t})^{m_0 - m} dt = 1 \\[1ex] \sqrt{E} \int_0^\infty m \cdot \Pr(n; n_0 e^{-t}) dt = \\[1ex] \sqrt{E} \int_0^\infty m \binom{n_0}{n} (e^{-t})^n (1 - e^{-t})^{n_0 - n} dt = 1 \end{cases}$$

That is, to find "total probability (=1) for units not shot" for each army, with infinite time as a precondition, surviving existing number of forces (n or m) at any time for the opposing army must be multiplied in advance by the probability for units not shot, Pr for each instance of fighting.

However, with regard to exchange rate E, it must be remembered that constant $\dfrac{1}{\sqrt{E}}$ for army m and constant $\sqrt{E}$ for army n are weighted as coefficients.

Therefore, to find the total probability for units not shot (survivors) for both armies, by way of weight correction, we must multiply $\sqrt{E}$ for army m and $\dfrac{1}{\sqrt{E}}$ for army n by "the probability for units not shot" obtained for each army at the end.

Therefore, regarding armies m and n, within initial number of forces $(m_0 + n_0)$ units, the probability that $(m + n)$ units are not shot, as the added total of probabilities for units not shot for both armies, can be obtained in the following manner. From now on, since we consider infinite time, the representation will be in the form of derived functions.

$$\frac{d}{dt}\{\Pr(m+n;\ m_0+n_0,\ e^{-t})\}$$

$$= n\binom{m_0+n_0}{m+n}(e^{-t})^{m+n}(1-e^{-t})^{(m_0+n_0)-(m+n)}$$

$$+ m\binom{m_0+n_0}{m+n}(e^{-t})^{m+n}(1-e^{-t})^{(m_0+n_0)-(m+n)}$$

$$= (m+n)\binom{m_0+n_0}{m+n}(e^{-t})^{m+n}(1-e^{-t})^{(m_0+n_0)-(m+n)}$$

Therefore: $(m+n)\dfrac{(m_0+n_0)!}{(m+n)!\{(m_0+n_0)-(m+n)\}!}$

$$= \frac{(m_0+n_0)!}{(m+n-1)!\{(m_0+n_0)-(m+n)\}!}(e^{-t})^{m+n}(1-e^{-t})^{(m_0+n_0)-(m+n)}$$

However, seen from losses of both armies, $\alpha = m_0 - n$ and $\beta = n_0 - n$, as they occur, surviving existing number of forces are $m = m_0 - \alpha$ and $n = n_0 - \beta$; thus,

$$\frac{d}{dt}\{\Pr(m+n;\ m_0+n_0,\ e^{-t})\}$$

$$= \frac{(m_0+n_0)!}{\{(m_0-\alpha)+(n_0-\beta)-1\}![\{(m_0+n_0)-\{(m_0-\alpha)+(n_0-\beta)\}]!}$$
$$\times (e^{-t})^{(m_0-\alpha)+(n_0-\beta)}(1-e^{-t})^{(m_0+n_0)-\{(m_0-\alpha)+(n_0-\beta)\}}$$

$$= \frac{(m_0+n_0)!}{\{(m_0+n_0)-(\alpha+\beta)-1\}+(\alpha+\beta)!}(e^{-t})^{(m_0+n_0)-(\alpha+\beta)}(1-e^{-t})^{(\alpha+\beta)}$$

$$(2.46)$$

Here, let's note the following equations.

$$(m_0 + n_0)! = \langle \beta \text{ fixed} \rangle \sum_{\alpha=0}^{m_0-m}(m_0 - \alpha)$$

$$\{(m_0 - \alpha) + (n_0 - \beta) - 1\}! \ f(\alpha, \beta)$$

$$+ \langle \alpha \text{ fixed} \rangle \sum_{\beta=0}^{n_0-n}(n_0 - \beta)$$

$$\{(m_0 - \alpha) + (n_0 - \beta) - 1\}! \ f(\alpha, \beta)$$

The upper limits of α and β cannot become m_0 and n_0; this is because there will be no survivors in either army and therefore no fighting. This means there must be a final single unit in both armies, and the upper limits of α and β become $(m_0 - 1)$ and $(n_0 - 1)$. In other words, the lower limits of armies m and n are both 1. Arranging the above equations

$$(m_0 + n_0)! = \langle \beta \text{ fixed} \rangle \sum_{\alpha=0}^{m_0-m}(m_0 - \alpha)$$

$$\{(m_0 - n_0) - (\alpha + \beta) - 1\}! \ f(\alpha, \beta)$$

$$+ \langle \alpha \text{ fixed} \rangle \sum_{\beta=0}^{n_0-n}(n_0 - \beta)$$

$$\{(m_0 + n_0) - (\alpha + \beta) - 1\}! \ f(\alpha, \beta) \qquad (2.47)$$

Here, $f(\alpha, \beta)$ is a special coefficient represented by the following recurrence formula.

$$f(\alpha, \beta) = (m_0 - \alpha) f(\alpha, \beta - 1) + (n_0 - \beta) f(\alpha - 1, \beta)$$

However, when $f(0,0) = 1$, the general equation will be as follows:

$$f(\alpha, \beta) = \prod_{i=0}^{\beta} \left[\sum_{\alpha_i=0}^{\alpha_{i-1}} (m_0 - \alpha_i) \right] \prod_{\gamma=0}^{\beta}(n_0 - \gamma)^{[\alpha_{\beta-\gamma}]-[\alpha_{\beta-\gamma+1}]}$$

(However, $\alpha_0 = m_0 - m$)

Shown from the surviving side,

$$(m_0 + n_0)! = \langle n \text{ fixed} \rangle \sum_{r=0}^{m_0-m}(m+r)\{(m+r)+n-1\}!$$

$$f(m+r,n) + \langle m \text{ fixed} \rangle \sum_{s=0}^{n_0-n}(n+s)$$

$$\{m+(n+s)-1\}!f(m,n+s)$$

Here, $f(m+r,n) = (m+r)f(m+r,n+1) + nf(m+r+1,n)$
$f(m,n+s) = mf(m,n+s+1) + (n+s)f(m+1,n+s)$
However, $r = 0,1,2,\text{L L},(m_0-m)$ $s = 0,1,2,\text{L L},(n_0-n)$
$f(m_o + n_0) = 1$

For example, when $m_0 = 5$ and $n_0 = 3$, the special coefficient chart will look as follows:

5-m=β	m\n	0	1	2	3	4
5-m=α		5	4	3	2	1
0	3	1	4(0)+3(1)=3	3(0)+3(3)=9	2(0)+3(9)=27	1(0)+3(27)=81
1	2	5(1)+2(0)=5	4(3)+2(5)=22	3(9)+2(22)=71	2(27)+2(71)=196	1(81)+2(196)=473
2	1	5(5)+1(0)=25	4(22)+1(25)=113	3(71)+1(113)=326	2(196)+1(326)=718	1(473)+1(718)=1,191

$\alpha = 2 \ (\therefore m = 3), \ \beta = 1 \ (\therefore n = 2)$

$(5+3)! = \langle \beta \text{ constant} \rangle \ [(5-0)\{8-(0+1)-1\}!f(0,1)$
$+ (5-1)\{8-(1+1)-1\}!f(1,1) + (5-2)\{8-(2+1)-1\}!f(2,1)]$
$+ \langle \alpha \text{ constant} \rangle \ [(3-0)\{8-(2+0)-1\}f(2,0)$
$+ (3-1)\{8-(2+1)-1\}f(2,1)]$

$$= [5 \cdot 6!(5) + 4 \cdot 5!(22) + 3 \cdot 4!(71)] + [3 \cdot 5!(9) + 2 \cdot 4!(71)]$$
$$= [18,000 + 10,560 + 5,112] + [3,240 + 3,408]$$
$$= [33,672] + [6,648] = 40,320$$

When $\alpha = 4$ (therefore m = 1) and $\beta = 2$ (therefore n = 1), this means armies m and n are each facing their final battle. That is, when β is fixed, the winning probability corresponding to the number of survivors, m, in army m, and when α is fixed, the winning probability corresponding to the number of survivors, n, in army n are affected.

$$(5+3)! = \langle \beta \text{ constant} \rangle \ [5 \cdot 5!(25) + 4 \cdot 4!(113) + 3 \cdot 3!(326)$$
$$+ 2 \cdot 2!(718) + 1 \cdot 1!(1,191)]$$
$$+ \langle \alpha \text{ constant} \rangle \ [3.3!(81) + 2.2!(473) + 1 \cdot 1!(1,191)]$$
$$= [15,000 + 10,848 + 5,868 + 2,872 + 1,191] +$$
$$+ [1,458 + 1,892 + 1,191] = [35,779] + [4,541]$$
$$= 40,320$$

The special coefficient chart must be solved according to initial values m_0 and n_0, and can be solved faster using a computer.

Here, by substituting (2.47) for (2.46), we can reduce the numerator and the denominator:

$$\frac{d}{dt}\{Pr(m+n;\ m_0+n_0,\ e^{-t})\}$$

$$= \left\{ \langle \beta \text{ constant} \rangle \left[\sum_{\alpha=0}^{m_0-m} (m_0 - \alpha) \frac{f(\alpha, \beta)}{(\alpha + \beta)!} \right] + \right.$$

$$\left. \langle \alpha \text{ constant} \rangle \left[\sum_{\beta=0}^{n_0-n} (n_0 - \beta) \frac{f(\alpha, \beta)}{(\alpha + \beta)!} \right] \right\} (e^{-t})^{(m_0+n_0)-(\alpha+\beta)} (1-e^{-t})^{(\alpha+\beta)}$$

The function chart based on this equation and based on a special coefficient chart, for example when $m_0 = 5$, $n_0 = 3$, is as follows:

$\alpha = 5 - m$		0	1	2	3	4
$\beta = 3 - n$	$\dfrac{m}{n}$	5	4	3	2	1
0	3	$\dfrac{1}{0!}e^{-8t}(1-e^{-t})^0$ $= e^{-8t}$	$\dfrac{3}{1!}e^{-7t}(1-e^{-t})$	$\dfrac{9}{2!}e^{-6t}(1-e^{-t})^2$	$\dfrac{27}{3!}e^{-5t}(1-e^{-t})^3$	$\dfrac{81}{4!}e^{-4t}(1-e^{-t})^4$
1	2	$\dfrac{5}{1!}e^{-7t}(1-e^{-t})$	$\dfrac{22}{2!}e^{-6t}(1-e^{-t})^2$	$\dfrac{71}{3!}e^{-5t}(1-e^{-t})^3$	$\dfrac{196}{4!}e^{-4t}(1-e^{-t})^4$	$\dfrac{473}{5!}e^{-3t}(1-e^{-t})^5$
2	1	$\dfrac{25}{2!}e^{-6t}(1-e^{-t})^2$	$\dfrac{113}{3!}e^{-5t}(1-e^{-t})^3$	$\dfrac{326}{4!}e^{-4t}(1-e^{-t})^4$	$\dfrac{718}{5!}e^{-3t}(1-e^{-t})^5$	$\dfrac{1{,}191}{6!}e^{-2t}(1-e^{-t})^4$

Here, infinite time, that is an infinite number of combats is presumed; therefore, both sides are integrated with respect to t from 0 to ∞. Here, the content inside the parentheses on the right side is treated as a constant, thus by substituting $e^{-t} = x$

$$\frac{d}{dt}(e^{-t}) = \frac{dx}{dt}, \quad -e^{-t} = \frac{dx}{dt}, \quad -x = \frac{dx}{dt} \quad \therefore dt = \left(-\frac{1}{x}\right)dx$$

When t varies from 0 to ∞, x simply varies from 1 to 0.

$$\therefore \int_0^\infty (e^{-t})^{(m_0+n_0)-(\alpha+\beta)} (1-e^{-t})^{(\alpha+\beta)} \, dt$$

$$= \int_1^0 x^{(m_0+n_0)-(\alpha+\beta)} (1-x)^{(\alpha+\beta)} \left(-\frac{1}{x}\right) dx$$

$$= -\int_1^0 x^{\{(m_0+n_0)+(\alpha+\beta)\}-1} (1-x)^{(\alpha+\beta)} \, dx$$

$$= \int_0^1 x^{\{(m_0+n_0)+(\alpha+\beta)\}-1} (1-x)^{\{(\alpha+\beta)+1\}-1} \, dx$$

And because this is a complete beta function,

$$= \beta\bigl[(m_0 + n_0) - (\alpha + \beta),\ (\alpha + \beta) + 1\bigr]$$

And because m_0, n_0, α, and β are all positive integers,

$$= \frac{\Gamma[(m_0 + n_0) - (\alpha + \beta)]\Gamma[(\alpha + \beta) + 1]}{\Gamma[\{(m_0 + n_0) - (\alpha + \beta)\} + (\alpha + \beta) + 1]}$$

$$= \frac{\{(m_0 - \alpha) + (n_0 - \beta) - 1\}!(\alpha + \beta)!}{(m_0 + n_0)!}$$

By substituting and rearranging the equation, and keeping in mind that since time is infinite, with regard to army m, $\sqrt{E}$, and with regard to army n, $\dfrac{1}{\sqrt{E}}$, are multiplied and weight-backed; thus:

$$Pr(m + n;\ m_0 + n_0,\ e^{-t})$$

$$= \left\{ \langle \beta\ \text{constant} \rangle\ \sqrt{E}\ \sum_{\alpha=0}^{m_0 - m}(m_0 - \alpha) + \langle \alpha\ \text{constant} \rangle\ \frac{1}{\sqrt{E}}\ \sum_{\beta=0}^{n_0 - n}(n_0 - \beta) \right\}$$

$$\times\ \frac{\{(m_0 - \alpha) + (n_0 - \beta) - 1\}!\, f(\alpha, \beta)}{(m_0 + n_0)!} \qquad (2.48)$$

Here, with respect to the ratio of winnings, the number of survivors for the opposing party is 1 (in other words, $\alpha = m_0 - 1$ and $\beta = n_0 - 1$ are fixed) and is the sum of the probabilities of men not shot up to the number of survivors (m or n) at least 1 above the initial number of men (m_0 or n_0) at the time of fighting. If the number of men not shot corresponding with whatever number of survivors are denoted as P_m and P_n, then the rate of winnings for armies m and n, $\sum P_m$ and $\sum P_n$.

Rate of victories for army m:

$$\sum P_m = \langle \beta = n_0 - 1 \rangle \sqrt{E} \sum_{\alpha=0}^{m_0-1} (m_0 - \alpha)$$

$$\times \frac{(m_0 - \alpha)! f(\alpha, n_0 - 1)}{(m_0 + n_0)!} \quad (2.49)$$

Rate of victories for army n:

$$\sum P_n = \langle \alpha = m_0 - 1 \rangle \frac{1}{\sqrt{E}} \sum_{\beta=0}^{n_0-1} (n_0 - \beta)$$

$$\times \frac{(n_0 - \beta)! f(m_0 - 1, \beta)}{(m_0 + n_0)!} \quad (2.50)$$

With respect to the number of men not shot corresponding to whatever number of survivors $m \; (= m_0 - \alpha)$ and $n \; (= n_0 - \beta)$, P_m, P_n, it is obvious that $m = n = 1$ (fixed condition), and when $t \to \infty$, the portions regarding the time variable t are calculated according to the initial condition and the fixed condition, which can then be abbreviated as $P(m, 1, \infty)$ and $P(1, n, \infty)$ and shown as follows:

$$P_m = m\sqrt{E} \; P(m, 1, \infty) \qquad P_n = \frac{n}{\sqrt{E}} \; P(1, n, \infty)$$

For example, when $m_0 = 5$, $n_0 = 3$, and $E = 1$, $P(m, n, \infty)$ looks as follows:

Here, the rate of winnings becomes directly the ratio of winning as shown in the following table:

	α= 5-m	0	1	2	3	4	Total win for army n
β= 3-n	m \ n	5	4	3	2	1	Total loss for army m
0	3	$\frac{7!(1)}{8!}=0.125$	$\frac{6!(3)}{8!}=0.053571$	$\frac{5!(9)}{8!}=0.026786$	$\frac{4!(27)}{8!}=0.016071$	$\frac{3!(81)}{8!}=0.012054$	
1	2	$\frac{6!(5)}{8!}=0.089286$	$\frac{5!(22)}{8!}=0.065476$	$\frac{4!(71)}{8!}=0.042262$	$\frac{3!(196)}{8!}=0.029167$	$\frac{2!(473)}{8!}=0.023462$	
Total win for army m / Total loss for army n	2 1	$\frac{5!(25)}{8!}=0.074405$	$\frac{4!(113)}{8!}=0.067262$	$\frac{3!(326)}{8!}=0.048512$	$\frac{2!(718)}{8!}=0.035615$	$\frac{1!(1,191)}{8!}=0.029539$	

Here, P_m and P_n as well as $\sum P_m$ and $\sum P_n$ look as follows:

Army m wins			Army n wins		
m	$mP(m,1,\infty)$	P_m	n	$nP(n,1,\infty)$	P_n
5	5x0.074405=0.372024		3	3x0.012054=0.036161	
4	4x0.067262=0.269047				
3	3x0.048512=0.145536		2	2x0.023462=0.046924	
2	2x0.035615=0.071230				
1	1x0.029539=0.029539		1	1x0.029539=0.0.29539	

Army m win ratio $\sum P_m$ 0.887376   Army n win ratio $\sum P_n$ 0.112624

Furthermore, when army m or n wins, how many men are expected to survive? Let's assume that 1 unit of enemy survives at the end of the battle and the number of survivors in one's own army (m or n) is a probability variable, then all we need to do is find the sum product of numbers not shot (P_m or P_n); i.e., expected values E(m) and E(n).

That is, when $m_0 = 5$, $n_0 = 3$, and $E = 1$, $E(m)$ and $E(n)$ looks as follows:

Army m wins			Army n wins		
m	mP_m	$m^2P(m,1,\infty)$	n	nP_n	$n^2P(1,n,\infty)$
5	5x0.372024=1.860119		3	3x0.036161=0.108482	
4	4x0.269047=1.076191				
3	3x0.145536=0.436607		2	2x0.046924=0.093849	
2	2x0.071230=0.142460				
1	1x0.029539=0.029539		1	1x0.029539=0.029539	

Expected value of army m: Expected value of army n:

$E(m) = 3.544916$ $E(n) = 0.231870$

The expected values of $E(m)$ and $E(n)$ from equations (2.49) and (2.50) are as follows:

Expected number of suvivors of army m when it wins:

$$E(m) = \langle \text{where } \beta = n_0 - 1 \rangle \sqrt{E} \sum_{\alpha=0}^{m_0-1} (m_0 - \alpha)^2 \frac{(m_0 - \alpha)! f(\alpha, n_0 - 1)}{(m_0 + n_0)!} \quad (2.51)$$

Expected number of survivors of army n when it wins:

$$E(n) = \langle \text{where } \alpha = m_0 - 1 \rangle \frac{1}{\sqrt{E}} \sum_{\beta=0}^{n_0-1} (n_0 - \beta)^2 \frac{(n_0 - \beta)! f(m_0 - 1, \beta)}{(m_0 + n_0)!} \quad (2.52)$$

However, when referring to (2.47) and (2.48), the only difference is the weighted product of $\sqrt{E}$ for army m and $\frac{1}{\sqrt{E}}$ for army n, and since the right side of (2.48) is equal to the left side of (2.47) divided by $(m_0 + n_0)!$.

For army m, if $\frac{1}{\sqrt{E}}$ is multiplied by $\sum P_m$, and in the case of army n, $\sqrt{E}$ is multiplied by $\sum P_n$, and the weight correction is applied, then evidently the sum of winning rates for both armies becomes 1.

That is $\dfrac{1}{\sqrt{E}}\sum P_m + \sqrt{E}\sum P_n = 1$ ∴ when $E=1$, $\sum P_m + \sum P_n = 1$

If one's own army is inferior, then how far should the exchange rate E be enhanced in order to gain parity in the fighting strength? First, let's assume E = 1 and calculate the winning rate. If E' is the exchange rate that yields parity in the fighting strength, and winnings for armies m and n are $\left(\sum P_m\right)'$ and $\left(\sum P_n\right)'$, then:

$$\dfrac{1}{\sqrt{E'}}\left(\sum P_m\right)' + \sqrt{E'}\left(\sum P_n\right)' = 1, \quad \left(\sum P_m\right)' = \left(\sum P_n\right)'$$

$$\dfrac{1}{\sqrt{E'}}\left\{\sqrt{E'}\sum P_m\right\} + \sqrt{E'}\left\{\dfrac{1}{\sqrt{E'}}\sum P_n\right\} = 1$$

$$\therefore \left(\sum P_m\right)' = \sqrt{E'}\sum P_m, \quad \left(\sum P_n\right)' = \dfrac{1}{\sqrt{E'}}\sum P_n$$

$$\therefore \sqrt{E'}\sum P_m = \dfrac{1}{\sqrt{E'}}\sum P_n, \quad \therefore E' = \dfrac{\sum P_n}{\sum P_m}$$

That is, E' must be set to the ratio of a winning rate when E = 1; then the winning will be

$$\left(\sum P_m\right)' = \sqrt{E'}\sum P_m = \sqrt{\dfrac{\sum P_n}{\sum P_m}}\sum P_m = \sqrt{\sum P_m \cdot \sum P_n}$$

$$\left(\sum P_n\right)' = \dfrac{1}{\sqrt{E'}}\sum P_n = \dfrac{1}{\sqrt{\dfrac{\sum P_n}{\sum P_m}}}\sum P_n = \sqrt{\dfrac{\sum P_m}{\sum P_n}}\sum P_n = \sqrt{\sum P_m \cdot \sum P_n}$$

This is the geometrical average of the winning rates of both armies when E = 1

$$\therefore \left(\sum P_m\right)' + \left(\sum P_n\right)' = \sqrt{\sum P_m \cdot \sum P_n} + \sqrt{\sum P_m \cdot \sum P_n}$$
$$= 2\sqrt{\sum P_m \cdot \sum P_n} \neq 1$$

According to the converted exchange rate E', the sum of winnings for armies m and n is no longer equal to 1. However, by introducing a new weight W from the next condition, we have:

$$\left(\sum P_m\right)' = \left(\sum P_n\right)' = \frac{1}{2}, \quad W\sqrt{\sum P_m \cdot \sum P_n} = \frac{1}{2}$$

$$\therefore W = \frac{1}{2\sqrt{\sum P_m \cdot \sum P_n}} = \frac{1}{\left(\sum P_m\right)' + \left(\sum P_n\right)'}$$

$$\therefore W\left[\left(\sum P_m\right)' + \left(\sum P_n\right)'\right] = 1$$

Therefore, generally, winning rates $\sum P_m$ and $\sum P_n$ for armies m and n for a given exchange rate E can be represented in the following manner.

Here, when E = 1, then W = 1.

$$W\left(\sum P_m + \sum P_n\right) = 1 \quad \text{However, } W = \frac{1}{\sum P_m + \sum P_n}$$

$$\sum P_m = \langle \text{where } \beta = n_0 - 1 \rangle \, W\sqrt{E} \sum_{\alpha=0}^{m_0-1}(m_0 - \alpha)\frac{(m_0 - \alpha)! f(\alpha, n_0 - 1)}{(m_0 + n_0)!}$$

$$= Wm\sqrt{E}\, P(m, 1, \infty)$$

$$\sum P_n = \langle \text{where } \alpha = m_0 - 1 \rangle \, \frac{W}{\sqrt{E}} \sum_{\beta=0}^{n_0-1}(n_0 - \beta)\frac{(m_0 - \beta)! f(m_0 - 1, \beta)}{(m_0 + n_0)!}$$

$$= W\frac{n}{\sqrt{E}} P(1, n, \infty)$$

In contrast to the previous example, when army m is inferior to army n, for example when $m_0 = 3$ and $n_0 = 5$, then the exchange rate from army m's perspective in order to gain parity and the expected values for survivors of both armies can be obtained as follows:

Winning ratio for both armies when $E = 1$

$$\sum P_m = 0.112624 \qquad \sum P_n = 0.887376$$

$$\text{Exchange rate } E' = \frac{0.887376}{0.112624} = 7.879102$$

$$\therefore \sqrt{E'} = 2.806974 \qquad \text{Again let } E' = E$$

$$W = \frac{1}{2\sqrt{0.112624 \times 0.887376}} = \frac{1}{2 \times 0.316133} = 1.5816615$$

Table of results, army m wins, army n is defeated:

m	$m\sqrt{E}\,P(m, 1, \infty)$		$W \cdot m\sqrt{E}\,P$ $(m, 1, \infty) = P_m$	$W \cdot m^2 \sqrt{E}\,P$ $(m, 1, \infty) = m P_m$
3	$3 \times 2.806974 \times \dfrac{3!(81)}{8!}$	$= 0.101502$	0.160537	0.481612
2	$2 \times 2.806974 \times \dfrac{2!(473)}{8!}$	$= 0.131716$	0.208324	0.416648
1	$1 \times 2.806974 \times \dfrac{1!(1,191)}{8!}$	$= 0.082915$	0.131139	0.131139

$$\left(\sum P_m\right)' = 0.316133 \qquad \sum P_m = 0.5 \qquad E(m) = 1.029399$$

Table of results, army n wins, army m is defeated:

n	$\dfrac{n}{\sqrt{E}}P(1, n, \infty)$			$W\dfrac{n}{\sqrt{E}}P$ $(1, n, \infty) = P_n$	$W\dfrac{n^2}{\sqrt{E}}P$ $(1, n, \infty) = nP_n$
5	$5x$	$\dfrac{1}{2.806974} \times \dfrac{5!(25)}{8!}$	$= 0.132536$	0.209620	1.048101
4	$4x$	$\dfrac{1}{2.806974} \times \dfrac{4!(113)}{8!}$	$= 0.095850$	0.151597	0.606389
3	$3x$	$\dfrac{1}{2.806974} \times \dfrac{3!(326)}{8!}$	$= 0.051848$	0.082004	0.246010
2	$2x$	$\dfrac{1}{2.806974} \times \dfrac{2!(718)}{8!}$	$= 0.025376$	0.040135	0.080271
1	$1x$	$\dfrac{1}{2.896974} \times \dfrac{1!(1,191)}{8!}$	$= 0.010523$	0.16644	0.016644

$$\left(\sum P_n\right)' = 0.316133 \quad \sum P_n = 0.5 \quad E(n) = 1.997415$$

That is, in contrast to a single combat, an army with initially fewer forces may enhance the exchange rate and gain parity in the winning rate, but the expected value for survivors will still be low.

It is not easy to increase the exchange rate, and even if it is increased to 7.8791, the expected value for survivors is only increased to 4.4396 (1.029399/0.231870). Still, in group-to-group battles and total wars, we can see the evidence that it is not a good idea to increase the exchange rate to compensate for the inferiority in number.

Let's calculate a couple of examples where the ratios of initial forces $m_0:n_0$ are equal, as shown in the following table:

Initial forces	When E=1				When the inferior side win ratio is (0.5)			
	Winning Probability		Expected value for Survivors		Exchange rate the inferior side has to increase	Corresponding value for Survivors		Expected survival value factor
$m_0: n_0$	ΣP_m	ΣP_n	E(m)	E(n)	E'	E'(m)	E'(n)	E(n)'/E(n)
5 : 3	0.8874	0.1126	3.5449	0.2319 7.8791	1.9974	1.0294	4.4396
10 : 6	0.9584	0.0416	7.4363	0.1337 23.0185	3.8797	1.6054	12.0092
25 : 15	0.9971	0.0029	19.4554	0.0164 339.3385	9.7564	2.7934	170.1693
50 : 30	0.99995	0.00005	39.4946	0.0004 21,059.083	19.7482	4.1421	10,530.0565

It is clearly evident here that as the number of initial forces grow, even when studied from the perspective of the theory of probability, the winning rate and the expected value for survivors rapidly approach results obtained from Lanchester's Square Law.

For example, when $m_0 = 50$, $n_0 = 30$, and E = 1, the winning of army m ($\sum P_m = 1$), the destruction of army n ($\sum P_n = 0$), and the number of survivors for army m ($m = \sqrt{m_0^2 - n_0^2}$) approach $\sqrt{50^2 - 30^2} = 40$.

However, for an inferior army to enhance the exchange rate to gain more than parity in the fighting strength, in contrast to Lanchester's Linear Law, the exchange rate is not simply derived from Lanchester's Square Law where $E > \left(\dfrac{n_0}{m_0}\right)^2$ or $E > \left(\dfrac{m_0}{n_0}\right)^2$, but it must be enhanced to a much greater degree. For example, in this case, since $m:n = 5:3$, normally the exchange rate must be increased to $E > \left(\dfrac{5}{3}\right)^2 = \dfrac{25}{9} = 2.7778$.

However, the more the initial forces grow, the more rapidly the lower limit of the exchange rate must increase to a very large number. This is a very important side of the analysis based on the theory of probability with respect to Lanchester's Square Law.

Therefore, in group-to-group battles and total wars, should an inferior army attempt to enhance the exchange rate in order to gain parity in the fighting strength, corresponding to the absolute value of the forces, an incredible exchange rate is required. Military people generally seek superior weapons to ensure their victory against the enemy. This was the case with General McArthur who was discharged by former President Truman when he requested the use of tactical nuclear weapons in the Korean war.

According to Lanchester's Square Law, when an inferior army increases the exchange rate to fight the enemy, $E > \left(\dfrac{n_0}{m_0}\right)^2$, regardless of the absolute value of the initial number of forces, it must be greater than the square of the ratio n_0/m_0. In the previous example, when the ratios were 5:3 and 50:30, the exchange rate must be greater than $\left(\dfrac{5}{3}\right)^2 = \dfrac{25}{9} = 2.7778$. This is a result of the construction based on the model of theory of certainty, but the analysis based on the theory of probability is more realistic.

In the case of single combats and duels, even based on the theory of probability, as the initial number of forces increases, there is a point of congruity with Lanchester's Linear Law in that the exchange rate that the inferior army must enhance approaches the ratio n_0/m_0; therefore, the concentration of the forces and the increase of the exchange rate received equal treatment. In group-to-group combats and total wars, through an analysis based on the theory of probability, it is increasingly more important to increase the concentration of forces compared to the enemy rather than being concerned with the increase of the exchange rate.

Summary

Armies m and n are engaged in a group-to-group combat or a total war; according to an analysis based on the theory of probability, the initial forces are m_0 and n_0, and the number of survivors are m and n.

Winning rate for army m:

$$\sum P_m = \langle \beta = n_0 - 1 \rangle \ W\sqrt{E} \sum_{\alpha=0}^{m_0-1} (m_0 - \alpha) \frac{(m_0 - \alpha)! f(\alpha, n_0 - 1)}{(m_0 + n_0)!}$$

Winning rate for army n:

$$\sum P_n = \langle \alpha = m_0 - 1 \rangle \ W \frac{1}{\sqrt{E}} \sum_{\beta=0}^{n_0-1} (n_0 - \beta) \frac{(n_0 - \beta)! f(m_0 - 1, \beta)}{(m_0 + n_0)!}$$

However: $E = \dfrac{b}{a}$ $\quad W\left(\sum P_m + \sum P_n\right) = 1$

Here, $f(\alpha, \beta)$ is a special coefficient represented by the following recurrence formula.

$$f(\alpha, \beta) = (m_0 - \alpha) f(\alpha, \beta - 1) + (n_0 - \beta) f(\alpha - 1, \beta)$$

However, we set $f(0, 0) = 1$

Expected value for survivors of army m:

$$E(m) = \langle \beta = n_0 - 1 \rangle \ W\sqrt{E} \sum_{\alpha=0}^{m_0-1} (m_0 - \alpha)^2 \frac{(m_0 - \alpha)! f(\alpha, n_0 - 1)}{(m_0 + n_0)!}$$

Expected value for survivors of army n:

$$E(n) = \langle \alpha = m_0 - 1 \rangle \ W \frac{1}{\sqrt{E}} \sum_{\beta=0}^{n_0-1} (n_0 - \beta)^2 \frac{(n_0 - \beta)! f(m_0 - 1, \beta)}{(m_0 + n_0)!}$$

Exchange rate that the inferior army must enhance:

When E=1, winning rates for armies m and n, $\sum P_n$ and $\sum P_m$, can be calculated (here, W=1).

The exchange rate $E = \dfrac{\sum P_n}{\sum P_m}$ $\left(\text{or} \quad E = \dfrac{\sum P_n}{\sum P_m} \right)$

For example, when $m_0 = 49$, $n_0 = 51$, and E = 1, the exchange rate the inferior army m must enhance $E = \dfrac{0.6353}{0.3647} = 1.7420$.

From the winning condition of Lanchester's Square Law, $E > \left(\dfrac{51}{49} \right)^2 = 1.0408^2 = 1.0833$, which compared to an analysis based on the theory of probability, is quite low. As initial forces m_0 and n_0 increase, even when the ratio of forces remain the same, the value of the exchange rate that the inferior army must enhance changes as it increases rapidly.

That is, in total wars, enhancing the exchange rate by increasing the efficiency of the weapons and skills to gain parity for an inferior army is not advantageous. Rather, increasing the concentration of forces over the enemy is a better approach.

Chapter 3

The Lanchester Strategy Model

3.1 Generalization of Lanchester's Square Law

3.1.1 Introducing the concept of suppy and demand

Both Lanchester's Linear Law and Lanchester's Square Law, which we studied in the previous chapter, concern the number of survivors once the initial number of forces are decided, even though there may be differences in the way battles are fought. In other words, conditions are set within individual battles, which have a limited range. There are some cases such as the battle of Iwojima, where in anticipation of a somewhat prolonged battle, additional forces were committed, while Japanese defenders had to fight in isolation and without support. In that sense, wars fought on the Pacific Islands were individual battles, and classic examples where Lanchester's laws are applicable.

However, in an individual battle, an army may face an eminent defeat, but with the arrival of supporting forces, the situation could suddenly reverse itself. Even though the initial forces may be inferior in number, if the man power supplies during the battle are large enough, the results could be different. Also, in a longer term, even though an army may lose in a limited, individual battle, it still may win in a broader war. Therefore, prior to the supply, on the production side, the training of the forces and the production of weapons must also be considered.

There are various terms describing fighting such as fight (a street fight) and combat (a single combat) to prolonged and large-scale battle (battle of Waterloo), but none of them connote the totality of global war (World War II).

In modern times, with total wars, the idea that professional soldiers fight the war at a faraway place and separate from the general population is not valid anymore.

But when a theory that has been applied to more or less continuous fighting, i.e., battles, is expanded and applied to full-scale wars, the modeling of a pair of differential equations could end up as a simplification so thorough that it almost cannot be expected to be applied to real-world situations. But it surely is effective to organize thoughts when comparing this model to reality. Members of the U.S. Navy Tactical Research Team established bold hypotheses in an effort to generalize and apply Lanchester's Laws to the process of war.

The first problem they faced was the unit of measure of fighting that correspond to quantities m and n. At any given moment, both armies carry a number of trained men, tanks, ships, and aircraft, and these forces are continuously committed to the fighting, and they are transported and supplied to the battlefield. The total fighting power of the forces is decided by the efficiency of the weapons and skills of each component. At a given stage of a combat process, one can very roughly approximate that a ship has the same fighting force as a division or two companies of fighter planes have the same value as a submarine.

Based on this gross approximation, each unit can be measured based on an arbitrary unit — for example, can be equated to x number of divisions. This is the same idea in measuring all sorts of energy in terms of kiloliters (kl) of crude oil, or in forecasting demand, measuring various models of cars in terms of a particular model.

It goes without saying that differences in tanks and submarines are quantitative as well as qualitative. Ignoring qualitative differences is great simplification; however, the fighting power in question is vast enough that qualitative differences are hidden by quantitative ones, and we can consider that the total fighting strength of a country at any given day and time can be measured numerically.

This fighting strength varies with time as it increases or decreases. When it increases, both armies are busy producing and supplying fighting power by training forces, manufacturing aircraft, and other means.

Let the rate of production and supply for army m be P and for army n be Q. P and Q are numbers of unit values — infantry divisions or equivalent battle ships, etc. — that armies m and n can train and equip annually with the year as the unit of time. Initially, we assume that P and Q are constants.

On the other hand, the fighting strength declines as the fighting continues. The rate of depreciation as studied in Lanchester's Square Law, with respect to both armies, is discounted by the fighting strength. At the same time, as could be imagined by considering the supply side, it must be remembered that considering the greater one's fighting strength, there is a part that operates on the attrition of the fighting strength.

3.1.2 Boulding's supply model (logistics)

K. E. Boulding, as introduced in Chapter 1 (1.3.1), in *Conflict and Defense; A General Theory*, appendix 12, has a very interesting reference to the supply model. He proposes a measure called the Loss of Strength Gradient [LSG]. With respect to a country's LSG, as the distance from the base increases, the military and political power is gradually decreased. Factors to determine that degree are very diverse and complex, and relates to geographical, psychological, and organizational engineering issues.

Boulding lists the following factors to explain the basic features of the problem and constructs the supply model:

a   Number of men working to maintain LSG
s   Unit distance from the base

h   Number of men at the front working directly to maintain the LSG, then:
k   Number of men required to maintain the supply line, that is, (a-h)
q   The basic ratio constant of this supply system. Since the number of men directly supporting the supply system is fewer that those working to maintain it, then $0 < q < 1$

The greater the number of men that must be supplied at the front, and the longer the supply line (s), the greater the number of men work on the supply (k=a-h).

Therefore, k is proportional to h and s, and the unit can be defined as the number of men required to supply one man at the front for each 1 km.

$$k = qsh = a - h \quad \therefore \quad h = \frac{a}{1+qs}$$

Here, LSG is the ratio of increment Δs versus Δh, then:

$$LSG = \frac{dh}{ds} = \frac{d}{ds}\left(\frac{a}{1+qs}\right) = a\frac{d}{ds}\left(\frac{1}{1+qs}\right)$$

$$\text{set} \quad 1+qs = u, \quad \text{then} \quad \frac{du}{ds} = q$$

$$\frac{dh}{ds} = \frac{dh}{du} \cdot \frac{du}{ds} = \frac{dh}{du}q = aq\frac{d}{du}\left(\frac{1}{u}\right) = aqu^{-2} = aq(1+qs)^{-2}$$

$$\therefore \quad LSG = \frac{aq}{(1+qs)^2}$$

Let's see what happens when the focus is on the number of men (h) who work directly at the front. The greater the number of steps from the front line, the greater the supply must provide not only for the front line but also the supply and sustenance ot the line itself.

The step 1 supplier to the front line must be supplied by the step 2 supplier, and so on. The following chart shows this relationship when s=5.

(Front Line)	h				
s=5	(qh)	Arrow shows the supply direction. Parentheses indicate the number of supplies to the next step. Lines indicate connections between suppliers.			
4	(qh) $q^2h =$	(q^2h)			
3	(qh) $q^2h+q^2h =$	$(2q^2h)$ $q^3h=$	(q^3h)		
2	(qh) $q^2h+q^2h+q^2h =$	$(3q^2h)$ $q^3h+2q^3h=$	$(3q^3h)$ $q^4h=$	(q^4h)	
1	(qh) $q^2h+q^2h+q^2h+q^2h =$	$(4q^2h)$ $q^3h+2q^3h+3q^3h=(6q^3h)$	$q^4h+3q^4h=(4q^4h)$	(q^5h)	
Suppliers	Step 1	Step 2	Step 3	Step 4	Step 5

(Front Line)	Total of suppliers at each step
s=5	qh
4	+) qh(1+q)
3	+) $qh(1+2q+q^2)=qh(1+q)^2$
2	+) $qh(1+3q+3q^2+q^3)=qh(1+q)^3$
1	+) $qh(1+4q+6q^2+4q^3+q^4)=qh(1+q)^4$
Suppliers	$k=qh\dfrac{(1+q)^5-1}{(1+q)-1}=h[(1+q)^5-1]$

Step 1 suppliers supply h men in the front line. Since qh men are needed for each step, the total number is 5qh. The latter step suppliers are always multiplied by q. The number of suppliers in the second step supply all firststep suppliers in each step and therefore is equal to q^2h; however, because of the connections, the combined number of men required to supply the front line is calculated as $q^2h+2q^2h+3q^2h+4q^2h=10q^2h$.

The number of suppliers in the third step is equal to q^3h; however, because of the connections, the combined number of men is calculated as $q^3h+3q^3h+6q^3h=10q^3h$. Similarly, the combined number of men in the forth step is calculated as $q^4h+4q^4h=5q^4h$, and that for the fifth step is calculated as q^5h, directly supplying the next step, step 4.

The total number of suppliers (k) is equal to $(1+q)^5$, that is:

According to the expansion of the binomial $(1+q)^5$,

$$k = 5qh + 10q^2h + 10q^3h + 5q^4h + q^5h$$
$$= h(1 + 5q + 10q^2 + 10q^3 + 5q^4 + q^5 - 1) = h\{(1+q)^5 - 1\}$$

However, as shown in the right column of the previous chart, the first term is qh and we have a geometric progression of the common ratio (1+q); therefore, k is a summation up to the term s, and since $q \neq 0$, then

$$a = h + k = h + qh\frac{(1+q)^s - 1}{(1+q) - 1} = h + h\{(1+q)^s - 1\} = h(1+q)^s$$

$$\therefore \quad h = \frac{a}{(1+q)^s}$$

Also, if only h (number of) men in the front line need to be supplied, then first suppliers alone are accumulated in each step, which means, k = sqh, a = h + k = h + sqh = h (1+sq), and h = a/(1+sq).

For example, if a = 1,000 and q = 0.1; that is, one man is needed to supply 10, then h, the number of men for each step that can be committed to the front line is calculated as in the following table:

No of steps	0	1	2	3	4	5	6	7	8	9	10	20
Front line troops only	1000	909	833	769	714	667	625	588	556	526	500	333
Front line and support troops	1000	909	826	751	683	621	564	513	467	424	386	149

When the front line is extended, the supply line is stretched, and the real distance approaches 20 steps, even when the front line is supplied, from 1000 men who can be committed to the fighting only 1/3 (333) can be directly committed to the combat; in the case where suppliers are supplied, this number drops to only 1/7, or only 147. This shows the critical importance of the supply problem in a combat situation.

In the US, after 1960, the Society of Logistics Engineering(SoLE) was established. Logistics is generally compared to Strategy, and encompasses a broader stratum than OR. In Japan, it competes with OR and has devoted followers such as Ishikawajima-Harima Heavy Industries and Suntory.

3.1.3 Generalized Lanchester Model

In relation to the fighting strength changes, the Lanchester model can be generalized by adding production and supply ratios P and Q, which are increasing factors, and introducing surviving forces n and m adopted from the Lanchester's square law, which are decreasing factors, and the efficiencies of the weapons and skills, a and b, in the following manner:

$$\frac{dm}{dt} = P - an - cm \qquad (3.1)$$

$$\frac{dm}{dt} = Q - bm - dn \qquad (3.2)$$

$$P, Q > 0, \ a, b, > 0, \ a, b \gg c, d$$

Here, c and d are proportional constants and may be positive, negative, or zero values.

This model resembles the Richardson model referred to as (1.10) and (1.11) in 1.3.1 of Chapter 1 to a great degree. It also resembles the predatory model as referred to in 1.2.1 of Chapter 1, which is an extension of the competition model that bloomed in the 1920s under the aegis of the U.S. Navy Operation Research Team and a cadre of drafted physicists, chemists, and mathematicians.

To solve the system of equations (1.10) and (1.11), we employ the differential operator $D\left(\frac{d}{dt}\right)$.

$$\begin{cases}\dfrac{dm}{dt}+cm+an=P\\ \dfrac{dn}{dt}+bm+dn=Q\end{cases}$$

$$\begin{cases}Dm+cm+an=P\\ Dn+bm+dn=Q\end{cases}$$

$$\begin{cases}(D+c)m+an=P\\ bm+(D+d)n=Q\end{cases}$$

Here, to eliminate variables from m side and n side:

$$\begin{cases}(D+c)(D+d)m+a(D+d)n=(D+d)P\\ \qquad abm+a(D+d)n=aQ\end{cases}$$

$$\begin{cases}b(D+c)m\qquad\qquad +abn=bP\\ b(D+c)m+(D+c)(D+d)n=(D+c)Q\end{cases}$$

$$(D+c)(D+d)m-abm=(D+d)P-aQ$$
$$(D+c)(D+d)n-abn=(D+c)Q-bP$$

$$\{D^2+(c+d)D+cd\}m-abm=DP+Pd-Qa$$
$$\{D^2+(c+d)D+cd\}n-abn=DQ+Qc-Pb$$

Since $DP=\dfrac{dP}{dt}$, and $DQ=\dfrac{dQ}{dt}$, both become zero

$$\{D^2+(c+d)D+(cd-ab)\}m=Pd-Qa \qquad (3.3)$$
$$\{D^2+(c+d)D+(cd-ab)\}n=Qc-Pb \qquad (3.4)$$

These equations differ from those in 2.3.2 of Chapter 2, and since the right sides of these equations are not generally zero, they are called inhomogeneous linear second-order differential equations with constant coefficients. When it is inhomogeneous, m (general solution) = m_c (cofunction) + m_0 (particular solution).

To find the cofunction, with regard to the term including variables, an auxiliary equation can be set up where the right side is zero; we then can follow the same procedure as in the previous chapter.

With respect to both equations, the auxiliary equation is,
$$\{D^2 + (c+d)D + (cd-ab)\}\ m(or\ n) = 0$$
therefore, when the characteristic root (eigen value) is r, the characteristic (eigen) equation,

$$r^2 + (c+d)r + (cd-ab) = 0$$

$$r = \frac{-(c+d) \pm \sqrt{(c+d)^2 - 4(cd-ab)}}{2}$$

$$= \frac{-(c+d) \pm \sqrt{c^2 + 2cd + d^2 - 4cd + 4ab}}{2}$$

$$= -\frac{(c+d)}{2} \pm \frac{1}{2}\sqrt{(c-d)^2 + 4ab}$$

$$= -\frac{c+d}{2} \pm \sqrt{\frac{(c+d)^2}{4} + ab}$$

$$= -\frac{c+d}{2} \pm \sqrt{\left(\frac{(c-d)}{2}\right)^2 + ab}$$

Here, $\dfrac{c+d}{2} = \lambda$, and $\dfrac{c-d}{2} = \kappa$, then $r = -\lambda \pm \sqrt{\kappa^2 + ab}$

and if we let $\sqrt{\kappa^2 + ab} = \mu$, then $r = -\lambda \pm \mu$

And since the root's discriminant is obviously positive, with two distinct real roots:
$$r_1 = \mu - \lambda, \quad r_2 = -(\mu + \lambda)$$

Thus, the cofactors are as follows:

$$m_c = C_1 e^{(\mu-\lambda)t} + C_2 e^{-(\mu+\lambda)t}, \qquad n_c = C_3 e^{(\mu-\lambda)t} + C_4 e^{-(\lambda+\mu)t}$$

Next, we find the particular solutions m_p and n_p. The right sides of (3.3) and (3.4) do not include variable t; therefore, assuming $m_p = X$, and $n_p = Y$ (where X and Y are arbitrary constants)

$$\frac{d}{dt}(m_p) = 0, \qquad \frac{d^2}{dt^2}(m_p) = 0$$

$$\frac{d}{dt}(n_p) = 0, \qquad \frac{d^2}{dt^2}(n_p) = 0$$

By substituting these in (3.3) and (3.4), and assuming that $(ab - cd) \neq 0$, then:

$$0 + (c+d)0 + (cd-ab)m_p = Pd - Qa$$
$$0 + (c+d)0 + (cd-ab)n_p = Qc - Pb$$

$$\therefore m_p = \frac{Qa - Pd}{ab - cd} = A, \quad n_p = \frac{Pb - Qc}{ab - cd} = B$$

Therefore, the general solutions for the system of differential equations (3.1) and (3.2) are as follows:

$$\begin{cases} m = \dfrac{Qa - Pd}{ab - cd} + C_1 e^{(\mu-\lambda)t} + C_2 e^{-(\mu+\lambda)t} & (3.5) \\ n = \dfrac{Pb - Qc}{ab - cd} + C_3 e^{(\mu-\lambda)t} + C_4 e^{-(\mu+\lambda)t} & (3.6) \end{cases}$$

Thus, $\dfrac{c+d}{2} = \lambda, \quad \dfrac{c-d}{2} = \kappa, \quad \sqrt{\kappa^2 + ab} = \mu$

Furthermore, with regard to (3.1) and (3.2),

$$\frac{dm}{dt} = m', \quad \frac{dn}{dt} = n'$$

and we have the following matrix.

$$\begin{bmatrix} m' \\ n' \end{bmatrix} = \begin{bmatrix} P \\ Q \end{bmatrix} + \begin{bmatrix} -c & -a \\ -b & -d \end{bmatrix} \begin{bmatrix} m \\ n \end{bmatrix}$$

Here, we can be certain that the characteristic roots (eigen values) of the characteristic equation are two distinct real roots.

In addition, finding the particular solutions from the initial conditions for constant terms C_1, C_2, C_3, and C_4.

Differentiating (3.5) and (3.6) with respect to t:

$$\begin{cases} \dfrac{dm}{dt} = C_1(\mu - \lambda)e^{(\mu-\lambda)t} - C_2(\mu + \lambda)e^{-(\mu+\lambda)t} & (3.7) \\[2mm] \dfrac{dn}{dt} = C_3(\mu - \lambda)e^{(\mu-\lambda)t} - C_4(\mu + \lambda)e^{-(\mu+\lambda)t} & (3.8) \end{cases}$$

Since the initial conditions (t=0) are $m = m_0$ and $n = n_0$, from (3.1) and (3.2), (3.5) and (3.6) as well as (3.7) and (3.8) can be represented as follows:

$$\begin{cases} m_0 = \dfrac{Qa - Pd}{ab - cd} + C_1 + C_2 & (3.9) \\[2mm] \left[\dfrac{dm}{dt}\right]_{t=0} = (\mu - \lambda)C_1 - (\mu + \lambda)C_2 = P - an_0 - cm_0 & (3.10) \end{cases}$$

$$\begin{cases} n_0 = \dfrac{Pb - Qc}{ab - cd} + C_3 + C_4 \\ \left[\dfrac{dn}{dt}\right]_{t=0} = (\mu - \lambda)C_3 - (\mu + \lambda)C_4 = Q - bm_0 - dn_0 \end{cases}$$

Let's first solve with respect to C_1 and C_2. By multiplying by $(\mu + \lambda)$ on both sides of (3.9) and eliminating C_2 from (3.10):

$$\begin{cases} (\mu + \lambda)\dfrac{Qa + Pd}{ab - cd} + (\mu + \lambda)C_1 + (\mu + \lambda)C_2 = (\mu + \lambda)m_0 \\ (\mu - \lambda)C_1 - (\mu + \lambda)C_2 = P - an_0 - cm_0 \end{cases}$$

$$(\mu + \lambda)\dfrac{Qa - Pd}{ab - cd} + 2\mu C_1 = P - an_0 + (\mu + \lambda - c)m_0$$

$$\therefore \quad 2\mu C_1 = (\mu + \lambda - c)m_0 - an_0 - (\mu + \lambda)\dfrac{Qa - Pd}{ab - cd} + P$$

$$= (\mu + \lambda - c)m_0 - an_0 - (\mu + \lambda)\dfrac{Qa - Pd}{ab - cd}$$

$$+ \dfrac{P(ab - cd) + Qac - Qac}{ab - cd}$$

$$= (\mu + \lambda - c)m_0 - an_0 - (\mu + \lambda)\dfrac{Qa - Pd}{ab - cd}$$

$$+ \dfrac{Qac - Pcd}{ab - cd} + \dfrac{Pab - Qac}{ab - cd}$$

$$= (\mu + \lambda - c)m_0 - an_0 - (\mu + \lambda - c)\dfrac{Qa - Pd}{ab - cd}$$

$$+ \dfrac{ab}{ab - cd}P - \dfrac{a}{ab - cd}Qc$$

Here,

$$\mu + \lambda - c = \mu + \frac{c+d}{2} - c = \mu - \frac{c-d}{2} = \mu - \kappa ,$$

$$\mu = \sqrt{\kappa^2 + ab} , \quad \mu^2 = \kappa^2 + ab$$

$$ab = \mu^2 - \kappa^2 , \quad ab = (\mu + \kappa)(\mu - \kappa) , \quad \therefore \mu - \kappa = \frac{ab}{\mu + \kappa}$$

Therefore,

$$\mu + \lambda - c = \frac{ab}{\mu + \kappa}$$

$$= \frac{ab}{\mu + \kappa} m_0 - \frac{ab}{b} n_0 - \left(\frac{ab}{\mu + \kappa}\right)\left(\frac{Qa}{ab - cd}\right)$$

$$+ \left(\frac{ab}{\mu + \kappa}\right)\left(\frac{Pd}{ab - cd}\right) + \frac{ab}{ab - cd} P - \frac{ab}{ab - cd} \cdot \frac{1}{b} Qc$$

Also, because $a = \dfrac{(\mu + \lambda)(\mu - \lambda)}{b}$

$$= \frac{ab}{\mu + \lambda} m_0 + \left(\frac{ab}{\mu + \lambda}\right)\left(\frac{Pd}{ab - cd}\right) + \left(\frac{ab}{\mu + \lambda}\right)\left(\frac{\mu + \lambda}{ab - cd}\right) P$$

$$- \left(\frac{ab}{\mu + \lambda}\right)\left(\frac{\mu + \lambda}{b}\right) n_0 - \left(\frac{ab}{\mu + \lambda}\right)\left(\frac{\mu + \lambda}{b}\right)\left(\frac{c}{ab - cd}\right) Q$$

$$- \left(\frac{ab}{\mu + \kappa}\right)\left(\frac{\mu + \kappa}{b}\right)\left(\frac{\mu - \kappa}{ab - cd}\right) Q$$

$$= \frac{ab}{\mu+\lambda}\left[m_0 + \frac{d}{ab-cd}P + \frac{\mu+\kappa}{ab-cd}P - \left(\frac{\mu+\kappa}{b}\right)n_0\right.$$
$$\left. - \left(\frac{\mu+\kappa}{b}\right)\left(\frac{c+\mu-\kappa}{ab-cd}\right)Q\right]$$

$$= \frac{ab}{\mu+\kappa}\left\{\left[m_0 + \frac{d+\mu+\kappa}{ab-cd}P\right] - \frac{\mu+\kappa}{b}\left[n_0 + \frac{c+\mu-\kappa}{ab-cd}Q\right]\right\}$$

$$\therefore C_1 = \frac{ab}{2\mu(\mu+\kappa)}\left\{\left[m_0 + \frac{d+\mu+\kappa}{ab-cd}P\right] - \frac{\mu+\kappa}{b}\left[n_0 + \frac{c+\mu-\kappa}{ab-cd}Q\right]\right\} = F$$

(3.11)

To find C_2, we substitute (3.9) and (3.11)

$$C_2 = m_0 - \frac{Qa - Pd}{ab - cd}$$
$$- \frac{ab}{2\mu(\mu+\kappa)}\left\{\left[m_0 + \frac{d+\mu+\kappa}{ab-cd}P\right] - \frac{\mu+\kappa}{b}\left[n_0 + \frac{c+\mu-\kappa}{ab-cd}Q\right]\right\}$$

$$= \frac{ab}{2\mu(\mu+\kappa)}\left\{\frac{2\mu(\mu+\kappa)}{ab}m_0 - \frac{2\mu(\mu+\kappa)}{ab}\cdot\frac{a}{ab-cd}Q\right.$$
$$+ \frac{2\mu(\mu+\kappa)}{ab}\cdot\frac{d}{ab-cd}P - m_0 - \frac{d+\mu+\kappa}{ab-cd}P$$
$$\left. + \frac{\mu+\kappa}{b}\left[n_0 + \frac{c+\mu-\kappa}{ab-cd}Q\right]\right\}$$

$$= \frac{\mu+\kappa}{b} \cdot \frac{ab}{2\mu(\mu+\kappa)} \left\{ \frac{2\mu}{a} m_0 - \frac{2\mu}{a} \cdot \frac{a}{ab-cd} Q + \frac{2\mu}{a} \cdot \frac{d}{ab-cd} P \right.$$

$$\left. - \frac{b}{\mu+\kappa} m_0 - \frac{b}{\mu+\kappa} \cdot \frac{d+\mu+\kappa}{ab-cd} P + n_0 + \frac{c+\mu-\kappa}{ab-cd} Q \right\}$$

$$= \frac{\mu+\kappa}{b} \cdot \frac{ab}{2\mu(\mu+\kappa)} \left\{ \left(\frac{2\mu}{a} - \frac{b}{\mu+\kappa} \right) m_0 + \frac{2\mu}{a} \cdot \frac{d}{ab-cd} P \right.$$

$$\left. - \frac{b}{\mu+\kappa} \cdot \frac{d}{ab-cd} P - \frac{b}{\mu+\kappa} \cdot \frac{\mu+\kappa}{ab-cd} P + n_0 - \frac{2\mu}{ab-cd} Q + \frac{c+\mu-\kappa}{ab-cd} Q \right\}$$

$$= \frac{\mu+\kappa}{b} \cdot \frac{ab}{2\mu(\mu+\kappa)} \left\{ \left[\frac{2\mu(\mu+\kappa)-ab}{a(\mu+\kappa)} \right] m_0 + \left(\frac{2\mu}{a} - \frac{b}{\mu+\kappa} \right) \left(\frac{d}{ab-cd} \right) P \right.$$

$$\left. - \left(\frac{b}{ab-cd} \right) P + n_0 + \frac{c+\mu-\kappa-2\mu}{ab-cd} Q \right\}$$

Here: $ab = (\mu+\kappa)(\mu-\kappa)$, $b = \frac{(\mu+\kappa)(\mu-\kappa)}{a}$ Thus:

$$= \frac{\mu+\kappa}{b} \cdot \frac{ab}{2\mu(\mu+\kappa)} \left\{ \left[\frac{2\mu-(\mu-\kappa)}{a} \right] m_0 + \left[\frac{2\mu-(\mu-\kappa)}{a} \right] \left(\frac{d}{ab-cd} \right) P \right.$$

$$\left. - \left(\frac{\mu+\kappa}{a} \right) \left(\frac{\mu-\kappa}{ab-cd} \right) P + n_0 + \frac{c-\mu-\kappa}{ab-cd} Q \right\}$$

$$= \frac{\mu+\kappa}{b} \cdot \frac{ab}{2\mu(\mu+\kappa)} \left\{ \left(\frac{\mu+\kappa}{a} \right) m_0 + \left(\frac{\mu+\kappa}{a} \right) \left(\frac{d}{ab-cd} \right) P \right.$$

$$\left. - \left(\frac{\mu+\kappa}{a} \right) \left(\frac{\mu-\kappa}{ab-cd} \right) P + n_0 + \frac{c-\mu-\kappa}{ab-cd} Q \right\}$$

$$\therefore C_2 = \frac{\mu+\kappa}{b} \cdot \frac{ab}{2\mu(\mu+\kappa)} \left\{ \frac{\mu+\kappa}{a} \left[m_0 + \frac{d-\mu+\kappa}{ab-cd} P \right] + \left[n_0 + \frac{c-\mu-\kappa}{ab-cd} Q \right] \right\}$$

$$= \frac{\mu+\kappa}{b} G \qquad (3.12)$$

Next, C_3, C_4, from (3.1), general solutions, (3.5), (3.6), and (3.7)

$$C_1(\mu-\lambda)e^{(\mu-\lambda)t} - C_2(\mu+\lambda)e^{-(\mu+\lambda)t} \qquad \left(\frac{dm}{dt} = P - an - cm\right)$$

$$= P - a\left[\frac{Pb-Qc}{ab-cd} + C_3 e^{(\mu-\lambda)t} + C_4 e^{-(\mu+\lambda)t}\right]$$

$$-c\left[\frac{Qa-Pd}{ab-cd} + C_1 e^{(\mu-\lambda)t} + C_2 e^{-(\mu+\lambda)t}\right]$$

$$= \left[P - a\left(\frac{Pb-Qc}{ab-cd}\right) - c\left(\frac{Qa-Pd}{ab-cd}\right)\right]$$

$$-(cC_1 + aC_3)e^{(\mu-\lambda)t} - (cC_2 + aC_4)e^{-(\mu+\lambda)t}$$

However, [...] is equal to zero because they contain particular solutions for m and n, thus:

$$\left[P - a\left(\frac{Pb-Qc}{ab-cd}\right) - c\left(\frac{Qa-Pd}{ab-cd}\right)\right]$$

$$= \frac{1}{ab-cd}(Pab - Pcd - Pab + Qac - Qac + Pcd) = 0$$

$$\therefore C_1(\mu-\lambda)e^{(\mu-\lambda)t} - C_2(\mu+\lambda)e^{-(\mu+\lambda)t}$$

$$= -(cC_1 + aC_3)e^{(\mu-\lambda)t} - (cC_2 + aC_4)e^{-(\mu+\lambda)t}$$

This means the coefficients of the first and second terms on the left and right sides become equal, thus:

$$C_1(\mu - \lambda) = -(cC_1 + aC_3), \qquad -C_2(\mu + \lambda) = -(cC_2 + aC_4)$$
$$aC_3 = -\{c + (\mu - \lambda)\}C_1 \qquad aC_4 = \{(\mu + \lambda) - c\}C_2$$
$$= -\{\mu - (\lambda - c)\}C_1 \qquad = \{\mu + (\lambda - c)\}C_2$$

Here, $\lambda - c = \dfrac{c+d}{2} - c = -\dfrac{c-d}{2} = -\kappa$ and from the (3.11),

thus: $\dfrac{(\mu + \kappa)(\mu - \kappa)}{ab} = 1$

$$aC_3 = -\{\mu - (-\kappa)\}C_1 \qquad aC_4 = \{\mu + (-\kappa)\}C_2$$
$$\therefore C_3 = -\frac{\mu + \kappa}{a}C_1 \qquad \therefore C_4 = \frac{\mu - \kappa}{a}C_2$$
$$= -\frac{\mu + \kappa}{a}F \qquad = \frac{\mu - \kappa}{a} \cdot \frac{\mu + \kappa}{b}G$$
$$\qquad\qquad\qquad\qquad = G$$

And particular solutions can be represented as follows:

$$\begin{cases} m = A + Fe^{(\mu-\lambda)t} + \dfrac{\mu + \kappa}{b}Ge^{-(\mu+\lambda)t} & (3.13) \\[1em] n = B - \dfrac{\mu + \kappa}{a}Fe^{(\mu-\lambda)t} + Ge^{-(\mu+\lambda)t} & (3.14) \end{cases}$$

However,

$$\lambda = \frac{c+d}{2}, \quad \kappa = \frac{c-d}{2}, \quad \mu = \sqrt{\kappa^2 + ab}$$

$$A = \frac{Qa - Pd}{ab - cd}, \quad B = \frac{Pb - Qc}{ab - cd}, \quad ab - cd \neq 0$$

$$F = \frac{ab}{2\mu(\mu + \kappa)} \left\{ \left[m_0 + \frac{d + \mu + \kappa}{ab - cd} P \right] - \frac{\mu + \kappa}{b} \left[n_0 + \frac{c + \mu - \kappa}{ab - cd} Q \right] \right\}$$

$$G = \frac{ab}{2\mu(\mu + \kappa)} \left\{ \frac{\mu + \kappa}{a} \left[m_0 + \frac{d - \mu + \kappa}{ab - cd} P \right] + \left[n_0 + \frac{c - \mu - \kappa}{ab - cd} Q \right] \right\}$$

Note that the solutions for the Richardson model in (1.3.1) of Chapter 1 are based on these particular solutions. With respect to the Lanchester's Square Law, in this equation, P, Q = 0, c, d = 0; that is, $\lambda = 0$, $\kappa = 0$, A=0, B=0, and $\mu = \sqrt{ab}$.

3.1.4 Relationship between fighting strength, production, and supply

In general, ab is greater than cd. Also,

$$\mu^2 - \lambda^2 = (\kappa^2 + ab) - \left(\frac{c+d}{2}\right)^2 = \left(\frac{c-d}{2}\right)^2 + ab - \left(\frac{c+d}{2}\right)^2$$

$$= ab + \frac{c^2 - 2cd + d^2 - c^2 - 2cd - d^2}{4}$$

$$= ab - \frac{4cd}{4} = ab - cd$$

As μ is also greater than λ, thus, $(\mu - \lambda) > 0$. Therefore, the second terms of (3.13) and (3.14) increase continuously, the third term decreases continuously.

As a result, if F determined by the initial conditions is positive (>0), army n becomes zero and army m wins. If F is negative (<0), army m becomes zero and army n wins.

If the efficiency of the weapons and skills for both armies are equal, and the rate of reduction that accompany supply is equal, then a=b; that is, exchange rate E=1 and c=d. Here, (3.13) and (3.14) are abbreviated as follows: Since $\lambda = c = d$, $\kappa = 0$, $\mu = a = b$,
$\mu - \lambda = a - c = b - d$, $\mu + \lambda = a + c = b + d$

$$\begin{cases} m = A + Fe^{(a-c)t} + Ge^{-(a+c)t} \\ n = B - Fe^{(a-c)t} + Ge^{-(a+c)t} \end{cases}$$

$$\begin{cases} m = A + Fe^{(b-d)t} + Ge^{-(b+d)t} \\ n = B - Fe^{(b-d)t} + Ge^{-(b+d)t} \end{cases}$$

Also,

$$A = \frac{Qa - Pc}{a^2 - c^2}, \quad B = \frac{Pa - Qc}{a^2 - c^2}$$

$$A = \frac{Qb - Pd}{b^2 - c^2}, \quad B = \frac{Pb - Qd}{b^2 - c^2}$$

$$F = \frac{1}{2}\left[\left(m_0 + \frac{P}{a-c}\right) - \left(n_0 + \frac{Q}{a-c}\right)\right]$$

$$F = \frac{1}{2}\left[\left(m_0 + \frac{P}{b-d}\right) - \left(n_0 + \frac{Q}{b-d}\right)\right]$$

$$G = \frac{1}{2}\left[\left(m_0 - \frac{P}{a+c}\right) + \left(n_0 - \frac{Q}{a+c}\right)\right]$$

$$G = \frac{1}{2}\left[\left(m_0 - \frac{P}{b+d}\right) + \left(n_0 - \frac{Q}{b+d}\right)\right]$$

Here we consider the constant F that determines which fighting strength becomes zero. The total fighting strength of either side is equal to the initial fighting strength plus the production/supply rate divided by the amount (a-c) or (b-d).

Depreciation constants c and d accompanying the supply do not just thwart the fighting power. It is important to use part of the fighting strength and build up the supply. The sign of constant F depends on which of these fighting strengths becomes the greatest.

Let a=b=2 (E=1), c=d=1, and let's consider a combination of several initial fighting strengths and productions/supplies. The four groups at the top of the figure corresponds to the case when $m_0 = n_0$ and the initial fighting strengths are equal, the four groups at the bottom of the figure corresponds to the case when $m_0 = 2n_0$ and the initial fighting strengths are 2 to 1.

The first two cases of (a) and (b) are when the initial fighting strengths and productions/supplies are equal the fighting ends up in a tie. The other cases are when the initial fighting power or either of production or supply, or both, are different, and after a time, which may vary in range, one of the armies, m or n army, will be defeated in the end. In particular, the last case, graph (h), is very interesting. This is when there is a final victory, but there is a difference of 1/2 in the initial fighting strength.

As a result, the initial disadvantage is hidden by 3 times greater production and supply. In the beginning, army n, which is inferior in the initial fighting strength, if reduced, and for a while, army n proceeds with superiority over army m. However, as soon as the initial fighting strength is covered by superior production and supply, then the advantage becomes rapidly decisive and the fighting power of army m is destroyed in a short period of time.

Generalized Lanchester Model

$$\frac{dm}{dt} = P - 2n - m, \quad \frac{dm}{dt} = Q - 2m - n$$

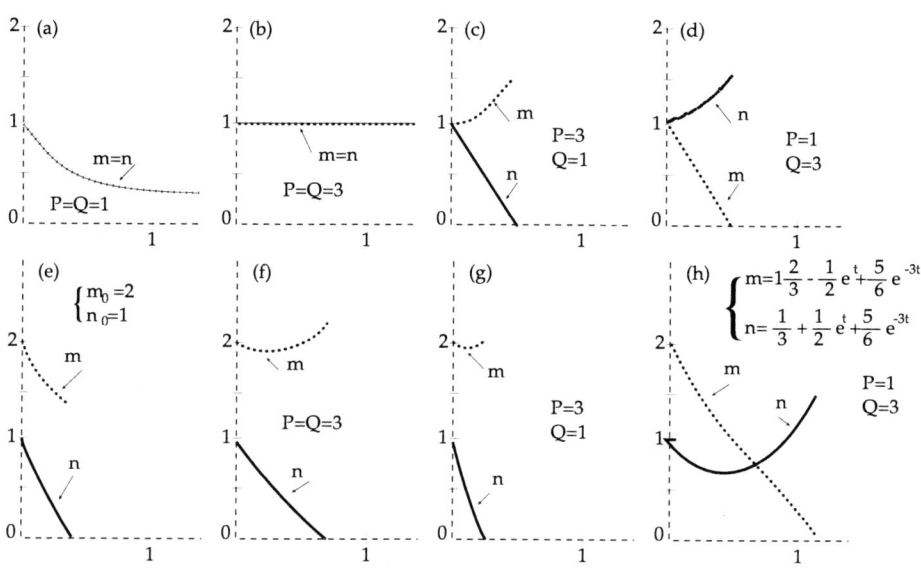

Now, let's examine the situation between the US and Japan on the eve of the Pacific War. The fighting strength at the beginning is estimated to be 5 to 1.

With respect to production and supply, professor Yoshio Ando of Tokyo University published a report after the war, shown in the table on the following page.

Comparing U.S. and Japanese Major Materials Production (in multiples of Japanese production)

	1929	1933	1938	1941
Oil	501.2	468.0	485.9	527.9
Iron Ore	416.8	55.6	37.5	74.0
Lead	208.0	37.9	31.3	27.4
Copper Solids	25.0	7.4	4.5	12.1
Steel	38.9	9.2	7.3	11.9
Zinc	26.0	9.5	7.5	11.7
Copper	12.4	3.1	5.3	10.7
Coal	16.1	10.5	7.2	9.3
Aluminum	—	—	8.7	5.6
Mineral Phosphate	254.7	72.3	45.2	—
Mercury	—	41.6	24.8	—
(Simple average)	166.6	71.5	60.5	76.7
(Geometrical average)	72.6	24.0	17.7	21.6

With respect to the production of important materials in 1941, the actual difference is said to be 1 to 77 on average. Even after excluding the oil multiple, the difference is still 1 to 22 based on the geometric average taken for a more even result.

After the war, Sadao Suzuki, the minister responsible for logistical planning, said: "People say we engaged in a reckless war without sufficient materials, but the reality is that we went to war because we didn't have enough materials and were forced into an economical embargo. It was the case of a cornered mouse nipping at a cat."

When the initial fighting strengths ($m_0 : n_0$) are 5 to 1, the calculations based on 2 cases of production/supply ratios (P : Q) of 1 to 77 and 1 to 22 are as follows: (see figure on following page)

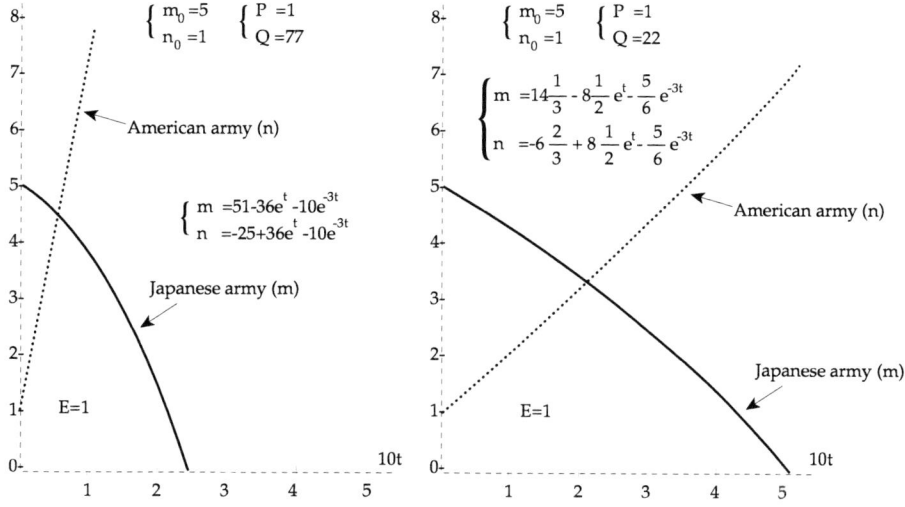

3.2 Separation of strategic and tactical components of strength

3.2.1 Attack and destruction against the production and supply

To leave the enemy's production and supply alone allows an increase in the fighting strength. Fighting on the battlefield alone is not everything. It is natural to think about attacking and destroying the production and supply. However, during World War I, the Allied Forces allowed some of the major German U-boats to escape, even though American supply ships were receiving indiscriminate attacks at the Atlantic Ocean and had sustained considerable damage.

In the second half of the war, the British front line was bogged down near the border of France, Luxembourg, and Germany. From here, all seven major German munitions plants in the Ruhr area were within the flying range for aerial bombing. The direct distance to a major munitions storage, Essen, and Hargen where two third of the storage battery used in U-boats were produced was only 280 km.

This was almost equal to the flying distance from the occupied Belgium's Ghent, where German Zeppelins were heading for London on bombing missions. Nevertheless, the chance to cripple the German army's military supply was sacrificed because of the aerial battles over the trench lines.

Besides, more than half of the aerial attacks were directed not at the industrial sites but at the enemy's artillery positions. The following facts suggest the broader indirect effects besides the direct military gains. A German artillery shell manufacturing plant that had never received any bombing was tormented by 53 cases of false alarms in August 1917 (the year before the end of the Great War) alone, and lost 3,000 tons of production. Further, as a fact triggering the reconsideration of the "principle of concentration" on the front line worshipped by the general headquarters, the German army frightened by the aerial bombing, redirected 20 flying companies, which was 3 to 4 times the number of British planes participating in the aerial attacks!

The same thing was true in the United States Immediately after the end of World War I, there was a great debate on how to shape the aerial fighting power of the country. General Billy Mitchel was an early advocate of an increased air force power and the establishment of an independent air force. He was too outspoken and as a result of criticizing the Army and Congress was court-martialed and expelled from the army.

In 1926, the Army Air Force was established with small fighter planes as their main force. However, in the late 1920s, the U.S. Army General Staff Office noticed that the army's bombers used in several exercises were becoming obselete, and although it was during the depression, they succeeded in convincing a reluctant Congress averse to any military outlays to agree to building a new bomber, and in 1930, submitted the design proposal for a new bomber to the aircraft manufacturers.

In 1934, a need for long-range bombers to protect the Hawaiian islands and Alaska as well as the mainland was identified with a goal of not just attacking but also in their operations against fleets. Bombers to be able to accommodate 900 kg of bombs and fly over 1,600 km at 300 km/hr, possibly increasing the load to over 3,500 km and the speed to 400 km/hr.

Boeing created Boeing 299 the following year in August 1935. This was the prototype model for the 4-engine propeller driven, 1,350-horsepower flying fortress B17.

In Japan after 1932, Rear Admiral Yamamoto developed the idea of attack planes for long-range naval operations, and the result was Mitsubishi's G3M1, called model 96, completed in 1935.

In 1939, the Nippon, a civilian version, succeeded in flying around the world. In 1937, these fighter planes participated in a one-way, 1,100-km attack from North Kyushu on mainland China across a stormy sea and through adverse weather, although they suffered quite a few losses, too. In December 10, 1941, model 96 and its newer model, called model 1 attacker, also engaged in attacking and sinking British battleships, Prince of Wales and Repulse.

The development of the next generation of model 96 attacker started in April 1937, completed in 1939, and was formally adopted as model 1 attacker in April, 1941. It had to carry 5 kl of fuel in order to load 800-kg of torpedoes and fly 3,700 km. Its streamlined design was eventually upgraded to carry 6.5 kl of fuel in order to fly 6,000 km, a longer range compared to the B17. However, its lack of fuel tank protection eventually lead to increased losses in action. As a result, a rubber protective shield was added, which proved to be fairly ineffective, and Admiral Yamamoto himself was later killed aboard the same model 1 fighter in April, 1943 during a command operation.

3.2.2 The B17, B29, and the birth of strategic air force

The World War II started on September 1, 1939. In November 1939, the U.S. Army began planning VLR (Very Long Range) bombing, and in January 1940, it submitted the plan to the aircraft manufacturers. The ambitious design aimed for a far more superior fighter bomber than the B17.

The initial goal was to run operations against possible German and Italian targets in South America; however, with the surrender of France, they were deployed in the North African theater. After the Casablanca meeting between Roosevelt and Churchill in January 1943, they were further diverted against Japanese forces in China and later to Mariana bases.

Model 97

Model 1

B 29

B 17

B 24

The VLR concept was first conceived in 1938, prototyped in September 1940, 250 airplanes were ordered in September 1941, and flew for the first time in September 1942. Thus Super-fortress B29 was developed, and the first volume airplanes appeared in September 1943. Boeing was able to manufacture B29 because of its success in creating a large, 55 liter engine. B17 crew still wore oxygen masks but the B29 allowed for free movement of the crew at the very high altitude of 10,000 m thanks to a special pressurized chamber structure. In contrast, Japanese interceptor crew were prone to loseing consciousness at such altitudes.

At the beginning of the Pacific War, B17s were deployed to the South Pacific Ocean; however, after repeated surprise attacks by Japanese Zeros, they were replaced by B24s. Existing B17 bombers began their mass migration and redeployment in the European theater.

Most of the B17s were flown with great success from their British base in bombing missions of German production and supply facilities.

Their first mission to northern France on August 18, 1942 consisted of 18 B17s. Their later missions included bombing of factories, storage facilities, and U-boat production and supply bases in mainland Germany. Based on the allies' hard-learned experience during World War I, the missions called for immediate sinking of any U-boat found, destruction of production plants, and of repair and supply bases. This was designed to reduce the overall number of U-boats operating in the Atlantic Ocean.

German U-boats began to lose ground beginning in the second half of 1943. It should be noted, however, that German Navy High Command recognized that the way to a decisive victory was in destroying the enemy's supply route. The Japanese navy, on the other hand, adhered to the principle of big battle ships and giant guns, and not paying enough attention to submarines.

US Bombers (WWII)

		Boeing B—29	Boeing B—17	Consolidated B—24
Types (model variations)		A, B	B, C, D, E, F, G	B, C, D, E, G H, J, L, M, N
Prototype production date (year/month)		1940/9	1935/7	1939/3
Volume production date (year/month)		1943/9	1937/11	1941/9
Volume production quantity (planes)		4,204	12,731	18,181
(model)		(A)	(G)	(J)
Total width	(m)	43.1	31.6	33.5
Total length	(m)	30.1	22.6	20.5
Total height	(m)	8.5	5.8	5.6
Wing surface	(m²)	161.5	132.0	97.4
Weight	(t)	32.4	16.4	16.6
Payload	(t)	22.1~31.6	8.5~13.1	13.0
Total weight	(t)	54.5~64.0	24.9~29.5	27.9
Engine (horsepower) (number)		2200 x 4	1350x4	1200 x 4
Speed (altitude m)		576 (7600)	462 (7600)	475 (7600)
Actual ceiling (aircraft climbing ceiling) (m)		10,000	10,850	8,500
Normal flying range (km) (bombs t)		6,600 (4.5)	3,200 (2.0)	3,400 (2.0)
Maximum flying range (km) (bombs t)		9,650 (7.25)	4,900 (1.0)	5,960 (1.0)
Maximum bomb payload (t)		9.0	4.9	3.6
Weapons (machine gun m/m)		12.7x12 20.0x1	12.7 x 13	12.7x10
Crew (men)		10~14	10	10

As a result, they never succeeded in either attacking the war ships or sinking commercial ships, and tragically ended up using their submarines as an inefficient means for transportation to isolated islands in the South Pacific.

Japanese Bombers (WWII)

	Mitsubishi 21 model 97(army)	Mitsubishi G4M model 1(navy)
Types (model variations)	1, 2	M1, M2. M3
Prototype production date (year/month)	1936 (11)	1939 (14)
Volume production date (year/month)	1940 (15)	1941 (16)
Volume production quantity (planes)	1,713	2,500
(model)	(2)	(M2)
Total width (m)	22.5	25.0
Total length (m)	16.0	20.0
Total height (m)	4.35	6.0
Wing surface (m^2)	69.6	78.13
Weight (t)	6.07	8.0
Payload (t)	4.0	4.5
Total weight (t)	9.71	12.5
Engine (horsepower) (number)	1,500 x 2	1,800 x 2
Speed (altitude m)	478 (4400)	440 (4600)
Actual ceiling (aircraft climbing ceiling) (m)	10,000	8,950
Normal flying range (km) (bombs t)	2,700 (1.0)	4,000 (0.8)
Maximum flying range (km) (bombs t)	4,000 (0.7)	6,060 (0.7)
Maximum bomb payload (t)	1.0	0.8
Weapons (machine gun m/m)	7.7 x 4	7.7 x 4
	13.0 x 1	20.0 x 2
Crew (men)	7	7

Intercepting Germans also flew FW190 and Bf109 fighters that compared well and stood up to the British Spitfire fighters. The result was that in October 1943, out of 291 B17 bombers on a bombing mission only 197 managed to return; 22 bombers suffered heavy damages and a total of 116 bombers were lost, raising the attrition rate to 40%.

In January 1944, the new Strategic Air Command (SAC) was established, and in March, in addition to 504 B17 bombers, 226 B24s were added, and a total of 730 bombers were sent to the first bombing mission of Berlin.

In the summer of 1944, the new rocket-powered Me163 fighter was introduced by Germany. It was capable of a top speed of 960 km/hr but had a short flying time of only 8 minutes. Japan also built its own version of the rocket fighter based on German's model. But the first aerial fighter to pose a serious challenge to the B17 bombers was Me262, the world's first jet fighter. It had a top speed of 870 km/hr, 200 km/hr faster than a propeller plane. Germany produced 1,433 of these jet fighters but it was already too late to change the course of the war. They first flew in August 1942; however, it was not until late in the war that Hitler ordered the production of their bomber versions.

Me 163

Me 262

Japan's homeland first came under bombardment in April 18, 1942. Sixteen B25 bombers ran the mission. They had a cruising range of less than 3000 km, and they flew from carrier Hornet and dropped their bombs in a surprise attack while on their way to China. This was the trigger that led to the battle of Midway.

The US strategic bombing began in earnest on June 16, 1944. They flew B29 bombers covering distances as far as 3,350 km and covered Japan's entire homeland.

Meanwhile, in 1941, a super bomber called Conveyer B36 was being planned with the capability of bombing Germany from North America in case Britain was occupied. It was designed to fly more than 12,000 km carrying a payload of 4.5 t. It was fitted with 6 engines and the diameter of its propellers was 5.6 m, but due to manufacturing difficulties, its maiden flight did not take place until August 1946, after WWII ended.

It was delivered to SAC the following year and came to symbolize the nuclear retaliatory power of the US in the ensuing East-West Cold War. It was capable of a top speed of 700 km/hr but was replaced with the new jet bomber B47 in 1958. Later, its successor, the B52 (introduced in 1952 with a top speed of 1,030 km/hr) was actually deployed during the Vietnam War and became widely known.

Later, as one of the United States main stays of the strategic nuclear power, an SST class Rockwell B1 was developed and was scheduled to be deployed after 1980; however, regardless of its superior attributes, with the emergence of ICBM, cruise missiles replaced all modes of transcontinental nuclear ordinance delivery, and the B52 became the last of the manned transcontinental bombers.

Nevertheless, the introduction of B17 and B29 bombers and the birth of the strategic bombing were decisive changes in the way wars were fought and the attack and destruction of enemy's production and supply capabilities were carried out.

Conveyer B36

Boeing B52

Rockwell B1

3.2.3 Strategic and tactical forces

When we generalized the Lanchester Model, we assumed that the production and supply ratios P and Q were constants. However, in the 1940s, with emergence of the strategic air force, the production and supply ratios could no longer be considered constant. An extended, large-scale model was needed to accommodate the supply demands of a new Europe and vast Pacific regions.

One country's production and supply capabilities are affected by the strength of an enemy's strategic attack forces, while it depends on the strength of its own defense system.

Let's call the component of the fighting strength for attacking and destroying the enemy's production and supply the "strategic forces," and the component of the fighting strength for protecting against enemy's attacks and for directly displaying on the battle field the "tactical forces." The relationship among these forces are as follows:

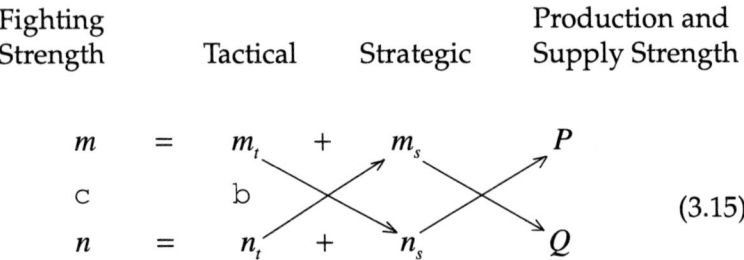

$$(3.15)$$

Fighting forces m and n are generally broken down to components shown in the above figure (3.15).

The strategic forces are directed to the destruction of the enemy's factories and supply bases. However, the efficiency of one's strategic forces is reduced by the size of the enemy's tactical forces.

To reduce the total production and supply forces of the enemy, as total war and probability war, Lanchester's Square Law is applied.

In the aerial warfare where the strategic air forces are reduced, Lanchester's First Law is applied. Both the strategic and tactical forces are affected by the production and supply forces; assuming that these effects are equal on both sides, a common ratio constant (β) can be introduced as follows:

Production and supply forces of army m = $P\left(1 - \beta \dfrac{n_s^2}{m_t}\right)$

Production and supply forces of army n = $Q\left(1 - \beta \dfrac{m_s^2}{n_t}\right)$

Furthermore, in a direct fighting situation, as discussed in the generalized Lanchester model, the size of the tactical forces committed leads to the attrition of the fighting strength.

Again, assuming these effects are equal on both sides, a common ratio constant (α) can be introduced as follows:

$$\begin{cases} \dfrac{dm}{dt} = P - \beta \dfrac{n_s^2}{m_t} P - \alpha(m_t + n_t) & (3.16) \\[2ex] \dfrac{dn}{dt} = Q - \beta \dfrac{m_s^2}{n_t} Q - \alpha(m_t + n_t) & (3.17) \end{cases}$$

3.2.4 Strategic and tactical forces: The generalized Lanchester model

Unfortunately, models (3.16) and (3.17) do not tie directly with the generalized Lanchester model as described in (3.1) and (3.2).

As in the case of Lanchester's square law, taking the ratio of both sides is not useful. This is because no rules are set up for dividing the fighting strength into the tactical and strategic forces, and both commanders must decide on the distribution of these forces.

Here, we try and take the differential with respect to time:

$$\frac{dm}{dt} - \frac{dn}{dt} = P - Q - \beta\left(\frac{n_s^2}{m_t}P - \frac{m_s^2}{n_t}Q\right)$$

Since, $m_s = m - m_t$, $n_s = n - n_t$

$$\frac{dm}{dt} - \frac{dn}{dt} = P - Q - \beta\left(\frac{(n-n_t)^2}{m_t}P - \frac{(m-m_t)^2}{n_t}Q\right) = L(m_t, n_t) \quad (3.18)$$

Thus there is the single function of m_t and n_t, $L(m_t, n_t)$

Deciding on the distribution of the tactical and strategic forces include numerous factors such as government policies, details of production circumstances, levels of science and technology, and so on. But in the end, each commander makes a decision to minimize losses to the tactical and strategic forces of their own army' and maximize those of the enemy's.

Here, the commander of army m strives to maximize $\left(\frac{dm}{dt} - \frac{dn}{dt}\right)$

and the commander of army n strives to minimize $\left(\frac{dm}{dt} - \frac{dn}{dt}\right)$

That is, for example, if $\left(\dfrac{dm}{dt}\right)$ for army m is 10, it is desirable that $\left(\dfrac{dn}{dt}\right)$ for army n is smaller than 10, 8, or even 5, and if $\left(\dfrac{dn}{dt}\right)$ is 10, it is also desirable that $\left(\dfrac{dm}{dt}\right)$ is greater than 10, 13, or 15.

On the other hand, if $\left(\dfrac{dn}{dt}\right)$ for army n is 10, it is desirable that $\left(\dfrac{dm}{dt}\right)$ for army m is smaller than 10, (8 or as low as 5), and if $\left(\dfrac{dm}{dt}\right)$ is 10, it is desirable that $\left(\dfrac{dn}{dt}\right)$ is greater than 10, 13, or 15.

Where m and n, the values for the surviving forces at any given time, depend on the changes immediately preceding them.

This means the commander of army m strives to distribute the tactical force m_t (i.e., the strategic force m_s) in order to maximize the difference. $L\left(=\dfrac{dm}{dt}-\dfrac{dn}{dt}\right)$ and the commander of army n strives to distribute the tactical force n_t (i.e., the strategic force n_s) in order to minimize the difference $L\left(=\dfrac{dm}{dt}-\dfrac{dn}{dt}\right)$

The "tug of war" between the two army commanders continues interminably. To solve this model, however, we need to apply Game Theory.

3.3 The principles of decision-making and the Game Theory

3.3.1 Certainty and uncertainty in relation to cause and effect

We live in an age of uncertainty. What we do and think could lead to totally unexpected results.

In 1661, British R. Boyle published "Skeptic Chemist," a compilation of alchemical concepts, and proposed the modern idea of chemical elements. Furthermore, in 1789, A. L. Lavoisier demonstrated the law of conservation of mass in *Principles of Chemistry*, and thus established the foundation for the modern chemistry. As we all know, burning hydrogen with oxygen results in water vapor, and this chemical reaction could be reversed, predictably, regardless of the time, location, and the experimenter, as shown in the following formula.

$$2H_2 + O_2 \Leftrightarrow 2H_2O$$

Chemistry, physics, and all other natural sciences follow the same principle of certainty in relation to cause and effect.

The opposite of the principle of certainty is that of uncertainty. This applies to such phenomena as solar and lunar eclipses in the days when their causes were unknown and they were shrouded in total mystery.

Thus, according to the theory of information by American scientist, C. E. Shannon, corresponding to the maximum entropy, or when there is a total lack of information. However, normally we try to approach the problem of cause and effect, albeit within a limited range, in a probabilistic manner. This is similar to the case when we deal with a toss of a coin.

One of the best examples is the ever-changing weather, where we tend to separate it into four major categories of "clear," "cloudy," "rain," and "snow," and based on scientific observations of such factors as the atmospheric pressure over a long period of time, we come up with a forecast.

When an event can be repeated, we verify it through experiments, collect data, and find the statistical probabilities. For example, the population death rate by age groups in a country is useful to determine the life insurance premiums.

Economics, where the fall in price and the rise in income create demand, linguistics, where depending on the link between sentences, there may be restrictions imposed by a preceding sentence, sociology, and anthropology all presuppose the principle of cause and effect based on the theory of uncertainty, where the occurrence of one event tend to lead to the occurrence of another.

When the mechanism or the system that links the cause and effect is difficult to understand, the concept of black box is employed.

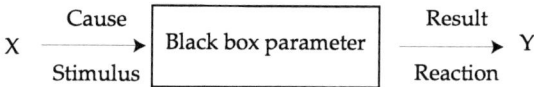

This concept is used in medicine, too, where the active drug and control are used in a double-blind test, and the results are submitted to stochastic examination.

It is important to closely examine the inside of the black box; however, the understanding of one thing brings on another new unknown. In the field of physics, *Uncertainty Principle* (1927) by W. K. Heisenberg (1902–1976) of Germany and the development of quantum mechanics greatly influenced other fields as well.

After the World War II, Bayesian statistics has given rise to, where in making decisions on military and financial affairs repetitions are not allowed, and thus subjective or weight is introduced to the classic Bayes principle of conditioned certainty and corrections are applied as new information is added and the expectation values are calculated. At the center of this discipline is professor R. Schlaifer (*Probability and Statistics for Business Decisions*, McGraw-Hill, Inc., 1959) who originally studied ancient Greek history but after his experience during the war, was not satisfied with Fisherian where Fisher maintained that all decisions should be deferred if there were no significant differences when an event was repeated, and the Quality Control (QC) school of thought as represented by A. Wald's sequential method of examination.

In the field of psychology, the IQ test based on the long-held view of man as a rational being and the intelligence as the all-mighty was devised by A. Binet of Paris University in 1905, and later revised by Professor L. M. Terman of Stanford University.

Another origin of the IQ test goes back to Professor R. M. Yerkes and his colleagues at Yale University who were commissioned to provide a method of quick selection of a large number of army volunteers to participate in WWI. This is called the "army test." Both of these methods have since been widely adopted in various forms by the educational systems and institutions, where intelligence and competence is measured in an objective and simplified manner; however, they also tend to categorize a person decisively as a result.

In 1913, Professor J. B. Watson of John Hopkins University proposed behaviorism, suggesting that the human personality is not just shaped by instincts and is not inborn but rather it is conditioned by a chain of stimuli and reactions similar to the process of learning. Although his extreme mechanical tendencies were negated, Professors E. C. Tolman of California University and C. L. Hull of Yale University advanced his general views into neobehaviorism as a modern, mainstream principle. The psychological process of mediating stimulus and reaction is understood as a black box, and specially in the field of social psychology where the group is the subject, the idea of "attitude" is adopted.

Attitude is defined as a behavior tendency, such as an act of kindness, hate, prejudice, and the like, that is repeated and carried on over a certain period of time and can be modified or reinforced through persuasion, education, and propaganda. Both cause and effect are variables, and the attitude that mediates them is also a variable and is treated as a parameter.

Attitude can be further classified in order of its changeability as opinion, perception, and custom. Public opinions and consumer surveys are all designed to gauge opinions and perceptions, in other words, attitudes, and attempt to find the right response; that is, depending on those parameters, they attempt to find the right stimulus for an expected reaction.

In the late 1930s, K. Horney and others introduced Neo-Freudians based on Freud's analysis of the psychological process of the black box. E. Dichter who followed K. Horney made a significant impact on the industrial world in the area of "motivation research" as known by V. Packard's "Hidden Persuader."

3.3.2 Game Theory as seen in the game of scissors-paper-rock

Decision making could be based on the principle of certainty or the principle of uncertainty, depending on the situation.

Based on the principle of certainty, if x (input, cause) is determined, then y (output, effect) is determined; therefore, x and y are each a function of another, and the solution is a deterministic one. This approach is sometimes used in entrance exams where the number of applicants exceed the admission capacity.

On the other hand, when testing the effectiveness of a substance under limited or finite experimental conditions after several screenings, the Fisherian probability approach is naturally adopted, and in quality control where the economics has the precedence, the method of "selection of random samples for inspection" is adopted. The same principle is also applied in the development of new products and taking surveys of consumer purchasing plans.

Here, to examine how the decision–making process works, let's take the simple example of the game of scissors-paper-rock. There are 2 players, A and B and three results of scissors, paper, and rock. If won, 100 yen is received from the other player; if lost, 100 yen is awarded to the other player; of course, no money is exchanged if the game is a tie. The pay-off matrix as viewed by player A is shown below:

A \ B	Rock	Scissors	Paper	Ratio of A's played hands
Rock	0	100	-100	p_1
Scissors	-100	0	100	p_2
Paper	100	-100	0	p_3
Ratio of B's played hands	q_1	q_2	q_3	

Ratios of A's played hands are represented as p_1, p_2, and p_3, and ratios of B's played hands are represented as q_1, q_2, and q_3. A's pay-off matrix L as a result of B's played hands is as follows:

When B plays rock, $\quad 0p_1 - 100p_2 + 100p_3 = L$
When B plays scissors, $\quad 100p_1 + 0p_2 - 100p_3 = L$
When B plays paper, $\quad -100p_1 + 100p_2 + 0p_3 = L$

With the condition that $p_1 + p_2 + p_3 = 1$, $\quad p_1, p_2, p_3 \geq 0$

Therefore, $p_3 = 1 - p_1 - p_2$

$$-100p_2 + 100(1 - p_1 - p_2) = L$$
$$100p_1 \qquad -100(1 - p_1 - p_2) = L$$
$$-100p_1 + 100p_2 \qquad = L$$

(I) $\quad -100p_1 - 200p_2 + 100 = L$
(II) $\quad 200p_1 + 100p_2 - 100 = L$
(III) $\quad -100p_1 + 100p_2 \qquad = L$

(II) − (III) $\quad 300p_1 - 100 = 0 \qquad 300p_1 = 100 \qquad \therefore p_1 = \dfrac{1}{3}$

(I) − (III) $\quad -300p_2 + 100 = 0 \qquad 300p_2 = 100 \qquad \therefore p_2 = \dfrac{1}{3}$

$$\therefore p_3 = 1 - \dfrac{1}{3} - \dfrac{1}{3} = \dfrac{1}{3}$$

In a similar manner, conversely, ratios of B's played hands are obtained 1/3 each. That is, the optimum play to maximize the gain and minimize the loss would be for both sides to play scissors, paper, and rock hands 1/3 each.

This has been proven by playing a computer against a human being. In the beginning, the human may keep winning, but as the number of plays add up, the computer eventually prevails. The reason is that a human being has certain peculiarities and idiosyncrasies.

In the game of scissors-paper-rock, adding the gains of the 2 players equals to zero. This is called a "zero-sum two-person game," and the starting point for the Theory of Games.

In 1923, J. L. von Neuman (1903–1957) of Berlin University proposed the Theory of Games as a mathematical analysis of the behavior of two parties in competition in which each side attempts to secure and maximize their own gain while constantly taking the behavior of the other party into account. He later moved to Princeton University in the United States and with cooperation from Professor O. Morgenstern (1900–78) completed 5 volumes of the *Theory of Games and Economic Behavior* in 1944.

Neuman's work begins with the 18th century's Adam Smith and his assertion that individuals need not pay attention to the behavior of others and all they need to do is comply with free market conditions, but he maintained that in the modern social economic system, large corporations have taken the form of monopoly and oligopoly and must make decisions while consciously taking the behavior of other competitors into account. Filling the gap between classic economic theory and modern reality, the Game Theory suddenly drew a great amount of interest.

3.3.3 Mixed-strategy game and basic solution

In the Game Theory, the playing hand is called strategy and it is constituted of 3 elements:

1. Gain and loss
2. Changes
3. Time

First, let's assume that company A's gain is company B's loss and company A's loss is company B's gain. Next, let's assume that company A can have 3 strategies and company B 4 strategies. When considering the Game Theory, we presuppose that both parties know all the strategies taken by the other one. For example, since with respect to A's pay-off matrix, the total gains and losses of A and B is fixed (in this case, 10), this is called a zero-sum two-person game, as described previously. Between 2 certain companies, in other words, the total of their top rankings and other market shares when added is also 100%; therefore, this becomes a zero-sum two-person game.

B strategies A strategies	(1.) Price increase	(2.) Deferment	(3.) Free gift	(4.) Price discount	(A's Probability)
(1.) Price increase	-5	▽ 30	-20*	5	p_1
(2.) Deferment	-20	-25 *	0	-15	p_2
(3.) Price discount	▽ 15	-10 *	▽ 25	▽ 30	p_3
(B's probability)	q_1	q_2	q_3	q_4	

In this case, if A takes (1), then B would naturally take (3) (*); if A takes (3) (▽), then B takes (2); if A takes (1) (▽), then the game returns to square one. If A takes (2), then B takes 2 (*); if A takes (1). If A takes (3), then B takes (2); if A takes (1), then the game again returns to square one and repeats.

On the other hand, if B takes (1), then A naturally takes (3); if B takes (2) ($*$), then A takes (1) (∇), and a similar situation as seen previously results. If B takes (2), then A takes (1), which is easily understandable. If B takes (4), then A takes (3) (∇), and a similar overlap as seen previously occurs.

That is, no matter what hands A and B deal, eventually, A mixes and deals (1) and (3), and B mixes and deals (2) and (3) alternately in round robin. Thus this strategy called a mixed-strategy, and the previous game of scissors-paper-rock is one example.

Here, examining ($*$) and (∇), ($*$) is attached to the minimum value of elements in each row and (∇) is attached to the maximum value of elements in each column. That is, ($*$) indicates desirability of B as viewed from A, and (∇) indicates desirability of A as viewed from B. Since these hands do not coincide, a round robin scenario results.

Here, A attempts to select probability ratios p_1, p_2, and p_3 so that regardless of what strategy B takes, at least L, the gains expectation value, or more precisely, the upper limit of L is maximized.

When B is (1), $\quad -5p_1 - 20p_2 + 15p_3 \geq L$ $\quad$ (i)
When B is (2), $\quad 30p_1 - 25p_2 - 10p_3 \geq L$ $\quad$ (ii)
When B is (3)$_\nabla$ $-20p_1 + 0p_2 + 25p_3 \geq L$ $\quad$ (iii)
When B is (4) $\quad 5p_1 - 15p_2 + 30p_3 \geq L$ $\quad$ (iv)

With $p_1 + p_2 + p_3 = 1$, $\quad p_1 \geq 0, \quad p_2 \geq 0, \quad p_3 \geq 0$

To eliminate one of the p_i ratios, $15 p_3$ in equation (i) corresponds to the minimum (∇) among the maximum values of p_i coefficients in each equation. To eliminate p_3, we substitute $p_3 = 1 - p_1 - p_2$

$$15 - 20p_1 - 35p_2 \geq L \qquad \text{(i)'}$$
$$-10 + 40p_1 - 15p_2 \geq L \qquad \text{(ii)'}$$
$$25 - 45p_1 - 25p_2 \geq L \qquad \text{(iii)'}$$
$$30 - 25p_1 - 45p_2 \geq L \qquad \text{(iv)'}$$

The p_2 coefficients are all negative; therefore, from the condition $p_2 \geq 0$, this could be a problem in maximizing L.

Here, the safest bet is $p_2 = 0$. Consequently,

$$15 - 20p_1 \geq L \qquad \text{(i)''}$$
$$-10 + 40p_1 \geq L \qquad \text{(ii)''}$$
$$25 - 45p_1 \geq L \qquad \text{(iii)''}$$
$$30 - 25p_1 \geq L \qquad \text{(iv)''}$$

The remaining p_1 coefficients include both positive and negative values; with respect to an absolute value size, (ii)' and (iii)' affect the expectation value L the most.

To eliminate p_1 from both equations

(ii)' ×9 $\quad -90 + 360p_1 \geq 9L$

(iii)' ×8 $\quad 200 - 360p_1 \geq 8L \quad \therefore 110 \geq 17L, \therefore L \leq \dfrac{110}{17}$

This gives us the upper limit of L.

To maximize L, assuming the equality, from equation (ii)'

$$-10+40p_1 = \frac{110}{17}, \quad 40p_1 = \frac{110}{17}+10 = \frac{110+170}{17} = \frac{280}{17}, \quad p_1 = \frac{7}{17}$$

$$\therefore \quad p_3 = 1-\frac{7}{17}-0 = \frac{10}{17}$$

$$p_1 = \frac{7}{17}, \quad p_2 = 0, \quad p_3 = \frac{10}{17}$$

Again, B attempts to select probability ratios $q_1, q_2, q_3,$ and q_4 so that regardless of what strategy A takes, at least M, the gains expectation value, or more precisely, the lower limit of M is minimized.

When A is (1): $\quad -5q_1 + 30q_2 - 20q_3 + 5q_4 \leq M \quad$ (i)
When A is (2): $\quad -20q_1 - 25q_2 + 0q_3 - 15q_4 \leq M \quad$ (ii)
When A is (3): $\quad 15q_1 - 10q_2 + 25q_3 + 30q_4 \leq M \quad$ (iii)

With $q_1 + q_2 + q_3 + q_4 = 1, \quad q_1 \geq 0, \quad q_2 \geq 0, \quad q_3 \geq 0, \quad q_4 \geq 0$

To eliminate one of the q_j ratios, note that $-10q_2$ in equation (iii) corresponds to the maximum ($*$) among the minimum values of q_j coefficients in each equation.

To eliminate q_2, we substitute $q_2 = 1 - q_1 - q_3 - q_4$

$$30 - 35q_1 - 50q_3 - 25q_4 \leq M \quad \text{(i)}'$$
$$-25 + 5q_1 + 25q_3 + 10q_4 \leq M \quad \text{(ii)}'$$
$$-10 + 25q_1 + 35q_3 + 40q_4 \leq M \quad \text{(iii)}'$$

Here the $q_1, q_3,$ and q_4 coefficients include both positive and negative values; with respect to an absolute value size, q_3 affects the expectation value M the most.

To eliminate q_3 from equations (i)' and (iii)' with large coefficients

(i)' ×7 $210 - 245q_1 - 350q_3 - 175q_4 \leq 7M$

(iii)' ×10 $-100 + 250q_1 + 350q_3 + 400q_4 \leq 10M$

$\therefore 110 + 5q_1 + 225q_4 \leq 17M$

From the given conditions, M is minimized when $q_1 = q_4 = 0$ and equality of the lower limit is established.

Therefore, returning to $M = \dfrac{110}{17}$ and (i)'

$30 - 30 \times 0 - 50q_3 - 25 \times 0 = \dfrac{110}{17}$ $\therefore q_3 = \dfrac{110 - 17 \times 30}{17 \times 50} = \dfrac{400}{850} = \dfrac{8}{17}$

Returning to (i),

$-5 \times 0 + 30q_2 - 20 \times \dfrac{8}{17} + 5 \times 0 = \dfrac{110}{17}$ $\therefore q_2 = \dfrac{110 + 20 \times 8}{17 \times 30} = \dfrac{270}{510} = \dfrac{9}{17}$

$\therefore q_1 = 0, \quad q_2 = \dfrac{9}{17}, \quad q_3 = \dfrac{8}{17}, \quad q_4 = 0$

The result of the probability calculations is exactly the same as when ($*$, ∇) are attached to the pay-off matrix. This is called the basic solution.

However, with respect to A, for example, when the price increase (p_1) is 7/17 and the price decrease (p_3) is 10/17, does this means that if there are 17 items, the price of the 7th item should be increased and the price of the 10th item decreased?

But this does not specify which item price to increase or decrease. Viewed from B, A seems to be inclined to discount with a weight of 4 to 6.

On the other hand, viewed from A, it could be generally said that B is deferring price (q_2) or giving away gifts (q_3) with a 50-50 weight, depending on the circumstances. Either way, in a mixed strategy, the basic solution seems to be not a totally satisfactory one.

3.3.4 Pure strategy game and saddle point/solution of equilibrium

In the same zero-sum game, in an A pay-off matrix as shown here, no matter what strategies A and B take, eventually, A settles into (3) discount and B into (4) discount.

B strategies A strategies	1. Price increase	2. Deferment	3. Free gift	4. Price discount
1. Price increase	-15	▽ 20	-20*	-10
2. Deferment	-30 *	-15	15	-5
3. Price discount	▽ 15	10	▽ 25	▽ 5*

That is, viewed from A, the maximum among minimum values ($*$) in each row considered by B, and the minimum among maximum values (∇) in each column considered by A agree. In other words, A is targeting the max-min value and B the min-max value.

Represented in symbols, if the rows are i and columns j, then:

$A:$ $\max[\min(-15, 20, -20, -10), \min(-30, -15, 15, -5),$
$\min(15, 10, 25, 5)]$
$= \max(-20, -30, 5) = \max_i \min_j f(i, j) = f(3, 4) = 5$

$B:$ $\min[\max(-15, -30, 15), \max(20, -15, 10), \max(-20, 15, 25)$
$\max(-10, -5, 5)]$
$= \min(15, 20, 25, 5) = \min_j \max_i f(i, j) = f(3, 4) = 5$

Therefore, when the max-min value and the min-max value of a certain matrix are equal, that matrix has a saddle point, or there is a point of equilibrium in the pay-off matrix. In other words, there is a solution of equilibrium rather than a probability solution.

This strategy is then called the pure strategy in contrast to mixed strategy.

The term saddle point refers to the fact that when looking at row (3) as the strategy taken by A, the value 5 is the minimum and when looking at column (4), this value 5 is the maximum value and is the summit.

The strategy to realize in this approach is called the optimum strategy, but in this case, it is a min-max strategy based on the min-max principle.

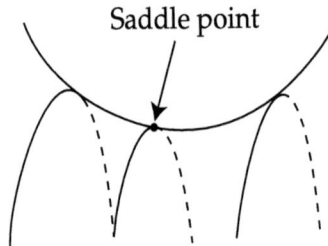

In a pure strategy where there is a saddle point, the results whether considered from B's standpoint min-max principle or A's standpoint max-min principle are the same; thus, it is normally represented by the former.

In the min-max strategy, maximum gains for the other party and minimum gains for one's own are considered; that is, the worst-scenario case is first considered; thereafter, an approach most advantageous to one's own is selected, which makes this decision - making method an extremely cautious one.

There is also a game called "Prisoners' Dilemma," where there are two players A and B and one side's gains is not the other side's loss; in other words, the total of gains and losses is not fixed. Two suspects that are known with certainty to be accomplices are captured and locked in separate rooms. Both suspects are separately notified of the punishments shown in the chart here.

A dilemma occurs because suspects are not sure how to respond, as they are also prevented from consulting with each other. Now let's assume that "remain silent" is "higher price," "testify to conspiracy" is "lower price," and suspects A and B are oligopolistic companies A and B.

Punishment for two prisoners

		Suspect B	
		Remain silent	Testify to conspiracy
Suspect A	Remain silent	2-year sentence for both suspects	10-year sentence for suspect A 6-month sentence for suspect B
	Testify to conspiracy	6-month sentence for suspect A 10-year sentence for suspect B	5-year sentences for both suspects

A game such as the game of "Prisoners' Dilemma" is called a non-zero-sum game, and the solution is hard to find without special conditions. In the game theory, the range is expanded to include 2xn-person game, 3x3 game, cooperative n-person game, and so on.

3.4 Lanchester strategy model and distribution of fighting strength

3.4.1 Application of the min-max principle

Let's list equation (3.18) from section 3.2.4 again here:

$$\frac{dm}{dt} - \frac{dn}{dt} = P - Q - \beta\left[\frac{(n-n_t)^2}{m_t}P - \frac{(m-m_t)^2}{n_t}Q\right] = L(m_t, n_t)$$

(3.18)

The commander of army m attempts to determine the tactical power m_t (i.e., the strategic power m_s) to maximize L. While the commander of army n attempts to determine the tactical power n_t (i.e., the strategic power n_s) to minimize L.

Therefore, based on the game theory, to achieve a solution of equilibrium, we adopt the pure strategy with the saddle point. However, we cannot avoid being restricted with respect to the conditions for obtaining a solution of equilibrium.

When an equilibrium is obtained, since there is a saddle point, viewed from one side, that is a maximum point, and viewed from the other side, that is the minimum point, and moreover, both coincide.

Thus, here, the max-min principle is applied to army m, and min-max principle is applied to army n. Specifically, in equation (3.18), first, army m targets the maximization; therefore, the other party's n_t is considered a constant. We take a first-order partial differential with respect to m_t, which is equal to a zero.

Similarly, army n targets the minimization; therefore, the other party's m_t is considered a constant. We take a first-order partial differential with respect to n_t, which is equal to zero. Since both must coincide, we have a system of equations. Furthermore, as maximum and minimum conditions, we take second-order partial differentials with respect to m_t and n_t, which are, respectively, less than and greater than zero.

$$\begin{cases} \dfrac{\partial L}{\partial m_t} = 0 \quad (3.19), \text{ Maximum condition} \\ \dfrac{\partial L}{\partial n_t} = 0 \quad (3.20), \text{ Minimum condition} \end{cases} \qquad \dfrac{\partial^2 L}{\partial m_t^2} < 0 \quad (3.21)$$

$$\dfrac{\partial^2 L}{\partial n_t^2} > 0 \quad (3.22)$$

3.4.2 Solving a system of partial differential equations

First, arranging equation (3.19),

P and Q are constants and therefore are eliminated

$$\dfrac{\partial L}{\partial m_t} = -\beta\left\{-\dfrac{(n-n_t)^2}{m_t^2}P + 2\dfrac{(m-m_t)}{n_t}Q\right\}$$

$$= \beta\left\{\dfrac{P(n-n_t)^2}{m_t^2} - \dfrac{2Q(m-m_t)}{n_t}\right\} = 0$$

$$Q \quad \beta \neq 0 \quad \therefore \quad \dfrac{P(n-n_t)^2}{m_t^2} - \dfrac{2Q(m-m_t)}{n_t} = 0$$

$$\therefore \quad Pn_t(n-n_t)^2 = 2Qm_t^2(m-m_t) \qquad \text{(i)}$$

Next, arranging equation (3.20),

P and Q are constants and therefore are eliminated

$$\frac{\partial L}{\partial n_t} = -\beta\left\{-2\frac{(n-n_t)}{m_t}P + \frac{(m-m_t)^2}{n_t^2}Q\right\}$$

$$= \beta\left\{\frac{2P(n-n_t)}{m_t} - \frac{Q(m-m_t)^2}{n_t^2}\right\} = 0$$

$Q \quad \beta \neq 0 \quad \therefore \quad \dfrac{2P(n-n_t)}{m_t} - \dfrac{Q(m-m_t)^2}{n_t^2} = 0$

$$\therefore \quad 2Pn_t^2(n-n_t) = Qm_t(m-m_t)^2 \qquad \text{(ii)}$$

To satisfy (i) and (ii) simultaneously, from (i)

$$(m - m_t) = \frac{Pn_t(n-n_t)^2}{2Qm_t^2}$$

Substituting this in (ii)

$$2Pn_t^2(n-n_t) = Qm_t\left\{\frac{P^2n_t^2(n-n_t)^4}{4Q^2m_t^4}\right\} = \frac{P^2n_t^2(n-n_t)^4}{4Qm_t^3}$$

$$\therefore \quad m_t^3 = \frac{1}{2^3}\cdot\frac{P}{Q}(n-n_t)^3$$

$$m_t = \frac{1}{2}\sqrt[3]{\frac{P}{Q}}(n-n_t)$$

Here, by defining $\sqrt[3]{\dfrac{P}{Q}} = \rho$, since $(n-n_t) = n_s$

Where ρ is called Lanchester's Strategic Coefficient.

$$m_t = \frac{\rho}{2}(n-n_t) = \frac{\rho}{2}n_s \qquad \text{(iii)}$$

Similarly, from (ii),

$$(n - n_t) = \frac{Qm_t(m - m_t)^2}{2Pn_t^2}$$

By substituting this in (i), since $(m - m_t) = m_s$

$$Pn_t\left\{\frac{Q^2m_t^2(m - m_t)^4}{4P^2n_t^4}\right\} = \frac{Q^2m_t^2(m - m_t)^4}{4Pn_t^3} = 2Qm_t^2(m - m_t)$$

$$\therefore \quad n_t^3 = \frac{1}{2^3} \cdot \frac{Q}{P}(m - m_t)^3 = \frac{1}{2^3} \cdot \frac{1}{\frac{P}{Q}}(m - m_t)^3$$

$$n_t = \frac{1}{2\rho}(m - m_t) = \frac{1}{2\rho}m_s \qquad (iv)$$

Furthermore, by substituting (iv) in (iii), and substituting (iii) in (iv)

$$m_t = \frac{\rho}{2}\left\{n - \frac{1}{2\rho}(m - m_t)\right\} \qquad n_t = \frac{1}{2\rho}\left\{m - \frac{\rho}{2}(n - n_t)\right\}$$

$$= \frac{\rho}{2}n - \frac{1}{4}m + \frac{1}{4}m_t \qquad = \frac{1}{2\rho}m - \frac{1}{4}n + \frac{1}{4}n_t$$

$$4m_t = 2\rho n - m + m_t \qquad 4n_t = \frac{2}{\rho}m - n + n_t$$

$$3m_t = 2\rho n - m \qquad 3n_t = \frac{2}{\rho}m - n$$

$$\therefore m_t = \frac{1}{3}(2\rho n - m) \quad (3.23) \quad \therefore n_t = \frac{1}{3}\left(\frac{2}{\rho}m - n\right) \quad (3.24)$$

Also, $m_s = m - m_t$, and $n_s = n - n_t$, From (iv) and (iii):

$$m_s = m - \frac{1}{3}(2\rho n - m) \qquad n_s = n - \frac{1}{3}\left(\frac{2}{\rho}m - n\right)$$

$$= m - \frac{2}{3}\rho n + \frac{1}{3}m \qquad = n - \frac{2}{3\rho}m + \frac{1}{3}n$$

$$= \frac{4}{3}m - \frac{2}{3}\rho n \qquad = \frac{4}{3}n - \frac{2}{3\rho}m$$

$$\therefore m_s = \frac{2}{3}(2m - \rho n) = 2\rho n_t \quad (3.25) \qquad \therefore n_s = \frac{2}{3}\left(2n - \frac{m}{\rho}\right) = \frac{2}{\rho}m_t \quad (3.26)$$

These solutions of equilibrium are collectively called Lanchester's Strategic Equations.

$$\begin{cases} m_t = \frac{1}{3}(2\rho n - m) \\ m_s = \frac{2}{3}(2m - \rho n) = 2\rho n_t \end{cases} \qquad \begin{cases} n_t = \frac{1}{3}\left(\frac{2}{\rho}m - n\right) \\ n_s = \frac{2}{3}\left(2n - \frac{m}{\rho}\right) = \frac{2}{\rho}m_t \end{cases}$$

$$\rho = \sqrt[3]{\frac{P}{Q}}$$

Note that when production (P) and supply (Q) are equal, and the committed fighting strengths are also equal, an equilibrium is achieved when the distribution is 3 to 1 for the tactical strength and 3 to 2 for the strategic strength. When there are no differences in the production and supply, as well as the total fighting strength, then it is important to note that, according to Lanchester's strategic equations, the solution is obtained by placing the weight on the strategic strength.

Here, the breakdown of the distribution of tactical and strategic forces of two armies, m and n, with equal fighting strengths when both possess similar information has become clear. It should be noted, however, that the solution here is for distribution to gain equilibrium and may not address the enemy's realities. In that sense, the solution of equilibrium found is a solution of certainty and not a temporary solution of stability. It is merely a reference solution for the judgment.

Furthermore, there are other issues such as the enemy's intention to commit its total fighting strength to the tactical force or to the strategic force, or more than anything else, the question of whether the total fighting strength is within the reach of equilibrium conditions.

3.4.3 Two equilibrium conditions

Both tactical and strategic strengths comprise parts of the fighting strength and therefore must assume positive values.

Thus in (3.23) and (3.24)

$$m_t = \frac{1}{3}(2\rho n - m) > 0 \qquad n_t = \frac{1}{3}\left(\frac{2}{\rho}m - n\right) > 0$$

This is exactly the same for (3.25) and (3.26)

$$\therefore 2\rho n - m > 0 \qquad \therefore \frac{2}{\rho}m - n > 0$$

$$2\rho n > m \qquad \frac{2}{\rho} > n, \quad \rho = \sqrt[3]{\frac{P}{Q}} \neq 0$$

$$n > \frac{1}{2\rho}m \qquad m > \frac{\rho}{2}n$$

$$\therefore \frac{\rho}{2}n < m < 2\rho n \qquad \text{Therefore}: \qquad \frac{1}{2\rho}m < n < \frac{2}{\rho}m \qquad (3.27)$$

Lanchester's strategic coefficient is involved here; however, as shown here, an upper range from the other party's fighting strength is decided, and when within that range, the solution of equilibrium is obtained. When below the lower limit, the fighting will be no match; when above the limit, one's own fighting strength will not be sufficient enough to face the enemy.

In other words, losing on the battleground is so obvious from the outlet that it would be foolish to engage in such a fight; therefore, other strategies must be conceived. Note that (3.27) is the first equilibrium condition in Lanchester's strategy model.

Next, let's consider the maximum condition (3.21) and the minimum condition (3.22). The previous section (3.4.2) was subjected to the first-order partial differential, shown as follows:

$$\frac{\partial L}{\partial m_t} = \beta \left\{ \frac{P(n-n_t)^2}{m_t^2} - \frac{2Q(m-m_t)}{n_t} \right\}$$

$$\frac{\partial L}{\partial n_t} = \beta \left\{ \frac{2P(n-n_t)}{m_t} - \frac{Q(m-m_t)^2}{n_t^2} \right\}$$

Furthermore, taking the second-order partial differential with respect to m_t,

$$\frac{\partial^2 L}{\partial m_t^2} = \beta \left\{ -2 \frac{P(n-n_t)^2}{m_t^3} + \frac{2Q}{n_t} \right\} = 2\beta \left\{ \frac{Q}{n_t} - \frac{P(n-m_t)^2}{m_t^3} \right\} < 0$$

Since $\beta > 0$, P, Q, m_t, n, n_t are positive numbers,

$$\frac{Q}{n_t} - \frac{P(n-n_t)^2}{m_t^3} < 0, \quad \frac{Q}{n_t} < \frac{P(n-n_t)^2}{m_t^3}, \quad m_t^3 < \frac{Pn_t(n-n_t)^2}{Q}$$

Here, regarding equation (i) of section (3.4.2):

$$m_t^3 < 2m_t^2(m-m_t), \quad m_t < 2(m-m_t), \quad m_t < 2m - 2m_t$$

$$3m_t < 2m \quad \therefore \quad m_t < \frac{2}{3}m \quad (3.28)$$

Similarly, taking the second-order partial differential with respect to n_t

$$\frac{\partial^2 L}{\partial n_t^2} = \beta\left\{-\frac{2P}{m_t} + 2\frac{Q(m-m_t)^2}{n_t^3}\right\} = 2\beta\left\{\frac{Q(m-m_t)^2}{n_t^3} - \frac{P}{m_t}\right\} > 0$$

$\beta > 0$, P, Q, m, m_t, n_t are positive numbers.

$$\frac{Q(m-m_t)^2}{n_t^3} - \frac{P}{m_t} > 0, \quad \frac{Q(m-m_t)^2}{n_t^3} > \frac{P}{m_t}, \quad n_t^3 > \frac{Qm_t(m-m_t)^2}{P}$$

Here, regarding (3.4.2) and (ii):

$$n_t^3 < 2n_t^2(n-n_t), \quad n_t < 2(n-n_t), \quad n_t < 2n - 2n_t$$

$$3n_t < 2n, \quad \therefore \quad n_t < \frac{2}{3}n \quad (3.29)$$

· For (3.28) and (3.29) to give a solution of equilibrium, both opposing armies must keep the distribution of tactical strength under 2/3 of the total fighting strength; in other words, at least more than 1/3 of the total fighting strength must be allocated to the destruction of the enemy's production and supply capabilities in order to maintain equilibrium. This is the second equilibrium condition in Lanchester's strategy model.

In summary, to rank with the enemy, prior to starting the fighting, first, these first and second conditions of equilibrium must be well-examined.

3.4.4 Relationship between the strategic and the generalized model

$$\frac{dm}{dt} = P - \beta \frac{n_s^2}{m_t} P - \alpha(m_t + n_t) \quad (3.16)$$

$$\frac{dn}{dt} = Q - \beta \frac{n_s^2}{m_t} Q - \alpha(m_t + n_t) \quad (3.17)$$

$$\frac{dm}{dt} = P - an - cm \quad (3.1)$$

$$\frac{dn}{dt} = Q - bm - dn \quad (3.2)$$

Where equations 3.16 and 3.17 represent the Strategic Model, and equations 3.1 and 3.2 represent the Generalized Model.

Since we obtained the solution of equilibrium for the Lanchester's strategic model, we must then clarify the relationship with the generalized Lanchester's model. We substitute Lanchester's strategic equations (3.23), (3.24), (3.25), and (3.26) into (3.16) and arrange:

$$\frac{dm}{dt} = P - \beta P \frac{\left(\frac{2}{\rho} m_t\right)^2}{m_t} - \alpha \left\{ \frac{1}{3}(2\rho n - m) + \frac{1}{3}\left(\frac{2}{\rho} m - n\right) \right\}$$

$$= P - \frac{4P\beta m_t}{\rho^2} - \frac{\alpha}{3}\left(2\rho n - n + \frac{2}{\rho} m - m\right)$$

$$= P - \frac{4P\beta m_t}{\rho^2} - \frac{\alpha}{3}(2\rho n - m) - \frac{\alpha}{3}(2\rho - 1)n - \frac{\alpha}{3}\left(\frac{2}{\rho} - 1\right)m$$

$$= P - \frac{\alpha}{3} \cdot \frac{8P\beta}{\rho\alpha} n - \frac{\alpha}{3}(2\rho - 1)n + \frac{\alpha}{3} \cdot \frac{4P\beta}{\rho^2 \alpha} m - \frac{\alpha}{3}\left(\frac{2}{\rho} - 1\right)m$$

$$= P - \frac{\alpha}{3}\left[\frac{8P\beta}{\rho\alpha} + 2\rho - 1\right]n - \frac{\alpha}{3}\left[\frac{2}{\rho} - 1 - \frac{4P\beta}{\rho^2 \alpha}\right]m$$

Collating with (3.1),

$$a = \frac{\alpha}{3}\left[\frac{8P\beta}{\rho\alpha} + 2\rho - 1\right] \quad (3.30), \qquad c = \frac{\alpha}{3}\left[\frac{2}{\rho} - 1 - \frac{4P\beta}{\rho^2\alpha}\right]$$

Similarly, we substitute Lanchester's strategic equations (3.23), (3.24), (3.25), and (3.26) into (3.17) and arrange:

$$\frac{dn}{dt} = Q - \beta Q \frac{(2\rho n_t)^2}{n_t} - \alpha\left\{\frac{1}{3}(2\rho n - m) + \frac{1}{3}\left(\frac{2}{\rho}m - n\right)\right\}$$

$$= Q - 4Q\rho^2\beta n_t - \frac{\alpha}{3}\left(2\rho n - n + \frac{2}{\rho}m - m\right)$$

$$= Q - 4Q\rho^2\beta \frac{1}{3}\left(\frac{2}{\rho}m - n\right) - \frac{\alpha}{3}\left(\frac{2}{\rho} - 1\right)m - \frac{\alpha}{3}(2\rho - 1)n$$

$$= Q - \frac{\alpha}{3} \cdot \frac{8Q\rho\beta}{\alpha} m - \frac{\alpha}{3}\left(\frac{2}{\rho} - 1\right)m + \frac{\alpha}{3} \cdot \frac{4Q\rho^2\beta}{\alpha} n - \frac{\alpha}{3}(2\rho - 1)n$$

$$= Q - \frac{\alpha}{3}\left[\frac{8Q\rho\beta}{\alpha} + \frac{2}{\rho} - 1\right]m - \frac{\alpha}{3}\left[2\rho - 1 - \frac{4Q\rho^2\beta}{\alpha}\right]n$$

Collating with (3.2),

$$b = \frac{\alpha}{3}\left[\frac{8Q\rho\beta}{\alpha} + \frac{2}{\rho} - 1\right] \quad (3.31), \qquad d = \frac{\alpha}{3}\left[2\rho - 1 - \frac{4Q\rho^2\beta}{\alpha}\right]$$

Incidentally,

$$b - c = \frac{\alpha}{3}\left\{\left[\frac{8Q\rho\beta}{\alpha} + \frac{2}{\rho} - 1\right] - \left[\frac{2}{\rho} - 1 - \frac{4P\beta}{\rho^2\alpha}\right]\right\}$$

$$= \frac{\alpha}{3}\left[\frac{8Q\rho\beta}{\alpha} + \frac{4P\beta}{\rho^2\alpha}\right] = \frac{4\beta}{3\rho^2}\left[2Q\rho^3 + P\right]$$

In addition:

$$\rho^3 = \left(\sqrt[3]{\frac{P}{Q}}\right)^3 = \frac{P}{Q} \quad \therefore \quad Q\rho^3 = P, \quad Q\rho = \frac{P}{\rho^2}, \quad Q\rho^2 = \frac{P}{\rho}$$

$$b - c = \frac{4\beta}{3\rho^2}[2P + P] = \frac{12P\beta}{3\rho^2} = \frac{4P\beta}{\rho^2} = 4Q\rho\beta$$

$$\therefore \quad b - c = 4Q\rho\beta \quad \therefore \quad c = b - 4Q\rho\beta \quad (3.32)$$

Similarly:

$$a - d = \frac{\alpha}{3}\left\{\left[\frac{8P\beta}{\rho\alpha} + 2\rho - 1\right] - \left[2\rho - 1 - \frac{4Q\rho^2\beta}{\alpha}\right]\right\}$$

$$= \frac{\alpha}{3}\left[\frac{8P\rho}{\rho\alpha} + \frac{4Q\rho^2\beta}{\alpha}\right] = \frac{4\beta}{3\rho}[2P + Q\rho^3]$$

$$= \frac{4\beta}{3\rho}[2P + P] = \frac{12P\beta}{3\rho} = \frac{4P\beta}{\rho} = 4Q\rho^2\beta$$

$$\therefore \quad a - d = 4Q\rho^2\beta \quad \therefore \quad d = a - 4\left(\frac{P\beta}{\rho}\right) = a - 4Q\rho^2\beta \quad (3.33)$$

As a result, the solution of equilibrium for Lanchester's strategic model go by way of (3.30), (3.31), (3.32), and (3.33) coefficients and can be docked with the generalized Lanchester's model. Particular solutions as shown in (3.13) and (3.14) can be calculated, and, for now, the total system of the Lanchester model is complete.

Summary:

Fighting strength matrix

		Fighting Strength		Tactical Strength		Strategic Strength		Production and Supply Strength
m	$=$	m_t	$+$	m_s				P
c		b						
n	$=$	n_t	$+$	n_s				Q

Lanchester strategy model

$$\begin{cases} \dfrac{dm}{dt} = P - \beta \dfrac{n_s^2}{m_t} P - \alpha(m_t + n_t) \\ \dfrac{dn}{dt} = Q - \beta \dfrac{m_s^2}{n_t} Q - \alpha(m_t + n_t) \end{cases}$$

Where α and β are ratio constants

Lanchester's strategic equations. (Solution of equilibrium)

$$\begin{cases} m_t = \dfrac{1}{3}(2\rho n - m) \\ m_s = \dfrac{2}{3}(2m - \rho n) = 2\rho n_t \end{cases} \qquad \begin{cases} n_t = \dfrac{1}{3}\left(\dfrac{2}{\rho}m - n\right) \\ n_s = \dfrac{2}{3}\left(2n - \dfrac{m}{\rho}\right) = \dfrac{2}{\rho} m_t \end{cases}$$

Lanchester's strategic coefficient:

$$\rho = \sqrt[3]{\dfrac{P}{Q}}$$

Conditions for equilibrium:

1: $\dfrac{P}{2} n < m < 2\rho n$ $\qquad \dfrac{1}{2\rho} < n < \dfrac{2}{\rho} m$

2: $m_t < \dfrac{2}{3} m$ $\qquad n_t < \dfrac{2}{3} n$

Generalized Lanchester coefficients conversion:

$$a = \dfrac{\alpha}{3}\left[\dfrac{8P\beta}{\rho\alpha} + 2\rho - 1\right] \qquad c = b - 4Q\rho\beta$$

$$b = \dfrac{\alpha}{3}\left[\dfrac{8Q\rho\beta}{\alpha} + \dfrac{2}{\rho} - 1\right] \qquad d = a - 4\left(\dfrac{P\beta}{\rho}\right) = a - 4Q\rho^2\beta$$

Generalized Lanchester model:

$$\begin{cases} \dfrac{dm}{dt} = P - an - cm \\ \dfrac{dn}{dt} = Q - bm - dn \end{cases} \qquad P, Q > 0, \ a, b > 0, \ a, b \gg c, d$$

Note that c and d can be positive, zero, or negative.

Particular solutions of the generalized Lanchester model:

$$\begin{cases} m = A + Fe^{(\mu-\lambda)t} + \dfrac{\mu+\kappa}{b} Ge^{-(\mu+\lambda)t} \\ n = B - \dfrac{\mu+\kappa}{a} Fe^{(\mu-\lambda)t} + Ge^{-(\lambda+\mu)t} \end{cases}$$

However: $\lambda = \dfrac{c+d}{2}$, $\kappa = \dfrac{c-d}{2}$, $\mu = \sqrt{\kappa^2 + ab}$

$$A = \frac{Qa - Pd}{ab - cd}, \qquad B = \frac{Pb - Qc}{ab - cd}, \qquad ab - cd \neq 0$$

$$F = \frac{ab}{2\mu(\mu + \kappa)} \left\{ \left[m_0 + \frac{d + \mu + \kappa}{ab - cd} P \right] - \frac{\mu + \kappa}{b} \left[n_0 + \frac{c + \mu - \kappa}{ab - cd} Q \right] \right\}$$

$$G = \frac{ab}{2\mu(\mu + \kappa)} \left\{ \frac{\mu + \kappa}{a} \left[m_0 + \frac{d - \mu + \kappa}{ab - cd} P \right] + \left[n_0 + \frac{c - \mu - \kappa}{ab - cd} Q \right] \right\}$$

CHAPTER 4

STRATEGY MODEL AND MARKETING APPLICATIONS

4.1. The principle and theory of the 40% market share

4.1.1 Military problems in relation to marketing

War is a clash of forces where the intelligence and resources of a country is challenged. In other words, all the intellectual powers and all the forces are directed toward the goal of winning by minimizing one's losses while maximizing those of the enemy's, or said differently, by making one's fighting strength plus while making that of the enemy's zero.

Operation Research (OR) with its inception during World War II was later adopted as the basis for Management Sciences, and with the popularity of computers, gave rise to Linear Planning (LP), business games, PERT/CPM, and various other methodologies. OR was originally designed to win the war; however, the objective of OR in business management, from the profitability standpoint, is to "minimize the costs and maximize the results," which has a tendency of emphasizing the internal management in relation to external factors.

When the overall economy shows a high growth rate, the economic pie also grows larger, but there is no guarantee that this condition could continue indefinitely. As the domestic and international competition becomes mores fierce, short of winning, one is doomed to defeat.

The know-how to win is the main theme in OR, and the expression "Remember to Lanchester" is its natural extension. In fact, the know-how to win remains only with the winner. Therefore, the United States upon its "retreat with dignity" from Vietnam produces the movie Midway (1976) to reawaken a sense of victory in commemoration of its bicentennial.

With respect to competition, the antitrust laws enable the supply of identical or similar products and services to the consumer from two or more suppliers. In the free market system, this means the exclusion of one supplier benefits the remaining, other suppliers.

The acquisition and maintenance of the consumer as a result over a certain period of time is shown by the market share. This certain period could be 6 months or a year, the areas of product and service and regional divisions may also be considered. In any case, the market share as a numeric value clearly shows the participating companies' competitive strength. And the market share does not necessarily correlate to the company's capital, number of employees, or age.

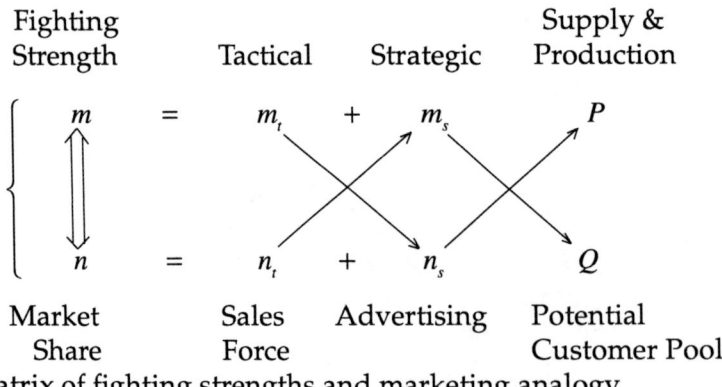

Matrix of fighting strengths and marketing analogy.

When correlating the fighting strength to the market share and competition between two companies, in this analogy, the production and supply require utmost handling. The result of composition of a corporation's tactical strength and strategic strength is reflected in the competitive strength and market share. If both sides abandon executing their own strategies against the other party's production and supply, in a competitive market environment, the production and supply will be automatically added to the other side as a "potential consumer pool."

Potential consumer pool: The strategy in a market environment aims not to destroy but to attract consumers. To that end, the power of product development and advertising is the key. Directly speaking, the strategy would have us destroying the production and supply, which are not factories and transportation centers. The tactics correspond to the number of sales offices, sales force, and capital. In other words, the tactics are direct competitive strength while the strategy is indirect competitive strength.

4.1.2 The science of market share — condition for the top position

One common variable in the fighting strength analogy with respect to the competitive strength and the market share is time. As we examined in the generalized Lanchester's model (3.1.4), even an initial inferior fighting strength could lead to victory if the production and supply are superior.

That is, fighting strength, production and supply have their own dimensions and are calculated separately. For example, according to Japan's 1978 Self–Defense White Paper, the number of self-defense army forces was 155,000 men, 86% of the fixed capacity of 180,000 men. In comparison, South Korea has 560,000 men in their army, 3 times greater the number in Japan. However, from the standpoint of production and supply, Japan has a GNP 20 times greater than Korea's (1977).

Therefore, in military terms, the ratios between fighting strength and production/supply are unequal. Or, $\dfrac{m}{n} \neq \dfrac{P}{Q}$

Deployment of military forces around Japan

	Army	Aircraft	Navy (ton)
Far-East Soviet Union	300,000	2,040	1,330,000
China	3,250,000	5,900	398,000
North Korea	430,000	630	44,000
Korea	560,000	340	78,000
US Forces	40,000	60	
Japan	155,000	430	174,000
US Forces	26,000	170	
Taiwan	330,000	300	183,000
US Forces	1,000		
Philippines	63,000	100	109,000
US Forces	14,000	70	
US 7th Fleet W. Pacific		160	550,000

From Japan's Self-Defense white paper 1978

Here, let's see the relationship between the market share and the potential consumer pool. For example, let's assume there are two companies with market shares of 20% and 10%. The absorption from the potential consumer pool for these two companies is 20% and 10%, respectively. In that sense, an existing cultivated market share defines the next market share over a short time period, a fact that can also be affirmed experimentally.

However, when the time period is 3-5 years, based on the life cycle of products, product development, merger and joint venture, business failure, and other reasons, the market share and competitive strength can go through ups and downs and reverse.

Therefore, in marketing, assuming companies continue to make the same degree of effort, the ratios between fighting strength and production/supply are equal. Or, $\dfrac{m}{n} \approx \dfrac{P}{Q}$

Thus, in the case of two companies, let's assume that one company has the top market share (m) and the remaining market share is (n). It is extremely advantageous to enjoy the top market share, which constitutes more than half of the market or 51% and greater.

To maintain the top position in the market, we must deal with the tactics and direct competitive strength m_t and the strategy and indirect competitive strength m_s, and the indirect competitive strength must be given a greater distribution than the direct competitive strength; that is, $m_s > m_t$. Based on Lanchester's strategy model:

$$m_s > m_t$$

$$\frac{2}{3}(3m - \rho n) > \frac{1}{3}(2\rho n - m)$$

$$4m - 2\rho n > 2\rho n - m$$

$$5m > 4\rho n$$

$$\frac{m}{n} > \frac{4}{5}\rho$$

$$\frac{m}{n} > \frac{4}{5}\sqrt[3]{\frac{P}{Q}}$$

$$\left(\frac{m}{n}\right)^3 > \frac{64}{125} \cdot \frac{P}{Q}$$

Since we can assume $\dfrac{m}{n} \approx \dfrac{P}{Q}$

$$\left(\frac{m}{n}\right)^2 > \frac{64}{125}$$

Since both m and n are positive numbers,

$$\frac{m}{n} > \frac{8}{\sqrt{125}}$$

233

Because m and n are market shares where m+n=1, n=1−m, we have:

$$\frac{m}{1-m} > \frac{8}{\sqrt{125}}$$

$$m\sqrt{125} > 8 - 8m$$

$$\left(8+\sqrt{125}\right)m > 8$$

$$m > \frac{8}{8+\sqrt{125}} \approx \frac{8}{8+11.1803} = \frac{8}{19.1803}$$

$$m > 0.4171$$

Here, the market share shown is 41.7% or greater as a condition for the top position. It seems that in a competitive state where several parties are engaged in the market share battle, a market share of 51% and greater is the condition for a stable position at the top. However, based on Lanchester's laws and the game theory, when there are 3 or more parties involved, to be the top competitor, it is clear that a target of 41.7%, not 51%, must be reached.

4.1.3 Why Kirin beer remains at the top

In 1950, Dai Nihon beer was split up by GHQ (General Headquarters of U.S. Occupation Forces in Japan) into two companies, Sapporo beer and Asahi beer, to avoid excessive concentration of economic power by any one company. There was also a third beer company by the name of Kirin beer. The market shares for Sapporo, Asahi, and Kirin in that year were 37.0%, 33.5%, and 29.5%, respectively.

In 1957, when the "Economic White Paper" declared the end of the post-war era, the total amount of beer production was 5,520,000 kl, and the market shares for Sapporo, Asahi, and Kirin in that year were 26.2%, 30.7%, and 42.1%, respectively, plus 1.0% for the newcomer, Takara.

Twenty-one years later, in 1978, the total amount of beer production was 44,300,000 kl, an increase of eightfold, and the market shares were: Kirin, 62.1%; Sapporo, 19.6%; Asahi, 12.0%; and Santory, another newcomer, 6.7%. Changes in the market share during those twenty years are shown in the following chart (see over).

As shown in the chart, a growth of eightfold over 20 years translates to an average annual growth rate of 11%. However, the gap between the listed companies indicates inevitable principles beyond reasons of negligence on the part of these companies in maintaining market share.

A common example of beer taste testing is the brand-name testing, in which various brands of beer are tested for their taste. Various tests conclude that no meaningful and consistent results have ever been reported that the testers had been able to accurately identify the beer by their brand name.

Another issue is the price, which remained 215 yen a bottle for all brands (1979). Other factors such as variation in the price due to seasonality, difficulty in obtaining the raw material, sales force, and back-up from the parent company are either irrelevant or of equal concern to all these companies.

By 1998, Asahi beer held the top position, with 39.9% in Japan, Kirin beer 38.8%, Sapporo beer 15.6% and Suntory beer 5.7%. The main reason is because of Asahi's concentration on the "Super-Dry" brand with a pungent taste against Kirin's brand "Lager" beer; Ichiban-Shibori or first pressing. Also, Asahi is well entrenched in super-market and convenience stores against Kirin's route sales to liquor stores. In addition, Asahi active advertising has been mores successful in capturing the younger generation.

Beer is also a special product that is consumed within a month of shipment. As a result, the amount of shipment can be almost directly translated to market share. This is not the case with other products that go through inventory, secondary processing, secondary sales, and a returned-item process, which require a time-lag revision to convert the factory-shipment volume to market share (see figure on following page).

Changes in the beer market share

Year		Kirin	Sapporo	Asahi	Suntory	Takara
(1957)	32	42.1	26.2	30.7		1.0
(1958)	33	39.9	27.5	30.9		1.7
(1959)	34	42.4	26.5	29.3		1.8
(1960)	35	44.7	26.0	27.2		2.1
(1961)	36	41.7	27.8	28.0		2.6
(1962)	37	45.0	26.4	26.4		2.2
(1963)	38	46.5	26.3	24.3	1.0	2.9
(1964)	39	46.2	25.2	25.6	1.2	1.9
(1965)	40	47.7	25.3	23.2	1.9	1.9
(1966)	41	50.8	23.8	22.1	1.7	1.5
(1967)	42	49.4	25.0	22.0	3.2	0.4
(1968)	43	51.3	24.4	20.1	4.2	
(1969)	44	53.3	23.3	18.9	4.5	
(1970)	45	55.4	23.0	17.2	4.4	
(1971)	46	58.9	22.1	14.0	4.1	
(1972)	47	60.1	21.3	14.1	4.5	
(1973)	48	61.4	20.3	13.6	4.7	
(1974)	49	62.6	19.6	13.1	4.8	
(1975)	50	60.8	20.2	13.5	5.5	
(1976)	51	63.8	18.4	11.6	6.2	
(1977)	52	61.9	19.6	12.0	6.5	
(1978)	53	62.1	19.6	11.6	6.7	

In the United States where positivism is revered, during 1970–1972, a joint project between Harvard Business School and Marketing Science Institute was conducted to survey 57 corporations on "how the marketing strategy could affect the profitability." The goal of this project was to identify and measure factors determining the Return on Investment (ROI). As a result, 37 factors were identified, among which the market share was the most significant.

To summarize their findings, when there is a 10% difference in the market share, a difference of about 5% in ROI was confirmed. Specially, the difference in two groups with one group with a market share exceeding 40% and another below 40% was the ratio of their R&D to sales. As market share increases, the R&D ratio slowly increases; however, after 40%, it declines sharply, which is a large amount in real dollars.

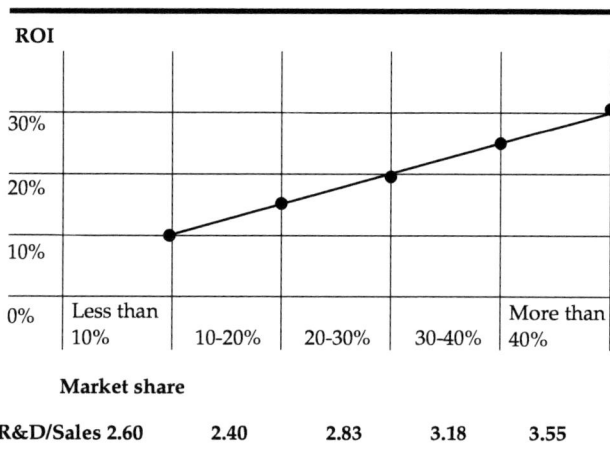

Relationship between the market share and pre-tax ROI

When the market share is less than 10%, the correlation with ROI is less clear. This 10% share is the minimum level for a business to be able to function in a market.

In the United States, Motorola's sales of TV sets during 1970–1973 fell to 6-7%; as a result, after suffering a loss of $20,000,000, early in 1974, it allowed itself to be bought out by Matsushita Electric, *Market share — a key to profitability* by R. D. Buzzell, B. T. Gale, and R.G.M. Sultan, Harvard Business Review, January–February 1975.

4.1.4 Why the Liberal Democratic Party stays in power

Why did Prime Minister Ohira come into power?

The analogy of market share and potential consumer pool is exactly the same as that of voting rate and eligible voters. A political party sells a product called "candidate," and must motivate the voting behavior (analogous to purchasing behavior). After the Kennedy versus Nixon campaign, in Japan as well as in the United States, the advertising agencies became key players in election campaigns.

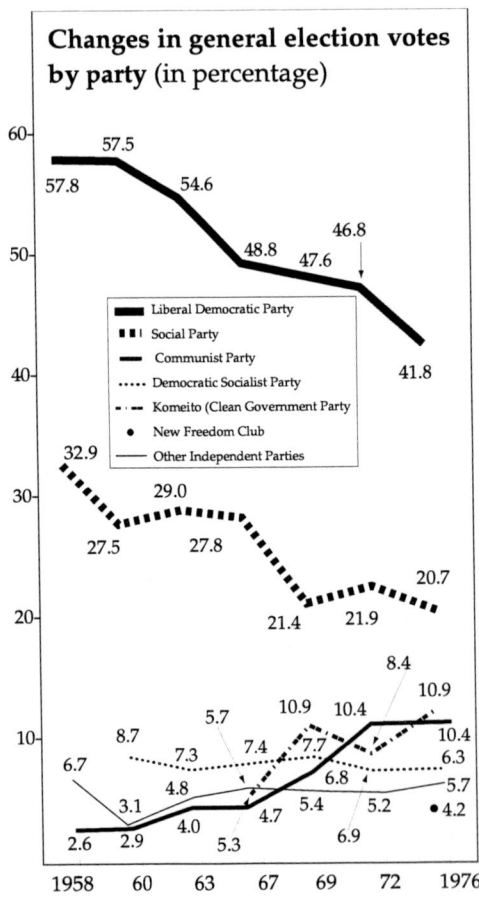

In the election of 1976, the Liberal Democratic Party (LDP) received 41.8% of the votes; it was 5% less than its previous share of 46.8%, but still it met the conditions for top ranking. During this time, New Freedom Club splintered from LDP and obtained 4.2% of the votes.

The following national campaign was in 1977. As a result of a Lockheed incident, the reversal of conservative and liberal parties seemed inevitable. However, the share of votes obtained by LDP on the national basis was 35.8% — 8.5%, less than the previous share of 44.3%. Locally, the share was 39.5% — unchanged from the previous share.

Since 1955, it has been said that the conservative and the Liberal Democratic Party were on a slow decline; however, partially due to the opposition parties' offensive, as long as the 41.7% level, which is the condition for maintaining the top position, is not broken, the LDP's political power will not be jeopardized.

In 1978, the most "uncertain" of times, the "reversal" victory of candidate Ohira was reported. Numbers don't lie and the fact was that it was no reversal. Candidate Ohira was bound to win.

	Number of votes for four candidates				
	Votes	Voting rate	Score	1st Rank	2nd Rank
Ohira	550,891	42.0%	748	26 (24)	17
Fukuda	472,503	36.1%	638	17 (14)	22
Nakasone	197,957	15.1%	93	2 (1)	6
Komoto	88,917	6.8%	46	2	2

Note: Inside ( ) are more than 40%

For 47 prefectures plus Tokyo, Hokkaido, Osaka, and Kyoto (the administrative division of Japan), the candidates scoring 1st rank and 2nd rank are proportionally distributed, with each score for about 850 party members as 1 point. Therefore, in all the prefectures plus Tokyo, Hokkaido, Osaka, and Kyoto, even if ranked 1st or 2nd, with respect to such rankings, there would be a gap in the score.

Ranking 1st then becomes a must. And since each candidate has both weak and strong areas, the campaign then must be fought by thoroughly concentrating on one's own strong areas and the other party's weak spots.

In the case of Ohira, within 47 prefectures plus Tokyo, Hokkaido, Osaka, nd Kyoto, there was a majority of 24 where he gained more than 40% and ranked 1st. Adding Yamanashi (39.7%) and Nagano (37.8%), there were 26 locations with 1st ranking and 17 locations with 2nd ranking. In the case of the opposing candidate Fukuda, within 47 prefectures plus Tokyo, Hokkaido, Osaka, and Kyoto, there were 14 locations where he gained more than 40% and ranked 1st.

Adding 3 more locations, there were 17 locations with 1st ranking and 22 locations with 2nd ranking. This resulted in candidate Fukuda's early withdrawal, and a victory for Prime Minister Ohira.

The beer shipment and the number of votes can be analyzed in detail over a short period of time with relative ease. In most other cases, the judgment and decision–making is normally conducted in the middle of a process that is in progress.

In the case of market share, depending on the data and invoice dates, the condition for the top ranking, which is a number greater than 41.7%, could have a floating point after the decimal point. It must be recognized, however, when the process is in progress, as a principle, the number to be targeted as a condition for securing the top ranking should be 40%.

In the case of candidate Ohira with 42% of the votes, he was not scoring 42% across all the prefectures together with Tokyo, Hokkaido, Osaka, and Kyoto. He scored a maximum of 96.6% in his home town of Kagawa and a minimum of 0.6% in the rival Gunma. The key is where to achieve the top-ranking condition and secure 40%.

In the beer market, in 1978, Kirin had a share of 62.1% of the total, but not in all parts of the country. As a matter of fact, Hokkaido has a share of only 4.56% of the overall beer consumption, which is mainly dominated by Sapporo beer. For one thing, Kirin does not own any plants north of Sendai.

Traditionally, Asahi beer is strong in western Japan, and while it has plants in Hakata, Kyushu, which is responsible for 9.72% of overall consumption, its share is only 11.6%. Here, Sapporo has 19.6% of the share and holds the top position. Suntory is naturally considered to be wise enough to limit its shipments to areas near its plants in Kanto and Kansai.

Even though the corporate size may be small, it is very important to segment the market by product, usage, territory, and distribution channel to secure a share of 40% and become number one.

Japan National Election Results 1978

	No. of Votes	Ohira	Fukuda	Nakasone	Komoto
		(%)	(%)	(%)	(%)
Hokkaido	49,925	13,279 (26.6)	23,233 (46.5)	6,874 (13.8)	6,539 (13.1)
Aomori	11,732	7,447 (63.5)	2,689 (22.9)	573 (4.9)	1,023 (8.7)
Iwate	21,216	15,101 (71.2)	3,946 (18.6)	928 (4.4)	1,241 (5.8)
Miyagi	12,644	4,458 (35.3)	5,947 (47.0)	1,435 (11.3)	804 (6.4)
Akita	13,454	7,756 (57.6)	3,203 (23.8)	1,218 (9.1)	1,277 (9.5)
Yamagata	13,906	5,903 (42.4)	5,545 (39.9)	1,356 (9.8)	1,102 (7.9)
Fukushima	23,904	14,314 (59.9)	5,418 (22.7)	2,897 (12.1)	1,275 (5.3)
Ibaragi	16,014	7,161 (44.7)	6,910 (43.1)	1,662 (10.4)	281 (1.8)
Tochigi	21,857	4,169 (19.1)	7,033 (32.2)	8,574 (39.2)	2,081 (9.5)
Gunma	68,609	357 (0.6)	55,133 (80.4)	12,988 (18.9)	109 (0.1)
Saitama	47,300	12,669 (26.8)	24,589 (52.0)	9,137 (19.3)	905 (1.9)
Chiba	31,593	4,117 (13.0)	23,847 (75.5)	1,981 (6.3)	1,648 (5.2)
Tokyo	85,201	26,032 (30.6)	37,283 (43.8)	16,570 (19.4)	5,316 (6.2)
Kanagawa	24,030	6,261 (26.1)	9,419 (39.2)	7,334 (30.5)	1,016 (4.2)
Niigata	38,140	28,441 (74.6)	5,091 (13.3)	4,296 (11.3)	312 (0.8)
Toyama	38,093	16,172 (42.5)	9,227 (24.2)	11,409 (30.0)	1,285 (3.3)
Ishikawa	30,592	13,527 (44.2)	11,659 (38.1)	946 (3.1)	4,460 (14.6)
Fukui	13,178	3,603 (27.3)	7,627 (57.9)	1,690 (12.8)	258 (2.0)
Yamanashi	18,187	7,205 (39.7)	7,118 (39.1)	3,638 (20.0)	226 (1.2)
Nagano	26,222	9,916 (37.8)	9,675 (36.9)	4,584 (17.5)	2,047 (7.8)
Gifu	52,766	18,325 (34.7)	20,543 (38.9)	13,013 (24.7)	885 (1.7)
Shizuoka	64,461	32,426 (50.3)	17,620 (27.3)	11,324 (17.6)	3,091 (4.8)
Aichi	37,161	13,228 (35.6)	14,598 (39.3)	6,626 (17.8)	2,709 (7.3)
Mie	17,743	7,918 (44.7)	3,370 (19.0)	3,235 (18.2)	3,220 (18.1)
Shiga	17,620	6,959 (39.5)	2,641 (15.0)	7,681 (43.6)	339 (1.9)
Kyoto	10,575	5,201 (49.2)	3,197 (30.2)	1,751 (16.6)	426 (4.0)
Osaka	35,840	14,576 (40.7)	14,793 (41.3)	4,466 (12.5)	2,005 (5.5)
Hyogo	35,811	8,112 (22.7)	9,393 (26.2)	6,148 (17.1)	12,158 (34.0)
Nara	18,240	7,254 (39.8)	8,918 (48.9)	1,470 (8.1)	598 (3.2)
Wakayama	15,646	4,283 (27.4)	8,798 (56.2)	2,241 (14.3)	324 (2.1)
Tottori	13,761	7,505 (54.5)	5,038 (36.6)	877 (6.4)	341 (2.5)
Shimane	18,048	9,931 (55.1)	3,860 (21.4)	4,051 (22.4)	206 (1.1)
Okayama	46,596	27,058 (58.1)	14,645 (31.4)	1,541 (3.3)	3,352 (7.2)
Hiroshima	43,661	36,063 (82.7)	5,599 (12.8)	1,107 (2.5)	892 (2.0)
Yamaguchi	34,731	9,973 (28.7)	22,635 (65.2)	1,170 (3.4)	953 (2.7)
Tokushima	12,645	5,110 (40.5)	1,106 (8.7)	1,720 (13.6)	4,709 (37.2)
Kagawa	46,996	45,341 (96.6)	531 (1.1)	255 (0.5)	869 (1.8)
Ehime	27,951	15,911 (57.0)	2,406 (8.6)	8,146 (29.1)	1,488 (5.3)
Kochi	9,073	3,183 (35.1)	3,492 (38.5)	1,241 (13.7)	1,157 (12.7)
Fukuoka	25,438	12,004 (47.2)	7,764 (30.5)	4,931 (19.4)	739 (2.9)
Saga	16,028	5,304 (33.1)	6,870 (42.9)	1,399 (8.7)	2,455 (15.3)
Nagasaki	22,022	7,118 (32.3)	4,408 (20.0)	2,015 (9.1)	8,481 (38.6)
Kumamoto	21,767	11,484 (52.8)	6,430 (29.5)	1,972 (9.1)	1,881 (8.6)
Oita	18,143	10,404 (57.3)	5,672 (31.3)	1,698 (9.4)	369 (2.0)
Miyazaki	9,851	3,370 (34.2)	2,870 (29.1)	3,335 (33.9)	276 (2.8)
Kagoshima	23,221	12,222 (52.6)	5,542 (23.9)	3,714 (16.0)	1,743 (7.5)
Okinawa	8,676	2,718 (31.3)	5,172 (59.7)	740 (8.5)	46 (0.5)
TOTAL	1,310,268	550,891 (42.0)	472,503 (36.1)	197,957 (15.1)	88,917 (6.8)

4.2 Shooting range theory: the weak and the strong

4.2.1 Inferiority fraction: the top ranker is also in danger

When the top ranker (m) exceeds the market share of 41.7%, it turns all the remaining players (n) against him; however, conversely, there is a case where the top ranker cannot counter the opposition from these players. That is, the top ranker stays in a precarious position — a case most common when a certain area of trading itself is in a period of high growth and the market condition for the top place is exceedingly competitive.

The competitive strength and market share of the top ranker (m) do not match those of other competitors (n); that is, they miss the lower limit of the first condition of equilibrium in Lanchester's strategy model.

$$m < \frac{P}{2}n$$

$$\frac{m}{n} < \frac{1}{2}P$$

$$\frac{m}{n} < \frac{1}{2}\sqrt[3]{\frac{P}{Q}}$$

In market competition, $\frac{m}{n} \approx \frac{P}{Q}$ thus:

$$\frac{m}{n} < \frac{1}{2}\sqrt[3]{\frac{m}{n}}$$

$$\left(\frac{m}{n}\right)^3 < \frac{1}{8} \cdot \frac{m}{n}$$

$$\left(\frac{m}{n}\right)^2 < \frac{1}{8}$$

Since m and n are positive, real numbers, $\dfrac{m}{n} < \dfrac{1}{\sqrt{8}}$
and, m and n are market shares, and since m+n=1, then n=1-m

$$\dfrac{m}{1-m} < \dfrac{1}{\sqrt{8}}$$

$$m\sqrt{8} < 1 - m$$

$$(1+\sqrt{8})m < 1$$

$$m < \dfrac{1}{1+\sqrt{8}} \qquad (4.1)$$

$$m < 0.2612$$

That is, when a top ranker has a market share of 26.1% or less, its position at the top is unstable.

In 1977, during the Miki administration, the Fair Trade Commission testified at the Diet that based on precedents from other countries it had set the alert line for the market monopoly by a corporation at 30% of the market share. Furthermore, it announced guidelines along with enforcement ordinances, related government ordinances, and regulations. Among them, as structural conditions, it listed the domestic annual revenue of a corporation exceeding 50 billion yen and the market share exceeding 50% for one company and 75% for two companies.

But Japan, based on its historical background, stands on the principle of regulating corporate abuses. In 1969, during the merger of Yahata Steel and Fuji Steel, the Fair Trade Commission issued the following report: Private monopoly as defined by the Antitrust Law is a "legal concept." It forbids specific actions that dominate or exclude business activities by other business operators, but it does not prohibit the existence of market dominance.

On that score, European countries stand on the principle of structural regulation, which is more severe in interpretation

For example, in Germany, the definition of the market dominance appears in the Cartel Law as follows:

(1) The corporation has 1/3 of the market share.
(2) Three corporations or more share a total of more than 50% of the market.
(3) Five corporations or more share a total of more than 2/3 of the market.

In England, the Antitrust Law was completely revised in 1974 and the monopoly share of the market was lowered from a previous 33% to 25%; the merger regulations were also further reinforced.

Economic laws are endorsed, established, and operated by the experience. Regardless of the stance they take, dominating the market means the elimination of instability and leadership for the top-ranking corporations. Lanchester's strategic model makes it clear that crossing the 26.1% level of instability for a top ranking corporation brings it into the "safety zone."

There are obvious cases where this concentration toward a select number of corporations is clearly undesirable. Energy companies are one example. Japan imports 99% of its oil from overseas and is largely dependent on major oil companies (foreign capital) for the most part; therefore, it has the licensing permission right with regard to refinement facilities for each of these companies and consciously diversifies the shares. Even the top-ranking Japan Petroleum has a 18-19% share.

4.2.2 Top position monopoly – absolute safety

Once a corporation has a 100% share, then the perfect monopoly is achieved. However, as long as Monopoly is not guaranteed to begin with, this in reality does not occur. The condition for absolute safety and top-position monopoly is that the top-ranker (m) faces all other competitors (n) and yields absolutely no share of the market.

Since the competitive strength and the market share of the top-ranker (m) overwhelms those of all other competitors, the upper limit of the first condition of equilibrium in the Lanchester's strategic model is exceeded:

$$2\rho n < m$$
$$2\rho < \frac{m}{n}$$
$$2\sqrt[3]{\frac{P}{Q}} < \frac{m}{n}$$

In market competition,
$$\frac{m}{n} \approx \frac{P}{Q} \text{ thus:}$$

$$2\sqrt[3]{\frac{m}{n}} < \frac{m}{n}$$

$$8\frac{m}{n} < \left(\frac{m}{n}\right)^3$$

$$8 < \left(\frac{m}{n}\right)^2$$

Since m and n are positive, real numbers:
$$\sqrt{8} < \frac{m}{n}$$

. m and n are market shares, and since m+n=1, then n=1-m

$$\sqrt{8} < \frac{m}{1-m}$$
$$\sqrt{8} - m\sqrt{8} < m$$
$$\sqrt{8} < (1+\sqrt{8})m$$
$$\frac{\sqrt{8}}{1+\sqrt{8}} < m \qquad (4.2)$$
$$0.7388 < m$$

That is, once a top ranker achieves a market share of 73.9% or greater, it has the absolute monopoly. We can also understand this experimentally.

In the Liberal Democratic Party preliminary election for the prime minister, as mentioned previously, the following candidates achieved a electoral share of more than 73.9% in the following areas. Along with the scoring points, the results are interesting indeed:

Inside ( ) are scores		Ohira	Fukuda	Nakasone	Komoto
Kagawa	50	96.6 (49)	1.1 (0)	0.5 (0)	1.8 (1)
Hiroshima	51	82.7 (44)	12.8 (7)	2.5 (0)	2.0 (0)
Gunma	73	0.6 (0)	80.4 (59)	18.9 (14)	0.1 (0)
Chiba	39	13.0 (6)	75.5 (33)	6.3 (0)	5.2 (0)
Niigata	42	74.6 (36)	13.3 (6)	11.3 (0)	0.8 (0)

4.2.3 Shooting range: Single combat and total war

So far, we studied the top-ranker (m) and all its other competitors (n); however, we can replace these with two certain companies (m and n). One side has 10% of the market share and the other 15%. Relatively speaking, we can consider 40% versus 60%.

In Lanchester's strategic model, generally, the fighting strength and production and supply are different. According to the first condition of equilibrium

$$\frac{\rho}{2}n < m < 2\rho n \quad \text{or,} \quad \frac{1}{2\rho}m < n < \frac{2}{\rho}m$$

In marketing, from the relationship between the competitive strength and market share and the potential consumer pool, the conditions for the inferiority fraction and top position monopoly are as follows:

$$\text{Inferiority Fraction, } m < \frac{1}{1+\sqrt{8}} \qquad (4.1)$$

$$\text{Top Monopoly Status, } \frac{\sqrt{8}}{1+\sqrt{8}} < m \qquad (4.2)$$

This means when a company dips below the inferiority fraction share, it will no longer be a match for the other opponents, but when a company moves above the top position monopoly share, then it no longer consider other opponents as a match. In other words, the shooting range is considered beyond all parties, and since with respect to the distance, the denominator is common in both, then it follows immediately that it is clearly beyond $\sqrt{8}$.

When the relative ratio of market shares between two companies is $\sqrt{8}$ =2.8284 or greater, then they are beyond the shooting range and their competitive strengths are not in equilibrium.

Conversely, once one's market share is $\sqrt{8}$ times the opponent's, then as long as the level of undertaking and efforts remain unchanged, the opponent will be of no challenge, at least for the time being.

However, this value is applicable to special local battles such as single-combat and duel situations $\sqrt{8}$, or 2.8 times, can be set to 3, since the process is in progress.

As an example, let's assume a large store opens up in a neighborhood, causing competition for a host of specialty stores. And let's assume that a competing electronic shop, dedicates the whole floor, which is three times the size of the area for electrical appliances in the large store, exclusively to audio products. The larger store obviously will never be able to make such a drastic product reorganization. This is a typical "differentiation" strategy for "the weak" (the specialty store) to combat "the strong" (the larger store).

When a group of products with different life cycles are marketed within a relative broad region, then Lanchester's Square Law of the total war applies, and the ratio of opposing fighting strengths and competitive strengths change to those of square roots. That is, since the ratio is now $1:\sqrt{8}$, then the original ratio of competitive strengths must be $1:\sqrt{\sqrt{8}}$ =1:1.6818. Since previously the process was in progress, we set $\sqrt{8}$ to 3; here, also, we may set $\sqrt{\sqrt{8}}$ to $\sqrt{3}$ because there is no significant difference.

As a result, when two certain companies are concerned, the judgment as to whether these companies are competitors (at least for the time being), we may make the following separation based on the basic type of the adopted battle and the relative ratio of shares in the segmented markets (regions):

In the case of single-battle

Relative ratio with $1:\sqrt{8}$ = 1:2.8284, becomes, 1:3

In the case of total war

Relative ratio: $1:\sqrt{\sqrt{8}}$ = 1:1.6818, becomes, $1:\sqrt{3}=1:1.7$

In reality, the combination of share contrast between two companies can be anywhere between 1% to 74%; however, the Lanchester's strategic coefficient ρ chart and (since the rest can be automatically calculated) the distribution ratio chart for the tactical force m_t and the strategic force m_s can be immediately calculated.

For example, in the case of the beer market, Kirin beer in 1978 had a share of 62% of the market, an invincible position. However, there are some blind spots such as the Hokkaido region. Sapporo beer has a share of 20% and Asahi beer 12% in that market.

Viewed from the perspective of Sapporo, $\rho=1.1856$ and $m_t : m_s = 14:86$, which indicates worthy competitors under advantageous conditions. Suntory (7%) is within the shooting range of Asahi beer, and viewed from Asahi beer, $\rho=1.1968$ and $m_t : m_s = 13:87$; that is, all three companies are ranked nearly the same in terms of competitive force ratios. Therefore, as the competition among these companies heats up, the differentiation strategy becomes a key to their future success.

4.2.4 Separation of attack target and competition target

Based on the idea of shooting distance, it is easy to find out if the enemy is worth fighting (for the time being). If the enemy is outside the shooting distance, fighting a superior force with conventional means is obviously bound to fail. In addition, engaging with an inferior enemy outside the shooting range could provide the real enemy with a chance to attack.

In the case of professional baseball, in 1978, in the Central League, 29 years after its inception, for the first time, Yakuruto won. It was not easy to win a pennant race of 130 plays. Here, let's find the differences between two famed managers, Nagashima and Hirooka.

Viewing the situation from the Giants' side, in 1977, they decisively distanced Yakuruto after 19 wins and 7 losses. In that year, Yakuruto was second overall; therefore, the Giants maintained with its immediate foe a ratio of 3:1 and kept it beyond the shooting range.

In 1978, the situation changed. After 7 ties, they won 9 and lost 10, and against the 3rd-ranking Hiroshima, they tied 5, won 10, and lost 11. That is, they lost to their immediate foes. In other words, praises should go to Yakuruto for their persistence and to Hiroshima for putting up a strong fight.

Number of spectators mobilized for the Central League

	1978	1 game average	1977	Increase or Decrease (%)
Giants	2,814,000	43,292	2,946,000	- 4.5
Yakuroto	1,810,000	27,846	1,610,000	+12.4
Chinichi	1,475,000	22,692	1,456,000	+ 1.3
Taiyo	1,437,000	22,108	825,000	+74.1
Hanshin	1,392,000	21,415	1,393,000	- 0.1
Hiroshima	1,060,000	16,308	8,84,000	+19.9
Total	9,988,000	25,610	9,114,000	+ 9.6

Similar wild patterns of wins and losses could also occur in the marketplace where companies are competing. Confusing the attacker and the competitor could unexpectedly provide the enemy with the chance to strike a finishing blow.

The difference between the attacker and the competitor is that the competitor is the player with the top market share. To be the top player in a market is not an easy task; therefore, it is important to always be aware of the competitor and try to study it. Imitation alone could lead a small player to being devoured by the top competitor.

The only time imitation is allowed or cannot be avoided is in the case of pricing. This is because the top competitor has pervasive sales and advertising power in the market place. As long as there is no significant product or service differentiation, attempting to compete with the top player through price discount could only lead to one's demise. It seems that actually the top-ranking player has the upper hand as it can take advantage of its vast information resources and copy any growth areas or marketing techniques and enter the market.

It is necessary to examine and recognize one's own position objectively in areas segmented by product, region, and so on. If one is in the top position, then one is the party to be taken note of and emulated by other competitors.

Therefore, the attacking target is the immediate enemy and a defeat by the second-ranker must be absolutely avoided. Any delay could only make the fighting harder. Consequently, constant attention must be paid to the second ranker and the top ranker must play preemptively the same trick the second-ranker would play in the market. The decisive factors would be information and a preemptive strike.

The second-ranker targets the top position; however, it must learn from the top ranker without becoming a copycat, and concentrate its all-out attack on its immediate enemy, the third ranker. It is very important to cultivate enough creativity not to be sucked into the top ranker's turf and machination.

The third-ranker must attempt to play the targeting competitor, first-ranker, against the second-ranker, while mustering all its political power to concentrate its attack against its immediate enemy, the forth-ranker.

The forth-ranker must avoid being directly entangled in the fighting among the upper ranks; it must use propaganda to join all the competitors ranking second and lower to attack the top ranker. In reality, it must focus to establish its own position in a completely differentiated field.

4.3 The change process of market share

4.3.1 Five patterns of market share

With respect to the top ranker's position (m), as it goes through the uncertain inferiority fraction (m<26.1%) to the top position (41.7%<m) and reaching the top, monopoly (73.9%<m), according to the Lanchester's strategic model, the market share can be divided into 5 patterns.

First, it is E (diversified type) where there are many new entrants. In terms of market share, it is less than 26%, and the ranking turnover can be fast and furious. Once this close competition is won, and a top-ranker with a maintained market share of 41.7% and more emerges, the pattern changes to D (top-position [run-away] type), and a certain order forms.

In the next phase, the top position will gain an almost unshakable status, and fighting for the market share will heat up between the second and third ranks.

Next, the second-ranker gains some market share, and the total share between the first and second-rankers exceeds 73.9%. The top two rankers reach the top, monopoly position. In this case, the first- and second-rankers are within the shooting range of $\sqrt{\sqrt{8}}\ (\approx \sqrt{3})$.

This pattern is C (relative oligopoly type). For example, relative oligopoly does not apply when the top ranker has 50% of the market share and the second ranker 24%. The typical example is when the top ranker has 44% and the second ranker a close 37% market share. Furthermore, in this pattern, normally the fighting between the second- and third-rankers become increasingly fierce even though the combined shares of the second- and third-rankers exceed that of the first-ranker.

The second-ranker after defeating the third and all other lower rankers, clears the 41.7% barrier, and along with the top ranker creates a dual rivaling pattern B (absolute oligopoly type). In this phase, the fight between the two parties could go on until either side falls or retreats, or they could be forced into cooperation for coexistence. In the latter case, the third-ranker could actually profit from the situation.

The last pattern is A (monopoly type) where the dominance of the market and a share of 73.9% or greater are achieved. The market-share competition starting with pattern E (diversified type) changes with time to D -> C -> B -> A. However, the process still bears a cyclicality where through merger, joint venture, antitrust laws, expiration of patent rights, and specially, as a result of technological innovation and new product development, it may return to pattern E (absolute oligopoly type).

There is also a possibility for pattern A (monopolistic oligopoly type) whereby changing through pattern B (absolute oligopoly type), only the fighting among second, third, and all other lower ranks increase, which leads to a runaway position for the top ranker with a market share in excess of 50%, a share greater than those of second- and third-rankers combined. The case of "beer" is a prime example of this pattern.

Five patterns of the market share based on Lanchester's strategic equations

	A ←	B ←	C ←	D ←	E
	Monopoly type	Absolute oligopoly type	Relative oligopoly type	Top-position [runaway] type	Diversified type
Company No. 1	75%	46%	44%	42%	25%
Company No. 2	11%	44%	37%	24%	22%
Company No. 3	7%	4%	11%	18%	20%
Company No. 4	4%	3%	5%	8%	15%
Company No. 5	2%	2%	2%	5%	10%
Company No. 6	1%	1%	1%	3%	8%
	100%	100%	100%	100%	100%
HH Index	.58	.41	.35	.28	.19

In reality, the five patterns of market share shown here reflect the changes in the market competition with respect to instant coffee in Japan over the last eight years, which I published in 1969.

In 1961, instant coffee was deregulated and more than 60 brands were introduced into the market, creating pattern E (diversified type). According to SCI (a consumer index panel research group), Morinaga Confectionery was the top ranking company.

In 1965, Nestle Japan (Nescafe brand) and Japan General Foods (Maxwell House brand) emerge and riding the wave of rapidly growing supermarket chains, Nescafe moves to pattern D (top-position [runaway] type).

In 1968, pattern C (relative oligopoly type) rapidly changed to B (absolute oligopoly type), resulting in a victory for both companies. With respect to pattern B (absolute oligopoly type), the cooperation between the two companies was quite limited, and as a result, based on the principle of retreat by one side, I presented pattern A (monopoly type).

Eventually, Maxwell House was defeated by Nescafe, and after 1970, it rapidly lost share. In 1973, it requested help from Ajinomoto and was reorganized as Ajinomoto General Foods (AGF). But the 75 to 25 barrier yielded once to the competition is too difficult to break.

General Foods, on the other hand, was marketing high-quality goods to Europe and second-rate coffee beans to south east Asia. In Japan, it switched to high-quality new Maxwell, but it failed to recall low-quality products already in stock. It also imported the highly successful "Jamaica" campaign from the United States to Japan, which did not go over well with Japanese consumers.

Nestle Japan, with its headquarters in Switzerland, has been doing business in Japan since 1913. Therefore, it has more than 40 years of marketing experience in Japan over Maxwell, a newcomer who started its Japanese business in 1955.

Looking at another market, shares of car models can be clearly documented by their registration. Here, we focus on the domestic market for compact cars and put the spotlight on limited regional markets. This is because car dealerships are organized mainly by car model in each city region.

For example, in Toyota City and Okazaki City, the Toyota share is dominant pattern A (monopolistic oligopoly type), which seems to be quite natural since they provide the location for the Toyota automotive plant.

However, in Toyohashi City, the pattern is C (relative oligopoly type). Generally, in Japan, when segmenting the market by region, this pattern C is quite commonplace.

Compact cars sold in 1977 (January to December)

	Toyota City/Okazaki City Number of registered cars	(%)	Toyohashi City Number of registered cars	(%)
Mark II	2,731		644	
Corona	2,00 5		471	
Carina	1,903		442	
Celica	746		138	
Chaser	337		28	
(Toyota)	(7,722)	66.5	(1,723)	37.8
Blue Bird	523		695	
Skyline	458		291	
Rorel	352		344	
Violet	208		400	
Auster	87		100	
Stanza	79		74	
Sylvia	69		38	
Fair Lady Z	65		40	
(Nissan)	(1,841)	15.9	(1,982)	43.5
Galan (Mitsubishi)	(948)	8.2	(240)	5.3
Accord (Honda)	(475)	4.1	(291)	6.4
Cupera. Cosmo	211		97	
Luche	107		59	
(Toyo Industries)	(318)	2.7	(156)	3.4
(Other)	(173)	1.5	(92)	2.0
(Foreign cars)	(130)	1.1	(72)	1.6
Total	11,607		4,556	

4.3.2 Fiercely fought absolute oligopoly (case of West Germany)

In market competition, when both the first and second rankers meet the conditions for the top position (runaway) — a scenario where pattern B (absolute oligopoly type) is the result — then a fierce fight between the two competitors is entailed until one side surrenders or is totally defeated. In Japan, a typical case is what occurred between Lion Toothpaste and Sunstar Toothpaste.

In the case of political parties' voting rate, the function of cooperation and compromise and change in the administration creates a settled pattern of two parties. After World War II, the late Yoshida Prime Minister is said to have encouraged having two major political parties, including the growth of Japan Social Party; however, today, there is no sign of that. In West Germany, in the 1960s, with the cold war winding down, the pattern has changed from C to B.

		1949	1953	1957	1961	1965	1969	1972	1976	1983
Votes (%)	C D U C S U	31.0	45.2	50.2	45.3	47.6	46.1	44.8	48.6	48.8
	S P D	29.2	28.8	31.8	36.2	39.3	42.7	45.9	42.6	38.2
	F. D. P	11.9	9.5	7.7	12.8	9.5	5.8	8.4	7.9	6.9
	Other	27.8	16.5	10.3	5.7	3.6	5.5	0.9	0.9	6.1
Number of seats	C D U C S U	139	243	270	242	245	242	225	243	244
	S P D	131	151	169	190	202	224	230	214	193
	F. D. P	52	48	41	67	49	30	41	39	34
	Other	80	45	17	0	0	0	0	0	27

*CDU., CSU : Christian Democratic Union, Christian Social Union
SPD: Social Party of Democracy   F.D.P.: Federal Democratic Party

In eight elections after World War II, the only time the majority of seats went to one party — CDU/CSU — was in the third election in 1957 under the Adenauer administration. Adenauer was prime minister from 1949 to 1963, and in 1966, he left CDU/CSU as prime minister. This gave birth to the coalition of the Federal Democratic Party and the Social Democratic Party with Brant as prime minister and Shale as foreign minister, when

SDP, lead by Berlin's mayor, Brant, gained more than 40% of the votes. In the recent election of 1976, the same coalition led by Schmit (SPD) as prime minister and Gensher (FDP) as foreign minister was born. In pattern B, a third party controls the casting vote. (Note: Election laws in Western Germany contain a major principle that excludes over-participation by minority parties which could create chaos.)

4.3.3 Concentration and the HH index

As the market share changes from pattern E to A, it goes without saying that the oligopoly by a small number of companies increases. In 1977, in revising the Antitrust Law, 26 industries were identified as highly oligopolistic. These included piano, beer, photographic film, dry copiers, butter, pane glass, and composite rubber. These included the case when the market share of one company exceeded 50% or the sum of market shares of two companies exceeded 75%.

Another standard adopted by the Fair Trade Committee is the HH index. This is shown by the square sum of market shares (decimal values) for companies in applicable industries. The closer the index approached 1, the greater the degree of oligopoly, and the closer to 0, the less the degree of oligopoly. The process of oligopoly can be graphed in time system.

The HH index was introduced by Hirschman, A.O. in 1945 in a theses called "The national strength and the trade structure — a strategy for economical development," and by Herfindahl, O.C. in a theses that analyzed the concentration of American steel industry.

When calculating the HH index for the 5 patterns of market share according to Lanchester's strategic model in the order from E to A, the results are 0.19 -> 0.28 -> 0.35 -> 0.41 -> 0.58, indicating an increase in oligopoly and concentration. However, for example, when getting past pattern E (diversified type); that is, when the shares are 32%, 31%, 4%, 2%, and 1%, the HH index becomes 0.29%, a higher value than pattern D (top-position [runaway] type).

In reality, once a company reaches the top-position (runaway) type, the position is maintained and it then tends to approach pattern C (relative oligopoly type) quite rapidly. The pattern based on Lanchester's strategic model that clarifies the position in the competition with a specific market share has a richer practicality. There is a sense that HH index suffers from being static.

With respect to the idea of the degree of concentration, at the end of the nineteenth century, Palate and Jeni in Italy devised an index to show inequity in income distribution.

Currently, the most common one is the Lorenz curve introduced by M.H. Lorenz, an American statistician, in 1906. He plotted the income on the x axis and the accumulated percentage of the income population on the y axis, and if all is distributed equally, the graph is plotted on a diagonal line.

However, in reality, because the distribution is biased toward fewer population, the graph has a bow shape. There is an area between the arrow and the line that is representative of the degree of concentration.

Presently, based on the normal distribution according to the theory of probability, since 68.3% of the total is within the range of ± 1 standard deviation and 95.4% of the total is within the range of ± 2 standard deviation, certain items are arranged in the order of their small and large sizes (values), and the accumulated percentage up to 70% is categorized as class A, the accumulated percentage up to 95% is categorized as class B, and the rest is categorized as class C, and this is known as "ABC Analysis" in order of importance. This ABC Analysis is commonly used for parts inventory management and defect rate management in quality control.

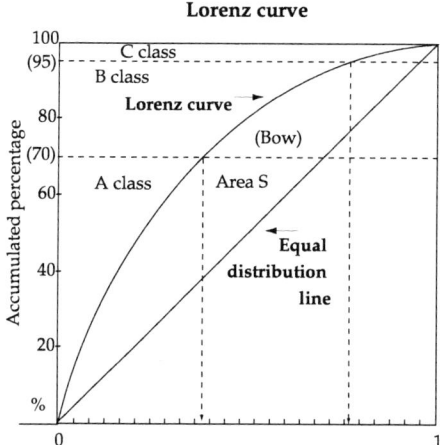

Lorenz curve

ABC Analysis in sales management so far seems to be exclusively used for availability of credit against a client and setting credit limits. From the marketing viewpoint, the judgment standard for the client rate of concentration according to the Lorenz curve is very important. The client rate of concentration is the bow-shaped area ratio against the triangle with the equal distribution line as the oblique line.

It is cumbersome to directly calculate the bow-shaped area (S); therefore, we first consider a rectangle with one side as unit 1, add a equilateral triangle of an area of 1/2 to the lower side and calculate this area, and then we can just subtract 1/2. We use Simpson's approximation method for definite integral to calculate the area. Generally, to find the area between x=a and x=b for the curve y=f(x), we use the following equation:

$$\int_a^b f(x)dx \approx \frac{h}{3}\left\{y_0 + y_{2n} + 4\sum_{i=1}^{2n-1} y_{2i-1} + 2\sum_{i=1}^{2n-2} y_{2i}\right\}$$

However, $h = \dfrac{b-a}{2n}$

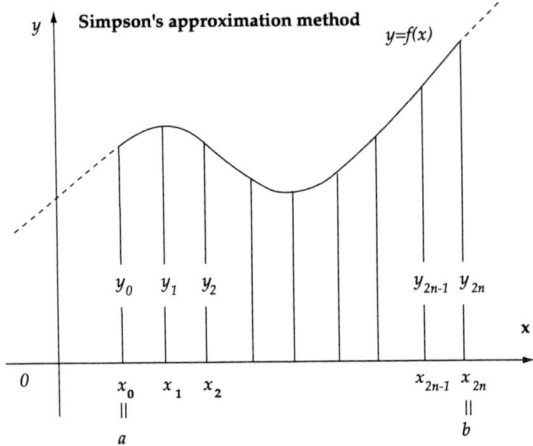

When applying this equation to the bow-shaped area (S), the number of items "N" must always be even N = 2n. First item is $x_0 = a = 0$ and the last item is $x_{2n} = b = 1$, thus $h = \dfrac{1}{2n} = \dfrac{1}{N}$.

Also, since we deal with accumulated percentage, $y_0 = 0$, $y_{2n} = 1$. The 2nd item in { } above, shows 4 multiplied by the sum of accumulated percentage for odd-numbered items, and the 3rd item shows 2 multiplied by the sum of accumulated percentage for even-numbered items. Therefore, the bow-shaped area (S) can be shown as follows:

$$S = \dfrac{1}{3N}\left\{1 + 4\sum_{i=1}^{2n-1} y_{2i-1} + 2\sum_{i=1}^{2n-2} y_{2i}\right\} - \dfrac{1}{2}$$

However, item number N = 2n

To specifically calculate the client concentration rate for company A, we first must calculate the bow-shaped area. Here, with respect to the number of items, there are 7 client stores — and odd number — we add a dummy X to make it 8 stores, an even number; we also let the average monthly trade be zero.

State of competition among three companies in the region

	Client	Average montly trade	%	Accumulation %	Rank
1	B	2,000	44.5	44.5	A
2	G	1,000	22.2	66.7	A
3	H	500	11.1	77.8	B
4	L	400	8.9	86.7	B
5	I	300	6.7	93.3	B
6	O	200	4.4	97.8	C
7	M	100	2.2	100.0	C
(8)	X	0	0.0	100.0	
	(Total)	4,500	100.0		

$$S = \frac{1}{3 \times 8} \left\{ \begin{matrix} 1 + 4(0.445 + 0.778 + 0.933 + 1.00) \\ + 2(0.667 + 0.867 + 0.978) \end{matrix} \right\} - \frac{1}{2}$$

$$= \frac{1}{24}(1 + 4 \times 3.156 + 2 \times 2.512) - \frac{1}{2}$$

$$= \frac{1}{24}(1 + 12.624 + 5.024) - \frac{1}{2}$$

$$= \frac{18.648}{24} - \frac{1}{2} = 0.777 - 0.5$$

$$= 0.277$$

The client concentration rate can be obtained by dividing the bow-shaped area by the area of this triangle, which is 0.5. The result is 0.554, which means company A's client concentration rate for this region is 55.4%.

Normally, the number of clients within a given region is not supposed to be this low. Based on an experiment, a 50% client concentration rate is the middle of the road and desirable; based on the ratio of ABC rank numbers, the approximate ratio approaches 1:2:2.

When the client concentration rate is too high or too low, there could be a problem with the competition. When the rate is too high and it exceeds 60%, the ABC ratio becomes 1:2:3; that is, too many "hanging fry" from group C. When the rate is too low and below 30%, the ABC ratio becomes 3:2:1; that is, with emphasis on group A, there is little difference among the groups.

4.3.4 The real market share in competition

The client concentration rate is based on one's own company's view and a self-management benchmark. It does not directly show the extent of competitive relationships. Let's assume that in a given region, company A, company B, and company C are in a competitive state, and there are 16 stores handling the same kind of products. Let's also assume that the following chart represents average monthly trades for these companies.

	Total	Company A	Company B	Company C
Average Monthly Trade (Yen)	17,800	4,500	5,200	8,100
Sales Share	100.0%	25.3%	29.2%	45.5%
ABC Analysis	42.2%	55.4%	42.2%	48.8%
Client Concentration rate per company		43.8%	62.5%	87.5%
Client store ratio		7/16	10/16	14/16

Rank	Accumulation %	Average Trade	Client	Av Mo Trade by Brand (10KYen)			Store Share Percentage			Store Share Factor		
				A	B	C	A	B	C	A	B	C
A	15.7 15.7	2,800	A		800	2,000		28.6	71.4		1	2.5
	29.7 14.0	2,500	B	2,000		500	80.0		20.0	4.0		1
	40.9 11.2	2,000	C		800	1,200		40.0	60.0		1	1.5
	52.1 11.2	2,000	D		1,400	600		70.0	30.0		2.3	1
	62.2 10.1	1,800	E		300	1,500		16.7	83.3		1	5.0
B	70.6 8.4	1,500	F		900	600		60.0	40.0		1.5	1
	78.5 7.9	1,400	G	1,000	100	300	71.4	7.2	21.4	3.3	(0.3)	1
	82.4 3.9	700	H	500		200	71.4		28.6	2.5		1
	85.8 3.4	600	I	300		300	50.0		50.0	1		1
	88.9 3.1	550	J		300	250		54.5	45.5		1.2	1
	91.7 2.8	500	K		300	200		60.0	40.0		1.5	1
	94.2 2.5	450	L	400		50	88.9		11.1	8.0		1
C	96.4 2.2	400	M	100		300	25.0		75.0	1		3.0
	97.9 1.5	250	N		150	100		60.0	40.0		1.5	1
	99.1 1.2	200	O	200			100.0			(1)		
	100.0 0.9	150	P		150			100			(1)	
Total: 100.0		17,800		4,500	5,200	8,100						
Percent:		100.0%		25.3%	29.2%	45.5%						

With respect to route sales, such as manufacturer, wholesale store, as well as sales and retail stores, that have the greatest share of the normal trading, including cosales, the following cases are commonly observed. The results of calculation of the total amount of the regional market, the analysis of ABC by company, client store ratios, and so on can be shown as follows:

The general shares within the regional market are A<B<C. In the ABC analysis, with respect to each company, the client concentration is the same as the example of company A; however, in the regional market, there is a

representation of the scale composition, and in this case, A rank is 5 stores, B rank is 7 stores, C rank is 4 stores, and the concentration (calculation procedure is the same) is 42.2%; it also shows that there are no extreme large-scale sales stores.

Company A's client concentration is the highest among the three companies, and based on the lowest client store ratio, we can surmise that the policy of concentration is emphatically adopted. B company's client concentration is average, and C company's client concentration is close to the standard rate of 50%, with a high client store ratio and among the three companies showing the most top-position stability.

Here, in the regional market, with respect to the comparison of total share alone, we notice that the competitive relationship is captured only in a cross-sectional manner and superficially. If three companies are independent entities, then clients A through P are also independent entities, residing in the whirlpool of expectations and bargaining as regards each company. In the offensive and defensive competition scene, the extent these three companies and clients are tied together is contingent on the issue of performance.

The degree of tie-up is, in a word, shown in the trading performance. That is, it is shown in the "in–store share" composition rate. In this case, this is an offensive and defensive battle over one client; therefore, it is a single combat, and with a range beyond the shooting range of $\sqrt{8} \approx 3$, the condition to defeat the enemy is sufficiently met. Looking at the in–store share factor, A company is 1 in market A rank (client B), 2 in B rank (clients G and L), a total of 3, none for company B, and C company is 1 in market A rank (client E) and 1 in C rank (client M), a total of 2.

To win the competition and increase the market share, there are two directions, one is horizontal, which increases the sales surface area, or the client store ratio. Another direction is vertical, which increases the sales volume, or the in–store share. This is also compared to a byobu screen. Byobu is useless if it cannot be opened horizontally; that is, if sales cannot be expanded. At the same time, without enough depth, it can easily break; that is, there would be little chance of winning against the competition.

Specially, if the condition to win with the in–store share of the client divided in A rank through the regional market (more than 3 times greater than the enemy) is met, then this could be the strongest tie possible. Let's assume that "A·A store ratio" is number 1 in A rank with the ratio of the number of stores meeting the condition to win through the regional market A rank client, and let the weight assigned be 0.5. Also, let's assign weight 0.5 to the "client store ratio" that shows the regional sales surface area.

The combination (addition) of these two shows the true market share in the competition scene, including the breadth and depth in the regional market. Today, the client store ratio is close to saturation, and when emphasis must be placed on A·A store ratio, then a weight of 0.6 may be assigned to A·A store ratio and a weight of 0.4 to the client store ratio.

Test-calculations with respect to companies A, B, and C, reveal that the real market share considering the competitive relationship, compared to the simple share of sales total and in regard to all weight distributions, of company A exceeds that of company B's, which means stronger competition.

	Company A		Company B		Company C	
Sales Share		25.3 %		29.2 %		45.5 %
a: (A.A Store Ratio)	(1/5)	20.0 %	(0/5)	0 %	(1/5)	20.0 %
b: (Client Store Ratio)	(7/16)	43.8 %	(10/16)	62.5 %	(14/16)	87.5 %
(0.5a + 0.5B)		31.9 %		31.3 %		53.8 %
(0.6a + 0.4b)		29.5 %		25.0 %		47.0 %

To find the real market share in the competition scene, what becomes necessary is not the real status of client stores in all regional markets, in-store share, or sample survey — so called, random sampling survey — but census data survey, which covers all subjects. Specially, in distribution channels where structural changes are rapid, this is referred to as "roller survey" and is very desirable. Also, in the monopoly marketing of automobiles, an analysis based on the Markov chain, where the "brand-royalty" is considered a probability process, is also attempted to find out the previous brandname during a trade-in.

Originally, the market share should be calculated based on numbers and values. The Fair Trade Commission during its revision of the Antitrust Law in 1977 made it clear in its guidelines that the market share must in principle be calculated based on numbers. However, the guideline calls for calculation based on price when the price difference is considerable and the practice of calculation of supply performance (record) based on price is stable. In the case of manufacturing, the market share is calculated as follows:

$$\text{Market Share} = \frac{\text{(Shipped Products)} - \text{(Exported Products)}}{\text{(Total Vol. of Shipped Products)} - \text{(Exports)} + \text{(Imports)}}$$

Here, "products" mean "certain products" and "same-kind products."

With respect to "certain products," regardless of digital or analog displays, or mechanical or electronic differences, functions and features of a watch remain the same, thus belonging to the "same-kind products" category.

Also belonging to this category are products such as board glass, which could be regular board glass or other variations such as polished board glass, but they all share common basic manufacturing facilities. Products that belong to the "similar products" include margarine and butter, instant coffee and regular coffee, steel pipes, etc. They are made of different materials and through different manufacturing methods but are closely related and can be substituted in their usage.

However, in the case of regional marketing, when segmenting a market, from the marketing standpoint, each company has different units of standard, which must be reflected in the display of prices.

4.4 Strategic area and tactical area in marketing

4.4.1 "The Law of Quantity," or the logic of the strong

After the war, the Lanchester Law was introduced to Japan in 1952. In the year before, "Methods of Operations Research," a compilation of the work of Operations Research in the United States during World War II, by P.M. Morse and G.E. Kimball was published. Three copies of this book were sent to Japan Science and the Technology League through Dr. W.E. Deming, who is well-known for his evangelism of quality control in postwar Japan.

The Japan Science and Technology League, with cooperation from the Defense Agency OR Group, published the first translated version of this book in 1955, and through 1963, seven editions were printed. Currently, this book is out of print.

Since then, Lanchester has been introduced in almost all the OR-related books; however, in the competitive arena, it first appeared around 1960. To promote the plan to double the national income, companies split by the occupation army had to reorganize in order to avoid excessive competition, allow more efficient distribution of resources, and be able to compete internationally.

To this end, "Showa Coterie Society," a group formed mainly by concerned academics and technocrats, published *Corporate Competition and Technology*. In this publication, one of the contributors, S. Okumura writes the following titled Lanchester's Law in Corporate Competition.

Competition takes different forms in its development stage but it is always governed by a single principle. With similar weapons and fighting methods, the one who initiates the combat with slightly greater strength will eventually win. Normally, the weak and the strong do not continue to grow and develop while maintaining their balance of power. As proof, the Lanchester Law is commonly taken up in the military science. The strong, when necessary, will continue to apply force until the weak is defeated.

This principle not only applies to the relationship between large corporations and small- and mid-size corporations but also between large corporations. In new industries and in the early phase, with the technology being equal, small- and mid-size companies are bound to fail with the passage of time.

For the small and mid-size companies to survive, they either have to join the larger companies or devise ways to eliminate or alleviate their competitive relationship with them. This means switching to products that the larger companies are not marketing, or provide the products with specialties, in effect turn the same products into different ones. Therefore, the real corporate competition is between large corporations. Again, according to the principle of competition, on the average, the one with slightly greater initial strength will eventually win.

This interpretation of Lanchester Law gave rise to a ruthless theory of the strong and the "Law of Quantity," which means the party with greater material resources will inevitably win.

4.4.2 Decision-making area and communication area

In the area of marketing, in 1966, professor Ikeda of Wakayama University studied the Lanchester model. According to him, a manufacturer's long-term goal is to win a final victory, and he divides a retailer into two categories: A primary retailer (affiliate stores that mainly market its own products and brands) and a secondary retailer (stores that also market other manufacturers' products and brands but wish to have them as affiliates).

Considering the former retailer to be tactical army m_t and the later strategic army m_s, after a certain period, for a retailer to gain total victory, we like to calculate the size of each retailer by calculating the optimum number of distribution through the equilibrium solution as follows.

Lanchester's strategic coefficient ρ is defined as:

$$\rho^3 = \frac{P}{Q} = \frac{\text{Target shipment capacity for one's own company in a region}}{\text{Shipment capacity for rivals competitive products in same region}}$$

Also, n is the number of sales retailers of other companies' rival products. He also introduces the profitability function H. Assuming that the against the profitability is 1 of a primary store, the profitability of a secondary store is 1/2, then:

$$H = \frac{m_t}{m} + \frac{1}{2} \cdot \frac{m_s}{m}$$

The final retail distribution rate is determined by applying the principle of distribution and maximizing the profitability within the distribution draft with the highest strategic winning percentage through a revision to maximize the profitability function against the retailer count (number of retailers) distribution draft (strategic primary draft) obtained by the equilibrium solution.

Terms used here are somewhat dated, but considering the corresponding relations of fighting strength, there are two points of difficulty with respect to the method of applicability against Ikeda's Lanchester strategy model.

First, affiliate stores are adapted to the tactical force and cosales stores are adapted to the strategic force; however, the strategic force should correspond to the "production and supply capability" of the other party.

Second, the production and supply capability can be translated into shipment capacity; however, it is not clear whether this relates to the affiliate stores, which are the tactical force, the co-sales stores, which are the strategic force, or the fighting force, which is the total of tactical and strategic forces; i.e., the total number of retail stores.

Furthermore, although the equilibrium solution based on the mini-maxi principle is mathematically the optimum solution, in reality, it is a solution that should be interpreted for conditions necessary to fight the enemy on an equal footing. Ikeda's proposal was nothing short of the mechanical misuse of the Lanchester strategy model, and a narrow approach that ignored its historical development.

In 1972, Dr. Nobuo Taoka published a series called "Lanchester Marketing Strategy," consisting of five volumes, and in 1975, a series called "Lanchester Reverse Marketing Strategy Series," consisting of three volumes.

These publications coincided with Nixon's Dollar Shock and the following Oil Shock, both periods of increasing market competition, which lead the books to be bestsellers. What Taoka is consistently emphasizing through his books is the negation of emotionalism and a "mind-over-matter" attitude in business affairs. He maintains that these are not lasting attributes; instead he presents the Lanchester Law as a rational alternative.

A Korean reporter once wrote the essence of Japanese rapid growth and international competitive strength was in Dr. Taoka's books. The books were later translated to Korean in 1975. After the Korean Lanchester Marketing Strategy Research Center was established in 1975, Dr. Taoka was twice invited to Korea for seminars in 1977.

Dr. Taoka's contribution is separating the strategic and tactical forces in the Lanchester strategy model into different areas. The strategic area is the invisible area of decision making, which includes pricing strategy, distribution strategy, advertising policy, product development, and so forth.

In contrast, the tactical strategy is mainly a visible area, which includes sales organization, sales force, and marketing force in general. Enemy's sales force behavior, marketing promotion activities, rate of rebates, posters, fliers, and other areas are visible and can be studied, and therefore belong to the tactical area.

4.4.3 Establishment of marketing tactical equations

In 1963, Professor Udell of Wisconsin University published the following chart according to a survey of 485 companies:

Importance of Marketing Activities and Competition Strategy

Marketing Activity (Total 485 Companies)	344 Industrial	52 Consumer Durable	89 Consumer Non-Durable
Marketing/Sales Management	28.3 (69.2%)	17.9 (47.6%)	17.0 (38.1%)
Advert Electronic Media	0.4 (0.9%)	4.0 (10.7%)	9.4 (20.9%)
Advert Print Media	5.1 (12.5%)	6.1 (16.1%)	6.6 (14.8%)
Sales Promotion (Show rebate)	3.9 (9.6%)	5.8 (15.5%)	6.9 (15.5%)
Label, Packaging	1.8 (4.5%)	3.5 (9.5%)	4.4 (9.8%)
Other	1.4 (3.3%)	0.2 (0.6%)	0.4 (0.9%)
Marketing Strategy (Total)	40.9 (100.0%)	37.5 (100.0%)	44.7 (100.0%)
Pre-service	7.0 (23.7%)	3.1 (12.8%)	2.8 (12.1%)
After-service	5.3 (17.7%)	3.5 (14.2%)	2.1 (9.2%)
Technology Innovation	10.2 (34.5%)	8.4 (34.1%)	8.8 (38.6%)
Market Research	4.6 (15.7%)	4.3 (17.8%)	6.2 (27.5%)
Design	1.8 (6.1%)	4.5 (18.7%)	2.2 (9.6%)
Other	0.7 (2.3%)	0.5 (1.9%)	0.7 (3.0%)
Product Strategy (Total)	29.6 (100.0%)	24.3 (100.0%)	22.8 (100.0%)
Transportation	2.4 (23.8%)	2.3 (12.2%)	4.4 (26.8%)
Inventory Control	2.9 (28.3%)	4.2 (22.7%)	3.8 (23.6%)
Route (Limited)	1.1 (10.5%)	2.7 (14.7%)	2.2 (13.6%)
Route (Optional)	1.3 (13.3%)	4.1 (21.7%)	2.4 (14.6%)
Assistance, Training	1.9 (19.0%)	5.1 (27.0%)	3.5 (21.4%)
Other	0.5 (5.1%)	0.3 (1.7%)	-
Distribution Strategy (Total)	10.1 (100%)	18.7 (100.0%)	16.3 (100.0%)
Pricing Strategy (Total)	19.0	19.0	16.0
Other	0.4	0.5	0.2
TOTAL	100.0	100.0	100.0

Dr. Udell, "The Perceived Importance of the Elements of Strategy," Journal of Marketing, Vol. 32 (January, 1968), pp. 34-40.

The importance according to producer goods and durable goods is somewhat different. However, compared to pricing, the marketing has a greater weight; specially, the evaluation of salespeople activity is salient. Dr. Udell maintains that sales activity is basically communication activity.

Some activities such as advertisement, billboards, catalogs, and so on are spatial communication between a sender and a receiver. On the other hand, visitation and contact by salespeople are temporal communication. Relatively speaking, in the case of consumer goods, the former has a higher weight, whereas in the case of producer goods, the later is more important.

In marketing, as part of the direct tactical force, the activity of salespeople; i.e., the fighting strength is measured in time units. The fighting strength, according to Lanchester's quantitative analysis, can be shown in the following manner. Also, refer to (2.1.3), where two basic types of the fighting strength were discussed.

In the case of single combat:

(Fighting strength) = (Efficiency of weapons) x (number of men)

And in the case of total war:

(Fighting strength) = (Efficiency of weapons) x (number of men)^2

In marketing, the efficiency of the weapons is the amount of damage that can be inflicted on the enemy per unit of time, and is represented as the size of impact and influence against the receiver, which can also be interpreted as the quality of the sales force. On the other hand, the number of men is the equivalent of the sales force, which is a quantitative factor.

The quality of a sales force here does not mean the personal aptitude or the personality trait, rather it means the capacity of communication or content to a recipient within a certain amount of time (10 minutes, 30 minutes, or the average communication time). This is commonly referred to as "documentation of communication procedure into manuals" or "standardization." It then goes on to say overstaying can be a negative factor.

The quantitative side, which can be changed by increasing or decreasing the number of salespeople, is "the number of visits" against the other party. Also, in the case of single combat, the competition is against one client or one customer, and in the case of total war, in a unit of regional market such as a business office or a branch office, the competition is against several customers and clients, and with respect to each company, several salespeople who are in charge engage in heated competition.

Therefore, the tactical equation in the sales and marketing can be arranged as follows:

(1) In the case of one customer or one client:

Fighting strength = (Average contact time per visit) x (Number of visits)

(2) In the case of regional market:

Fighting strength = (Average contact time per visit) x (Number of visits)^2

The problem is how to maximize the fighting strength in comparison to the attack target in market competition. This can be achieved by either increasing (Average contact time per visit) or (Number of visits); however, in the case of regional market, it is obviously more advantageous to increase (Number of visits).

This means, the strong with a greater number of salespeople engages in total war, and generally, opens several agencies and adopts the open territory method of competition. And the weak with a smaller number of salespeople engages in single combat with focal concentration, and it naturally emphasizes Average Contact Time per Visit over Number of Visits on the quantitative side.

Also, there are differences according to the product and the nature of service. For example, in the case of producer goods such as cement, machinery, construction consultants, and so on, the clients are well established, and on average, there are 3 to 6 people who make purchasing decisions. Thus, appointment-based visits and rational sales talks based on estimates become necessary, and as a result, (Average contact time per visit) must be increased, including the off-business entertainment, refering to model (1).

In the case of consumer goods such as foods, cosmetics, and so on, the contrasting model (2) is adopted. A prime example of this model used in advertising is TV's concentrated spot commercials. When the number of votes in an election campaign is concerned, the broader the territory, the greater the chance of total war and the application of model type (2).

4.4.4 Customer retention and new market development

There is a jinx in the restaurant business that holds if the business is left unattended, the number of customers will decrease by 20% annually. This means that after five years, the store could go bankrupt. Therefore, every business must not only maintain its clients but at the same time develop new ones. Customers could also easily lose their interest in a product or service. Aside from losing customers, there is no guarantee that a business continues to receive orders from customers.

All this means is that for companies to acquire and maintain a certain market share, they must constantly consider the balance between the order rate including the falling customers and orders from customers newly developed in order to cover the lost share.

Here, to determine this relationship, let the number of existing customers per one salesperson be (x_R) and the number of prospect (projected) new (to be developed) customers per one salesperson be (x_N).

T: Total labor time per month (minute)

k: Customer contact time ratio per month against total labor time (%). This is also called fighting strength ratio

P_R: Fighting strength per month against existing customers (target contact time) (minute)

P_N: Fighting strength per month against new customers (target contact time) (minute)

O_R: Average order ratio per month from existing customers (%). This maintains the month-to-month actual client store ratio

O_N: Average order ratio per month from new customers (%)

The above element values must be extracted from actual behavior record data. To that end, there is no need to add new attempts. Business journals are recorded in every company, all one has to do is to change the viewpoint and rearrange the available data.

At the same time as considering the fighting strength against continuous (existing) clients and new clients, orders not being placed by existing clients are covered by those from new clients. This will lead to the following system of equations that include x_R and x_N.

$$\begin{cases} P_R \cdot x_R + P_N \cdot x_N = T \cdot k \\ (1 - O_R) \cdot x_R = O_N \cdot x_N \end{cases}$$

As an example,

T: 12,000 minutes, 1 day 10 hours, operating 20 days
k: 35%

P_R: 110 minutes $\qquad$ P_N: 100 minutes
O_R: 95% $\qquad$ O_N: 10%

In this case,

$$\begin{cases} 110\ x_R + 100\ x_N = 12,000 \times 0.35 \\ (1 - 0.95)\ x_R = 0.1\ x_N \end{cases}$$

After arrangement,

$$\begin{cases} 110\ x_R + 100\ x_N = 4{,}200 \\ 0.05 x_R - 0.1\ x_N = 0 \end{cases}$$

$$\begin{cases} 110\ x_R + 100\ x_N = 4{,}200 \\ 50\ x_R - 100\ x_N = 0 \end{cases}$$

$$\therefore\quad 160\ x_R = 4{,}200$$

Thus:

$$\begin{cases} x_R = 26.25 \\ x_N = 13.125 \end{cases}$$

That is, in this case, for each salesperson, the number of continuous clients per month is intended to be 26 and the number of new or prospective clients to be 13, or about half. Furthermore, there are actually important ABC ranks with respect to continuous clients, and since the order density would be different, visiting schedules must be planned according to the state of competition for each occasion.

The laws of physics cannot select those who fit. Similarly, when considering the planning of a strategy and applying tactics in a competitive landscape, the Lanchester Law is not "the law of Quantity" that applies only to the strong, but can be compared to the principle of lever in which a small force can move a large object, and can be claimed for the weak as well.

Chapter 5

Marketing development and establishment of strategy and tactics

Marketing is a practical subject. Allowing rigid logic and theory to run ahead of itself as well as jumping to any conclusion must be strictly avoided. The admonishment of "the distribution revolution theory" in the 1960s that lead to the extinction of retailers must be clearly understood. Lanchester law as well as the Lanchester strategy model belong to the phenomenological model, and although based on the certainty model, they are in constant need of a reality check.

But the fact remains that in many companies, Lanchester law and the Lanchester strategy model are established as a guiding principle for the marketing strategy and tactic.

To address these issues, I would like to introduce and examine the following three case studies.

5.1 The law as seen in newspaper circulation market share

With a hundred years of history, newspaper circulation has reached penetration of almost 100% among households. In the absence of any major differentiation among circulating newspapers, a cutthroat competition is bound to unfold among them. The circulation of newspapers and their market share can be best estimated according to the ABC (Audit Bureau of Circulation) Report.

Newspaper Circulation and Market Share (Morning Edition)

		1973		1974		1975	
		Jan-Jun	Aug-Dec	Jan-Jun	Aug-Dec	Jan-Jun	Aug-Dec
National	Asahi	6,296,261 (30.7%)	6,442,598 (31.0%)	6,479,495 (32.4%)	6,551,352 (31.7%)	6,650,343 (32.2%)	6,736,901 (32.2%)
	Yomiuri	6,097,047 (29.8%)	6,208,909 (29.9%)	6,413,901 (32.1%)	6,401,064 (30.9%)	6,322,347 (30.7%)	6,523,625 (31.2%)
	Mainichi	4,836,817 (23.6%)	4,821,169 (23.2%)	3,824,050 (19.1%)	4,467,980 (21.6%)	4,346,181 (21.1%)	4,302,202 (20.5%)
	Sankei	1,824,205 (8.9%)	1,835,266 (8.8%)	1,795,514 (9.0%)	1,776,820 (8.6%)	1,785,309 (8.7%)	1,817,728 (8.7%)
	Nikkei	1,436,376 (7.0%)	1,448,052 (7.0%)	1,483,549 (7.4%)	1,49,479 (7.2%)	1,512,862 (7.3%)	1,550,409 (7.4%)
Regional	Hokkaido	804,715	806,943	818,681	813,445	821,823	820,047
	Chunichi	1,656,514	1,687,336	1,724,196	1,696,780	1,708,060	1,689,779
	Nishinihon	645,000	611,826	638,257	612,717	626,368	616,931

(Note: Yomiuri does not include Chubu Yomiuri in Aichi, Gifu, and Mie prefectures.)

Japanese national newspapers consist of Asahi, Yomiuri, Mainichi, Sankei, and Nihon Keizai (Nikkei). Nikkei, however, mainly targets industry and commerce and has a different readership compared with the other four general newspapers.

From 1973 to 1975, looking at the table, the shares of Asahi, Yomiuri, and Nikkei are rising, but the shares of Mainichi and Sankei are falling. Combining the shares of the 3rd ranker, Mainichi, and the 4th ranker, Sankei, still it falls short of the 1st and 2nd rankers. This indicates a sudden transition from a diverse pattern of 3 top runners to a relative oligopoly model.

Specially, in the middle of oil shock during 1974, Mainichi drops suddenly by one million copies. This seems a result of its weak financial position, and this is why in a recession, the true mettle of company in terms of its market share is tested.

Sankei is not selling in Hokkaido and Kyushu; therefore, its status as a national newspaper is arguable. It is also not completely a regional newspaper in its home region of Kansai. In the second half of 1975, the (newspaper) market shares in Osaka were in the following order: Yomiuri, 27.8%; Asahi, 25.5%; Mainichi, 20.8%; Sankei, 19.9%; and others, 6.0%. From the E (diversified type) development standpoint, the severity of Yomiuri' attack is discernible.

Regional newspapers consist of three: Hokkaido, Chunichi, and Nishinihon. Doshin in Hokkaido and Chunichi in Nagoya present A' model (monopolistic oligopoly type), which means they have more shares than all others below them combined. In the second half of 1975, Doshin's share in Hokkaido was 55.3%, surpassing that of the second ranker, Yomiuri's 12.8%, and those of Asahi's and Mainichi's. For Sankei this meant a full retreat with no chance of reentering the market.

Chunichi had a share of 67.1% in Aichi prefecture in the second half of 1975, the strongest penetration into any regional market in Japan. With 1,680,000 copies, it is on par with the national Sankei and Nikkei. Yomiuri would have lost if it had targeted Chunichi; therefore, naturally, the only option was to eat Mainichi's share.

The same regional paper, Nishinihon with its base in Fukuoka prefecture, had a share of 29.5% in the first half of 1975. It is reversing to pattern E (diversified type) as it is closed in by the second ranker, Asahi, and the third ranker, Yomiuri. Compared with Chugoku Newspaper in Hiroshima, with a share of 51%, it is outnumbered, but Nishinihon's sales areas are west of Ongagawa, Fukuoka City and along Nagasaki Main Line, and thus has a weak sales force in Kitakyushu City and along Nippo Main Line.

Yomiuri, a national paper, began its expansion in earnest after 1955, and has reached a remarkable market share, surpassing Mainichi. This is because unlike Hokkaido and Nagoya, there were no number one, or local newspapers of the top-position (runaway) type.

Circulation and Market Share in Kyushu (July to December 1995)

	National Newspapers				Regional Papers	Local Papers
	Asahi	Yomiuri	Mainichi	Nikkei	Nishinhon	
Fukuoka	296,306 (22.0%)	268,787 (19.9%)	212,048 (15.7%)	45,914 (5.4%)	398,122 (29.5%)	Evening Fukunichi 128,000 (9.5%)
Saga	25,734 (10.4%)	23,928 (9.7%)	19,796 (8.0%)	4,792 (1.9%)	58,789 (23.8%)	Saga 114,300 (46.2%)
Nagasaki	69,324 (18.6%)	35,309 (9.5%)	42,576 (11.3%)	9,447 (2.4%)	73,651 (19.7%)	Nagasaki 140,000 (37.9%)
Kumamoto	57,100 (14.9%)	47,713 (12.4%)	39,149 (10.2%)	10,753 (2.8%)	32,711 (8.5%)	Kumamoto Daily 197,064 (51.2%)
Ohita	61,929 (19.8%)	33,907 (10.8%)	41,061 (9.6%)	8,183 (2.6%)	25,263 (8.1%)	Ohitagodo Daily 142,463 (45.5%)
Miyazaki	58,176 (22.2%)	25,215 (9.6%)	31,701 (12.1%)	7,929 (3.0%)	14,957 (5.7%)	Miyazaki Daily 123,141 (47.0%)
Kagoshima	44,185 (11.0%)	35,191 (8.8%)	24,082 (6.0%)	11,219 (2.8%)	9,679 (2.4%)	Kagoshimashinpo 59,716 (14.9%) Minaminihon 217,361 (54.1%)
Okinawa	1,988 (-)	(-)	(-)	2,021 (-)	(-)	Okinawa Times 128,409 (60.1%) Ryukushipo 81,363 (38.1%)

In Okinawa, which is out of the reach of national papers, Okinawa Times and Ryukyushinpo divide the market share; however, other than Fukuoka, in all other prefectures, one local regional newspaper has all others including the second ranker on down outside the shooting range in a total war, presenting the top-position (runaway) type.

Numbers for Nagasaki newspaper are estimates; however, although Nagasaki newspaper is closest to the second ranker, Nishinihon in relative terms, the gap is: 1.92 times, where $1.92 > \sqrt{\sqrt{8}} \approx \sqrt{3}$.

All this means that local newspapers are small but have a strong punch, and national newspapers are large but have their weaknesses.

The reason that local newspapers are strong is because they are of the top-position (runaway) type, and number one in regional markets. On the other hand, the reason other newspapers such as Mainichi and Sankei have management problems is not unrelated to their falling market shares.

Not only in its native home, Tokyo, and Osaka, but also in other regions, because there is no one single top region, it brought about diversification of its own force.

Although the total number of copies for the five national newspapers remains unchanged, the fact that there are differences between their market shares means that the rule of market share works thoroughly in the competitive landscape.

5.2 Regulations against super stores in Matsumoto City, and the ratio of city modernization and store floor space

In the beginning of 1973, Nikkei Ryutsuu Journal published an article titled "Super Stores' Share (Sales Floor Space) Passes the 26% Line: The Arrival of Real Competition Era." This special article surveyed fifty major commercial cities, and the 26% line meant breaking out of Lanchester's strategy model E (diversified type), and with respect to sales floor space, which is a store's basic "fighting strength," when a super store's sales floor space exceeds 26% of the total sales floor space for all other local stores, this means the courtship between the super stores and other local stores is over. Once passed beyond this critical state, the nature of competition changes and the focus moves to the competition among super stores.

In this article, it was mentioned that although the rate of population growth in those commercial cities had slowed down, the ratio of super store floor space was high at 60% in Machida City (Tokyo), 53% in Hachioji City, and 45% in Hirakata City (Osaka). Within the next two years, Hachioji. Isetan had to withdraw, and in February 1979, the entry of furniture maker, Taishodo, took their place. There is also the market retreat of Midoriya from Tachikawa City (Tokyo) and Jasco from Tsudanuma in Narashino City (Chiba prefecture). Still, on top of all this, more super retail stores are planned for new commercial zones, targeting also cities with populations of 40,000 to 50,000, causing friction with local shopping districts across the country.

Nagano prefecture is divided into several commercial zones. The commercial zone with Matsumoto at its center has a population of 440,000 (August 1976).

In 1976, Matsumoto had a population of 187,000 and 2,900 retailers with a total annual revenue of 91,900,000,000 yen (excluding restaurants) and 150,000 m^2 of sales floor space. Super stores such as Jasco, Hayashibe, and Inoue department store had already five stores and 16,000 m^2 of sales floor space. The space ratio for the super stores was approximately 11%, lower than the ratio for each of its commercial zone (city).

Then there was a plan for Itoyokado to open a super store in Matsumoto, which drew fierce demonstrations in the spring of 1976. But even among the demonstrators, there were some local merchants with plans of opening stores as tenants and joining forces after the opening of the department store.

Matsumoto City Map

Note: Shaded areas indicate heavy pedestrian traffic.

After 1972, Matsumoto City drafted a plan called "Regional Plans for Modernizing Commerce," and began implementing part of it; however, it soon became evident that the resources at the disposal of super stores vastly exceeded those of the city, and the city was left with no alternative but to revise the plan. The center of the new plan, called "City Center Commercial District Plan," included the following three items:

1. Renovation of shopping district in front of the Matsumoto train station

The renovation plan was drafted in 1975, and beginning in 1976, with a fund of 800,000,000 yen and a loan of 2,800,000,000 yen the construction started and was scheduled for completion by 1978. However, additional modernization for the appropriation of 475 stores, the appropriation of an area of 59,000 m^2, and 4,600 m^2 per year was to be carried out as planned.

2. Renovation of National Railway Matsumoto Train Station and creation of an open space in front of the station.

Funds of 1,400,000,000 yen with the start date of April 1977 and the completion date of September 1978.

3. Bus terminal construction

Starting in September 1976 and completing in March 1978, a shopping center is to be added, and as an anchor store, approval of Itoyokado's entry with a fund of 4,000,000,000 yen and floor space of 27,804 m^2. The sales floor space would be 11,309 m^2 for Itoyokado, 2,570 m^2 for Matsuden store (Sanai) — a total of 13,879 m^2.

With respect to the entry of Itoyokado, a special committee was set up to objectively examine the impact of such a super store on commercial activities and the final report was published after a year of study in March 1977.

In calculating the maximum permissible level of a super store in this study, pattern E (diversified type) based on the Lanchester strategy model was employed as a standard. According to this model, the detachment condition was 26%.

In this study, to estimate the total sales amount, first, the total amount of retail business sales up to 1985 (1974 – 1985) based on available statistical results was projected using three different methods, next, among them the results were narrowed down to super-store-related businesses, and the average value of the three methods was found, and finally, it was divided by the annual sales floor efficiency ratio (488,000 yen/m^2).

Retail Business, Sales Forecast (Billion Yen)

Year	1974	1975	1976	1977	1978	1979	1980	1981	1982	1983	1984	1985
1. Macro Frame	65.5	68.2	73.6	79.1	84.5	89.5	95.3	104.1	113.0	121.6	130.5	136.3
2. Growth Forecast	65.5	69.8	74.3	79.1	84.2	89.7	95.5	101.2	107.3	113.7	120.5	127.7
3. Demand Forecast	67.9	75.3	82.7	91.4	99.9	108.3	109.8	117.1	124.6	135.0	143.8	155.8
Average	66.3	71.1	76.9	83.2	89.5	95.8	100.2	107.5	115.0	123.4	131.6	139.9

Note: Limited to super-store related businesses only

The projected total retail business sales is based on the Macro Frame method (1). The projection (2) is based on the Impact Model (planning model based on dynamic industry-related analysis) proposed by a research group called "Policy Making Forum," which consists of economists, social scientists, government and private economists. This model strives for a welfare state economy and projects a growth rate on an optimum course of 6.5% during 1976 – 1980, 6.0% during 1981 – 1985, and 5% after 1986.

Both models (1) and (2) stipulate that among 91,900,000,000 yen of Matsumoto City retail business annual sales based on a 1974 commerce statistical study, the super-store-related sales is to be 65,500,000,000 yen with a ratio of 71.3%.

Model (3) projects a Micro view based on the product sales study results for a ratio of 34.85% with respect to the total retail business annual sales in 1974, a pace moving unchanged through 1979; furthermore, it projects a ratio of 37% beyond 1980 following an increase in the income level. It also projects 91,900,000,000 yen for the super-store-related sales with a ratio of 73.9%, and 67,900,000,000 yen in 1974.

Store Area of existing retail businesses that can be expanded (in 1,000 m²)

Year	1974	1975	1976	1977	1978	1979	1980	1981	1982	1983	1984	1985
a. Total store area	135.8	145.6	157.5	170.4	183.4	196.3	205.3	220.2	235.6	252.0	269.6	286.6
b. Allowed (= a×26.1%)	35.5	38.0	41.1	44.5	47.9	51.3	53.6	57.5	61.5	65.8	70.4	74.9
b' Existing area	15.3	15.3	16.1	16.1	16.1	16.1	16.1	16.1	16.1	16.1	16.1	16.1
b" New area	20.2	22.7	25.0	28.4	31.8	35.2	37.5	41.4	45.4	49.7	54.3	58.8
c. Existing retail area	118.7	118.7	118.7	118.7	118.7	118.7	118.7	118.7	118.7	118.7	118.7	118.7
d. Expansion (= a-b-c)	-18.4	-11.1	-2.3	7.2	16.8	26.3	33.0	44.0	55.4	67.5	80.5	93.0
e. Local store expansion	1.8	7.1	11.7 (+4.6)	16.6 (+4.9)	21.6 (+5.0)	26.3 (+4.7)	33.0	44.0	55.4	67.5	80.5	93.0
f. Super store expansion	0	4.5	11.0	19.0	27.0	35.2	37.5	41.4	45.4	49.7	54.3	58.8
Local store total area (= c + e)	120.5 88.7%	125.8 86.4%	130.4 82.8%	135.3 79.4%	140.3 76.5%	145.0 73.9%	151.7 73.9%	162.7 73.9%	174.1 73.9%	186.2 73.9%	199.2 73.9%	211.7 73.9%
Super store total area (= b' + f)	15.3 11.3%	19.8 13.6%	27.1 17.2%	35.1 20.6%	43.1 23.5%	51.3 26.1	53.6 26.1%	57.5 26.1%	61.5 26.1%	65.8 26.1%	70.4 26.1%	74.9 26.1%

Total store area is the total sales or retail business divided by 488,000 yen/square meter

The so-called super-store permissible floor space (b) is obtained by multiplying the total store space (a) for each year by 26.1%, the standard coefficient, which is the detachment condition for Lanchester's strategy model E (diversified type). (b"), the new tolerance, is obtained by subtracting the existing (b').

However, the increasable space is obtained by subtracting c, the current local retail businesses store space (d=a-b-c). In the period of 1974 – 1976, this amount is negative.

Furthermore, through 1976, when this report was created, the local businesses modernization plan was underway, and the appropriation store space was implemented for 1,800 m² in 1974, 7,100 m² in 1975, and projected for 4,600-5,000 m² beyond 1981 (e). Thus, based on the permissible super-store sales floor space of 26.1%, although the new value, (b"), is already factored into calculation, modification (f) was still necessary, and based on the space (area) unit, in effect, the new superstore permissible value, which exceeds 19,000 m² after 1977, seems a more likely projection.

As a result, while complying with Lanchester's strategy model, through 1977, the report follows the revised new permissible space against super stores, and after 1979, as calculated, it concluded that the ratio of total local businesses floor space versus that of super stores would settle at 73.9 to 26.1.

In April 1978, Itoyokado opened with fanfare on schedule. The sales forecast for the first year was set conservatively to 4,910,000,000 yen and the annual sales floor efficiency to 434,000 yen/ m².

While the invasion of a super store breaks the stagnation of the local shopping district, it also creates a threat. In the process of finding a compromising proposal to allow peaceful coexistence among all stores, in the case of Matsumoto City, the selection of Lanchester's strategy model is indeed noteworthy.

Through this approach, the local shopping district clearly showed self-responsibility to modernize in a quantitative and measurable manner, and the super stores side accepted a certain measure of self-discipline to contain unchecked urges of invasive and excessive business practices. Similar attempts have also been discussed in other cities such as Kobe and Takamatsu.

5.3 Studying the conformity between customer visitation and receiving order planning, the equations of tactics

Setting a clear attack target belongs to the realm of sales strategy; however, once the attacking party is identified, the issue then becomes how to concentrate the fighting strength more than the enemy. However, when considering a single salesperson, the monthly total labor time is not only limited but it is also trending down. Customers and clients are also of various sizes and market shares; new clients must also be developed, and visiting only the friendly clients could play into the enemy's hands.

Although there are various restrictive conditions, visitation and receiving-order planning must be drafted and implemented with respect to customers and clients; an ad-hoc approach does not lend itself to sustained growth, it also erodes the desire to face the competition. Here, the regional customers and clients are ranked according to ABC analysis, and along with the results of the analysis of the behavior of the producer goods and consumer goods salesperson, we attempt to examine the elements of visitation and receiving-order planning. And we construct those to build a system of equations of tactics, and see if they actually hold. If they hold, mathematically, coordination is obtained, and at least, the visitation and receiving-order planning meet the real-world conditions.

Among continuous customers and clients, let the A rank number be x_A, B rank number be x_B, C rank number be x_C, and the number of newly developed customers and clients be x_N. Then the total number of sales force in charge will be $(x_A + x_B + x_C + x_N)$.

(1) Client contact time

We mentioned maintaining customers and developing new ones in (4.4.4); however, based on the equations of tactic that show the fighting strength, the elements are (the average contact time per visit) and (the number of visits). Let the former be t_A, t_B, t_C, t_N (unit is minute), and the former be V_A, V_B, V_C, V_N (unit is number of visits/month).

The conditions are, similarly, the monthly total labor time T (minute) and the client contact time ratio and fighting strength ratio k (%), thus:

$$t_A V_A x_A + t_B V_B x_B + t_C V_C x_C + t_N V_N x_N = T \cdot k \qquad \text{(i)}$$

It should be noted that the monthly total labor time, T, is the product of the average daily labor time, and the number of working days in a month, d, or $T = \bar{t} d$.

(2) Actual client rate

Similarly, following (4.4.4), if the average order rates per month are O_A, O_B, O_C, O_N, then as a condition, when compensating the lost continuous customers and clients with new orders, we have the following equation:

$$(1 - O_A)x_A + (1 - O_B)x_B + (1 - O_C)x_C = O_N x_N \qquad \text{(ii)}$$

(3) Number of visits

Even when just taking the customers' and clients' circumstances out of consideration, as long as there is a limit to the number of clients visited daily, the total number of visits per month, F, becomes a condition. Since this is equal to the sum product of the number of accounts (clients) by rank and the corresponding number of visits (times/month), then:

$$V_A x_A + V_B x_B + V_C x_C + V_N x_N = F \qquad \text{(iii)}$$

It should be noted that the monthly total number of clients visited, F, is the product of the average daily number of clients visited, $\bar{v}$ and the number of working days in a month, d, or $(F = \bar{v} d)$.

By the number of visits we mean, for example, 6 visits in a week, which could be one visit every day or two visits every other day. By the number of clients visited, we mean, for example, on a daily basis, even if the subject (client) is visited over again, we count each visit separately.

Therefore, in the same unit period, a month for example, the sum product of the number of visits and accounts coincide with the number of clients. With respect to planning, the number of visits is easier to plan and implement, and the conditions are easier understood when viewed from the side of the number of clients visited.

(4) The number of receiving-orders

Here, let's consider the rate of increase for receiving-orders. And let's say that we want to increase a receiving-order rate of 70% from a customer to 75% or 80%. For that, efforts to win the competition and concentration of the fighting strength become necessary.

According to the equations for tactic, the fighting strength, P, with respect to one customer or client, is represented as the product of the average contact time per visit, t, and the number of visits, v. However, with respect to the number of visits, which represents the quantitative side of the equation, visitor's discretion is allowed. Since the receiving-order ratio increase per increase in the number of visits per a unit period of time (a month for example, (τ)), is proportionate to the fighting strength, then the following differential equation can be obtained. (Note: Since the visitation values are discrete, they are subject to differentiation. Here, as a die's expected value is 3.5, we consider V to be continuous).

$$\frac{\frac{dO}{d\tau}}{\frac{dV}{d\tau}} = \frac{dO}{dV} = CP, \qquad \therefore \quad \frac{dO}{dV} = CtV$$

Where C is a constant.

Since an indefinite number of constituents comprises the regional market, we can separate the variables and take an indefinite integral:

$$O = Ct\frac{1}{2}V^2 + C_o \qquad C_o \text{ is a constant}$$

With respect to the integral constant, when the initial condition V=0; that is, when not visiting, the average contact time, t=0, and there is no need to consider it. When multiplying both sides by N, the number of customers and clients in the regional market, we have the number of receiving-orders emerging.

$$N \cdot O = C \frac{1}{2} t V^2 \cdot N$$

The right side of the above equation resembles very closely to the lift force formula (2.1.1) from aerodynamics:

$$L = C_L \frac{1}{2} \rho V^2 \cdot S \quad \text{(Lift Force)}$$

Where: C_L is the lift force coefficient
ρ is the air density
V is the velocity
S is the surface area of the wing

An aircraft slowly increases its velocity through the thrust of its engine and eventually takes off. The same analogy applies to lifting market share by increasing the number of visits and raising the number of orders.

The lift coefficient is dependent on the wing shape and is determined by air tunnel experiments. However, in the case of ordering of products and services, the receiving-order coefficient (C) must be found from the actual records of repeated commercial activities according to ABC ranks and new clients, not experiments.

Returning to the case of a single salesperson, the left side of the equation for the emerging number of receiving-orders is the sum product of the number of customers according to ranks and new clients and each receiving-order rate. The right side is the sum product of the receiving-order coefficient according to ranks and new clients, the average contact time per visit, and the number of visits. With this as the fighting strength condition for the left side of the emerging number or receiving-orders, we then have:

$$O_{AxA} + O_{BxB} + O_{CxC} + O_{NxN} = C_{AtA}V_A + C_{BtB}V_B + C_{CtC}V_C + C_{NtN}V_N \quad \text{(iv)}$$

(5) System of equations for tactics in 4 variables

By arranging the equations in the previous section we have the following system of linear equations in 4 variables:

$$t_A V_{AxA} + t_B V_{BxB} + t_C V_{CxC} + t_N V_{NxN} = \bar{t}dk \quad \text{(i)}$$
(Client contact time)

$$(1-O_A)x_A + (1-O_B)x_B + (1-O_C)x_C - O_{NxN} = 0 \quad \text{(ii)}$$
(Actual client store share)

$$V_{AxA} + V_{BxB} + V_{CxC} + V_{NxN} = \bar{v}d \quad \text{(iii)}$$
(Number of visits)

$$O_{AxA} + O_{BxB} + O_{CxC} + O_{NxN} = C_A t_A V_A + C_B t_B V_B + C_C t_C V_C + C_N t_N V_N \quad \text{(iv)}$$
(Number of receiving-orders)

This system of equations has four dimensions with the number of clients per salesperson (per month) according to ABC ranks and new clients as an unknown variable (x_i). When the number of clients is known but the number of visits (V_j) is not, then this system of equations has three dimensions; that is, the number of equations is reduced by one and therefore the general solution cannot be obtained and its conformity cannot be confirmed. In this case, we temporarily let the new client (x_N) be 1 and with three dimensions we can then find the relative value. The three and four dimension equations are normally solved by computers.

(6) Analysis of salesperson behavior

Average daily labor time $\bar{t}$, average daily number of visits $\bar{v}$, contact time ratio/ fighting strength ratio, k, receiving-order rate by rank, receiving-order coefficient, and values of other elements of visitation and receiving-order planning must be confirmed firsthand and then compiled.

This author, after 1974, analyzed sales activities of 262 salespeople from 7 producer-goods companies and 139 salespeople from consumer-goods companies, a total of 401 salespeople, to obtain a single test value.

This behavior analysis was done after the oil shock, therefore it reflects some of the restructuring and streamlining of companies surveyed. This report is based on a detailed and thorough analysis of individual salespeople behavior on a daily basis over a period of one month.

Producer goods and consumer goods can be categorized separately, and there are differences according to business type and company history. Averaging the results from 7 producer-goods companies and 8 consumer-goods businesses, we can see the average daily labor time is almost equal regardless of the product line, 10 hours, 22 minutes (622 minutes) and 10 hours, 15 minutes (615 minutes), respectively. The averages are based on company and business units rather than samples, or salesperson unit, to avoid leaning toward characteristics of companies with a large number of sales force.

The daily average number of visits ($\bar{v}$) is 3.41 for the producer-goods companies and 6.96 for the consumer-goods companies, and the average contact time is 1 hour, 36 minutes. For the producer-goods companies, the emphasis is on the average contact time, and for the consumer-goods companies, the daily number of visits is emphasized.

With respect to the daily average contact time, which is the product of these two averages, in the overtime composition ratio, the travel (time on the road) from the business outside the company is excluded, and the calculation is based on the active visits, passive visits, overtime entertainment (of clients), and other accumulated total (on average, the producer goods is 32.7% and the consumer goods is 41.3%) multiplied by the daily average labor time.

Primarily, with respect to the contact time, the active visits must be increased; however, responding to customer complaints and providing service as part of the passive visit is essential to securing orders.

In the case of producer-goods companies, the ratio of entertainment (of clients) outside the company is higher than that of the consumer-goods companies.

Here, the important point is the travel time (time on the road) ratio, which is close to 30% for both producer-goods and consumer-goods companies. There are many reasons such as traffic and the like, but this time must be reduced to less than 20% at the most. Also, in the active visits, sales means signing an agreement, and for the producer-goods companies, this is zero because agreements are signed through agencies.

Other standard values related to various elements of the visitation and order planning are derived from the behavior analysis.

The receiving-order rate (share) is route sales for both producer-goods and consumer-goods companies, which means they are not spot sales, and new sales include the old lost customers, which in both cases, no significant differences can be observed. On average, the target receiving-order rate is approximately 70%.

Analysis of Salesperson Performance Characteristics (one month period)

Sector			Industrial Products						
Product			Sheet glass	Pumps	Valves	Bridge	Steel	Interior	Fittings
Survey year/month			74/9	75/3	74/8	75/9	75/9	75/9	75/3	Average
Number of samples			25	23	165	5	6	5	33	7 firms
Survey region			Osaka	National	National	Osaka	Osaka	Osaka	Osaka	
(1) Monthly labor time			Minutes							
(2) Monthly work days			Day							
(3) Number of visits/month			Visit							
(4) Average daily work time			9h 54m	9h 55m	9h 54m	10h 00m	11h 37m	11h 23m	9h 54m	10h 22m
(5) Average number of daily visits			4.1	4.3	2.6	2.2	3.0	3.9	3.8	3.41
(6) Average contact time per visit			41m	41m	1h 03m	1h 25m	1h 36m	1h 13m	0h 45m	1h 00m
(7) Daily average contact time			2h 50m	2h 57m	2h 43m	3h 08m	4h 49m	4h 46m	2h 51m	3h 23m
Time Structure Ratio Percentage	External Company Activities	Active — Sales	0 %	0	0	1.9	7.8	6.4	0	
		Active — Sales promotion	12.2	18.9	-	4.7	10.9	9.2	-	
		Active — Product promotion	7.2	0.5	-	6.5	4.4	2.8	-	
		Active — Survey information	3.0	1.1	-	7.1	7.3	2.1	-	
		Active — Develop new clients	1.3	2.0	1.0	1.0	0.9	2.3	5.2	
		Active — Subtotal	23.7	22.5	21.5	21.2	31.3	22.8	24.5	23.9
		Passive — Bill collection	0.5	0.6	-	0.2	1.4	0.7	0.1	
		Passive — Complaints review	1.1	1.3	-	1.9	0.4	0.5	0.5	
		Passive — Service	0	0	-	0.6	0.2	0	0	
		Passive — Delivery	0.1	2.5	-	0	0	0.1	0.2	
		Passive — Subtotal	1.7	4.4	1.8	2.7	2.0	1.3	0.8	2.1
		Other — Entertainment	2.9	0.6	1.5	1.8	3.1	9.2	1.0	2.9
		Other — Other	0.3	2.2	2.6	5.6	5.1	8.6	2.5	
		Other — Subtotal	3.2	2.8	4.1	7.4	8.2	17.8	3.5	6.7
		Travel	23.1	32.4	20.8	29.9	32.6	28.9	38.5	29.5
		TOTAL	51.7	62.1	48.2	61.2	74.1	70.8	67.3	62.2
	Internal Activities	Meetings	7.4	4.7	11.4	10.8	1.3	6.9	3.9	
		Documentation	7.1	8.0	-	14.6	17.6	13.9	21.2	
		Customer visits	2.1	0.5	-	4.1	0.1	1.9	0.7	
		Shipping/receiving	9.3	4.0	-	0	0	0	0	
		Claims	0.8	2.4	-	0	0	0.5	0	
		Training	0.3	1.1	-	0	0	0.2	0	
		Other	15.3	9.9	-	3.2	1.0	0.4	0	
		TOTAL	42.3	30.6	45.1	32.7	20.0	23.8	25.8	31.5
		Break	6.0	7.3	6.7	6.1	5.9	5.4	6.9	6.3

Note: at the symbol - in above table, not sufficient data

Analysis of Salesperson Performance Characteristics (excludes travel time)

			Consumer Products					
Food	Electrical	Cosmetics	Drug			Household		
75/3	75/9	75/9	76/1	76/2	76/3	76/3	76/3	Average
24	6	6	12	17	15	26	33	5 firms
Osaka	Kobe	Tokyo	Tokyo	Osaka	Sapporo	Tokyo	Osaka	8 offices
Minutes								
Day								
Visit								
9h 32m	10h 31m	10h 32m	11h 18m	12h 00m	9h 24m	9h 12m	9h 36m	10h 15m
8.5	9.8	9.5	10.5	9.7	2.7	2.7	2.3	6.96
25m	31m	34m	25m	30m	1h 14m	1h 09m	1h 54m	36m
3h 30m	5h 07m	5h 24m	4h 21m	4h 47m	3h 21m	3h 07m	4h 22m	4h 14m
21.9	10.0	17.0	11.9	14.8	14.4	12.3	21.1	
6.6	32.0	26.6	17.3	8.5	6.1	7.1	6.1	
0.3	1.6	2.4	0.6	0.7	1.7	4.4	0.1	
1.0	0.2	0.5	1.5	8.7	1.6	2.2	4.6	
0.4	1.4	1.0	1.5	1.3	0	0.2	0	
30.2	45.2	47.5	32.8	34.0	23.8	26.2	31.9	34.0
1.5	0.8	0.8	0.7	0.5	0.8	0.3	0.6	
0.5	0.5	0.4	0.6	0.3	2.1	0.6	0.2	
0.5	0.4	0.3	1.0	2.0	1.8	1.5	1.9	
0.9	0.5	0.1	1.4	1.3	0.8	2.1	0.4	
3.4	2.2	1.6	3.7	4.1	5.5	4.5	3.1	3.5
0.1	0	1.2	0	0.5	1.4	0.2	1.7	0.6
3.0	1.3	1.0	2.0	1.2	5.0	3.0	8.7	
3.1	1.3	2.2	2.0	1.7	6.4	3.2	10.4	3.8
35.3	35.7	33.5	35.6	31.7	25.0	25.0	17.5	29.9
72.0	84.4	84.8	74.1	71.5	60.7	58.9	62.9	71.2
5.4	2.6	4.0	4.4	7.0	8.3	3.8	6.4	
11.5	6.7	4.1	10.4	12.7	13.7	16.3	10.7	
0.3	0	0	0.1	0.1	1.1	1.4	1.3	
1.3	0	0	3.1	3.2	1.7	0.7	1.4	
0.1	0	0	0.3	0.1	1.2	0	0	
0.5	0	0	0.1	0	0.1	3.1	0	
1.5	0.7	0.2	2.5	0.8	5.3	8.2	10.1	
20.6	10.0	8.3	20.9	23.9	31.4	33.5	29.9	22.3
7.4	5.6	6.9	5.0	4.6	7.9	7.6	7.2	6.5

		Producer Goods	Consumer Goods
Average contact time per visit:	t_A	60	40
	t_B	40	30
	t_C	30	20
	t_N	80	40
Number of visits per month:	V_A	3	6
	V_B	1	2
	V_C	0.5	1
	V_N	2.5	5
Order rate % per month:	O_A	100	100
	O_B	90	90
	O_C	80	80
	O_N	60	60
Order coefficient:	C_A	0.1	0.05
	C_B	0.2	0.1
	C_C	0.6	0.3
	C_N	0.065	0.13

With respect to receiving-order coefficient, the value for the continuous customer is two times greater in the case of producer goods than in the case of the consumer goods. However, in the case of top A-ranking clients, the receiving-order rate is high but the receiving-order coefficient is low, because there is no more room to increase the order rate. In the case of newly developed clients, the receiving-order coefficient is also low, which is expected; however, in contrast to the case of continuous customers, the producer goods rate is half of the consumer goods rate, which means difficult entry (participation) as a result of established, fixed supplied customers.

(7) The case of producer goods

In the case of producer goods, the average labor time, $\bar{t}$, is 622 minutes and the average contact ratio in business activities outside the company, excluding travel time, is 32.7%, or approximately 33%. The monthly average operating days is 24. The daily average number of visits, $\bar{v}$, is 3.41, or approximately 3.5. We approximate the numbers because in marketing planning, fractions and percentages should be kept simple and easy to understand.

Therefore, with the number of clients per salesman as a variable, we have the following system of equations:

$$\begin{cases} 60 \times 3x_A + 40 \times 1x_B + 30 \times 0.5x_C + 80 \times 2.5x_N = 622 \times 24 \times 0.33 \\ (1-1)x_A + (1-0.9)x_B + (1-0.8)x_C - 0.6x_N = 0 \\ 3x_A + x_B + 0.5x_C + 2.5x_N = 3.5 \times 24 \\ x_A + 0.9x_B + 0.8x_C + 0.6x_N = 0.1 \times 60 \times 3 \\ \qquad\qquad + 0.2 \times 40 \times 1 + 0.6 \times 30 \times 0.5 + 0.065 \times 80 \times 2.5 \end{cases}$$

After arranging:

$$\begin{cases} 180x_A + 40x_B + 15x_C + 200x_N = 4926 \\ 0.1x_B + 0.2x_C - 0.6x_N = 0 \\ 3x_A + x_B + 0.5x_C + 2.5x_N = 84 \\ x_A + 0.9x_B + 0.8x_C + 0.6x_N = 48 \end{cases}$$

The solutions are $x_A = 11.34$, $x_B = 13.13$, $x_C = 23.52$, and $x_N = 10.03$, a total of 58.03.

That is, A rank, 10; B rank, 15; C rank, 25; new clients, 10; a total of 60 clients or thereabouts are assigned monthly.

For the sake of simulation, against the enemy attack, and under current conditions, let's only double $V_A = 3 \rightarrow 6$, $V_B = 1 \rightarrow 2$, $V_C = 0.5 \rightarrow 1$, and $V_N = 2.5 \rightarrow 4$

The result will be the following system of equations:

$$\begin{cases} 360x_A + 80x_B + 30x_C + 320x_N &= 4926 \\ 0.1x_B + 0.2x_C - 0.6x_N &= 0 \\ 6x_A + 2x_B + 1x_C + 4x_N &= 84 \\ x_A + 0.9x_B + 0.8x_C + 0.6x_N &= 90.8 \end{cases}$$

The solutions are then $x_A = -33.70$, $x_B = -12.90$, $x_C = 137.40$, and $x_N = 43.65$. Since negative values are impossible, the solutions are incompatible in the real world, which means such an increase in visitation planning is nonsense.

Next, let's change the average contact time per visit, and relatively emphasize the A rank and new clients: $t_A = 60 \rightarrow 90$, $t_B = 40 \rightarrow 30$, $t_C = 30 \rightarrow 20$, and $t_N = 80 \rightarrow 90$.

The result will be the following system of equations:

$$\begin{cases} 270x_A + 30x_B + 10x_C + 225x_N &= 4926 \\ 0.1x_B + 0.2x_C - 0.6x_N &= 0 \\ 3x_A + x_B + 0.5x_C + 2.5x_N &= 84 \\ x_A + 0.9x_B + 0.8x_C + 0.6x_N &= 53.625 \end{cases}$$

The solutions then are $x_A = 5.59$, $x_B = 38.12$, $x_C = 9.91$, and $x_N = 9.67$, a total of 63.29. That is, under current conditions, this increase in contact time is realistic.

(8) The case of consumer goods

In the case of consumer goods, the average labor time, $\bar{t}$, is 615 minutes and the average contact ratio in business activities outside the company, excluding travel time, is 41.3%, or approximately 40%. The monthly average operating days is 24. The daily average number of visits, $\bar{v}$, is 6.96, or approximately 7. Therefore, with the number of clients per salesman as a variable, we have the following system of equations:

$$\begin{cases} 40 \times 6x_A + 30 \times 2x_B + 20 \times 1x_C + 40 \times 5x_N = 615 \times 24 \times 0.4 \\ (1-1)x_A + (1-0.9)x_B + (1-0.8)x_C - 0.6x_N = 0 \\ 6x_A + 2x_B + x_C + 5x_N = 7 \times 24 \\ x_A + 0.9x_B + 0.8x_C + 0.6x_N = 0.05 \times 40 \times 6 \\ \qquad\qquad +0.1 \times 30 \times 2 + 0.3 \times 20 \times 1 + 0.13 \times 40 \times 5 \end{cases}$$

After arranging we obtain:

$$\begin{cases} 240x_A + 60x_B + 20x_C + 200x_N = 5904 \\ 0.1x_B + 0.2x_C - 0.6x_N = 0 \\ 6x_A + 2x_B + x_C + 5x_N = 168 \\ x_A + 0.9x_B + 0.8x_C + 0.6x_N = 50 \end{cases}$$

The solutions are $x_A = 9.20$, $x_B = 24.00$, $x_C = 16.80$, and $x_N = 9.60$, a total of 59.60.

That is, A rank, 10; B rank, 25; C rank, 15; new clients, 10; a total of 60 clients or thereabouts are assigned monthly. The difference with the case of the producer goods is that the number of B and the number of C ranking clients are interchanged; the reason is not clear at this juncture.

Again, for the sake of simulation, with respect to the number of visits, we relatively emphasize the B rank: $V_A = 6$ (unchanged), $V_B = 2 \to 3$, $V_C = 1$ (unchanged), and $V_N = 5 \to 4$.

The result will be the following system of equations:

$$\begin{cases} 240x_A + 90x_B + 20x_C + 160x_N = 5904 \\ 0.1x_B + 0.2x_C - 0.6x_N = 0 \\ 6x_A + 3x_B + x_C + 4x_N = 168 \\ x_A + 0.9x_B + 0.8x_C + 0.6x_N = 47.8 \end{cases}$$

The solutions then are $x_A = 11.86$, $x_B = 9.73$, $x_C = 26.21$, and $x_N = 10.36$, a total of 58.16. That is, under current conditions, this increase in the number of visits is realistic.

On the other hand, if we decrease across the board, $t_A = 40 \to 30$, $t_B = 30 \to 20$, $t_C = 20 \to 10$, and $t_N = 40 \to 30$, then:

$$\begin{cases} 180x_A + 40x_B + 10x_C + 150x_N = 5904 \\ 0.1x_B + 0.2x_C - 0.6x_N = 0 \\ 6x_A + 2x_B + x_C + 5x_N = 168 \\ x_A + 0.9x_B + 0.8x_C + 0.6x_N = 35.5 \end{cases}$$

The solutions then are $x_A = 78.70$, $x_B = -1134.00$, $x_C = 1090.80$, and $x_N = 174.60$. Since negative values are impossible, the solutions are incompatible in the real world, which means such a decrease in contact time under current conditions is totally meaningless.

There are many cases of simulation. The above examples highlight attempts to increase the contact time per visit in the case of producer goods and to raise the number of customer visits in the case of consumer goods.

It should be noted, however, that the element values here are derived from a small number of analyses, and need to be further refined. In that sense, this evaluation has merely touched the beginning of the science of competition.

5.4 Consequences

As the 1980s begin, as a result of low growth and stagflation, the competition both domestically and internationally seems to increase even more.

In February 1959, major oil companies lowered their price to combat excess supply and price discount competition. In 1960, Exxon lowered their price for a second time, which led to the founding of the Organization of Petroleum Exporting Countries (OPEC). However, OPEC remained largely under the influence of major oil companies until 1969, when a coup brought Khaddafi to power in Libya.

The 1960s is symbolized by the Apollo Project proposed by President Kennedy that resulted in man's first moon landing by Apollo 11 in July 1969. In Japan, the Ikeda administration announced the doubling of income, which was greatly helped by the price of oil at one dollar per barrel.

In the 1970s, the Apollo Project, which originally called for 20 launches, ended after the launch of Apollo 17. The total cost of the project was $24 billion. In 1971, the United States, after deciding to back out of Vietnam, announced the floating exchange rate system for the dollar. This is the so-called Nixon Shock.

In September 1973, the oil shock created worldwide recession and a negative real growth rate in Japan (1975). In the following years, public investing expanded as large amounts of government bonds were issued to combat domestic recession caused by U.S.-Japan trade and currency war and higher yen. In 1979, a second oil shock further raised the price of oil.

In the meantime, the American oil import has steadily increased from 1,500,000 barrels a day in the early 1970s to 6,000,000 in 1979. This means an increase of 350,000,000 liters annually, or about 1.3 times more than Japan's annual import of 270,000,000 liters (1978).

Japan heavily depends on export. Among the total annual production of 9,300,000 compact cars, almost half is shipped overseas. However, the U.S. Big Three have spent $70 billion, or more than what was spent for the Apollo Project, in the area of compact-car manufacturing. GM is already selling its 2000-c.c. X-Model car, and in the 1980s, is going to introduce the sub-2000-c.c. J-,T-, and S-Model cars.

In the 1979 elections, the Liberal Democratic Party (LDP) gained 44.6% of the votes, an increase over its previous share, and although its number of seats was reduced by one to 248, it still remains firmly Japan's ruling party.

Overseas, the Thatcher cabinet was established following a victory by conservatives in the British elections. The Conservative Party obtained 43.9% (previously, 35.7%) of the votes and gained 339 seats, 21 seats over the majority. The defeated Labor Party obtained 36.9% (previously, 39.3%) of the votes.

INDEX

A·A store ratio, 265
ABC analysis, 259
ABC report, 277
acquisition value, 4
actual client rate, 288
aircraft in WWI, 57
antitrust law, 230, 244, 266
Appollo project, 301
Asahi beer company, 234
attitude, 202
auxiliary equation, 171
average contact time, 279, 287

Baysian statistics, 201
behaviorism, 202
behavior analysis, 292
Bernoulli, D., 32
beta function, 143, 151
billboard, 272
binomial, 132
binomial distribution, 108, 112, 140
black box, 23, 201-3
Boer War, 43
Boulding, Dr. K. E., 21, 165

cartel law, 244
catalog, 272
catenary, 78
cause and effect, 23, 200
characteristic value, 71, 171
Clausewitz, Karl von, 56
client, 287
client concentration, 263
client contact time, 287

client store ratio, 265
coefficient chart, 148, 150
co-function, 70, 171
combat, group to group, 52
combat, hand to hand, 55
compatibility, 298, 300
concentration, 36, 244, 257
continuous fixed-rate, 6, 10, 61
continuous fixed-sum, 3, 10, 61
concentration, law of, 36
consumer goods, 299
conversion, 5
correspondence of fighting strength, 196, 230
corporate abuses, 243-4
customer, 230, 287
customer pool, 230, 232

deterministic cause and effect, 201-3
defense white paper, 231
Deming, Dr. W. E., 267
depreciation, 5
depreciation constants, 182
differentiation, 249, 251
differential operator, 73, 169
differentiation strategy, 247
diversified type, 279, 281
diversionary tactics, 65
driving force, 32, 290
documentation, 272
double blind test, 201
duel model, 51

efficiency of weapons, 41, 58, 60, 65, 92, 94, 98, 272
entropy, 200

equilibrium solution, 218
expected value, 28, 112, 154, 203, 207
exchange rate, 60, 80, 65, 94-5, 157, 162
expected value for survivors, 129, 135, 137, 153-4, 158, 161

fair trade commission, 243, 257, 266
feint operation, 65
fighting force, 272, 275, 287
fighting strength, 45, 51, 55, 196
Fisherian probability, 203
Fuji steel company, 243
fundamental solution, 72
function solution, 203

game of scissors, paper, rock, 203
game theory, 200, 203, 205-6
gamma function, 143
generalized model, 169
general solution, 4, 8, 14, 22, 70, 170
global war, 164
GNP, 231

HH index, 258
Hideyoshi, General, 51
hyperbolic function, 78, 81

incomplete beta function ratio, 116
initial conditions, 18, 22, 60, 75, 89, 173
initial value, 4
investment profitability, 237

Kármán, T. van., 53
Kimball, Dr. G. E., 53, 60, 69, 130
Kirin beer company, 234
Koopman, Dr. B. O., 53, 60, 69, 87

Lanchester, F, W., 31
Lanchester's linear law, 54, 60, 64, 131
Lancherster's N-squared law, 35, 67, 69, 138
Lanchester strategy coefficient, 216, 218, 225, 248, 269
Lanchester strategy equation, 218, 222, 225
large-scale retailer, 281, 286
Law of quantity, 106, 267, 268, 276
Liberal Democratic Party, 238
lift coefficient, 34
lifting force, 33, 290
linear equation, 3, 27
linear programming, 29
Lockheed incident, 238
logarithmic differential, 7
Lorenz curve, 259
loss ratio, 139
loss of strength gradient (LSG), 165-6

market competition, 230, 273
market monopoly, 243
market share, 205, 230, 233, 236, 240, 242, 253, 257, 264, 278, 290
Markov chain, 266
Matsushita electric corporation, 237
maxium value, 212, 215
Maxwell house company, 253
Midway, battle of, 106, 193
military force, 94
minimum value, 212
min - max strategy, 212, 229
monopoly, 244
monopoly right, 244

monopolistic oligopoly, 252, 279
Morgenstern, O., 205
Morse, P. M., 53, 130, 267
motivation research, 202-3
Motorola corporation, 237

Napoleon, 47
natural logarithm base, 6
Nelson, Admiral Lord, 47
Nelson's memorandum, 47
Nestle corporation, 253
Neuman, J. L. von, 205
number of suvivors, 62, 82, 84
number of visits, 273, 288
number of visited clients, 287
Nobonaga, General, 51
non zero sum game, 213

oligopoly, 252
OPEC, 301
order coefficient, 290
operations research, 229, 267
optimum solution, 87

Pacific War, 94
partial sum, 116, 132
particular solution, 4, 8, 65, 96, 141, 170
pay-off matrix, 204, 206, 211, 213
Prandtl, L., 35
predator model, 14
prisoner's dilemma, 212
producer goods, 297
probability model, 28
probability solution, 203, 210
probabilistic cause and effect, 200-1
pure strategy, 212

polynomial, 19, 133

radio active decay, 11
recurrence formula, 147
regional market, 264
remaining book value, 4, 6
Richardson, L. F., 20, 23, 93, 180
Richardson model, 21
ROI, 237
roller survey, 266
route sales, 293
Runge-Kutta method, 18

saddle point, 212, 214
salesperson, 271-2, 274, 287, 290, 292
Sapporo beer company, 234
segmentation, 240, 248, 266
separation of variables, 4, 8, 289
Schlaifer, R., 201
shooting range, 249
simulation, 298, 300
Simpson's method, 259
single combat, 55, 64
Smith, Adam, 205
Smith, J. M., 20
special coefficient, 148, 150
standardization, 272
statistical probability, 201
strategic air command, 187, 194
strategy, 1, 206, 270
strategic strength, 232, 268, 270
structural model, 24
structural regulation, 243
store share, 264
supply line, 164, 168
survival rate, 58, 128, 154

system of differential equations, 14, 21, 58, 68, 90, 172
system of equations, 275-6
system of identities, 114, 118

tactics, 1, 271
tactical strength, 196, 230, 268, 270
Taoka, Dr. N., 270
the strong (company), 267, 276
the weak (company), 247, 276
total war, 86
top position, 233, 238
Trafalgar, battle of, 47

Udel, Dr., 271
uncertainty principle, 201

victory rate, 152
vortex, 33
voting rate, 238, 256, 302

weapon efficiency, 41, 51, 63, 98, 181, 272
weapon exchange rate, 80
wing-edge vortex, 34
winning probability, 115
winning rate, 115, 117, 123, 149, 161
WW I aircraft, 57
WW II aircraft, 190-1

Yahata steel company, 243

zero sum game, 205
zero sum two person game, 206